KNIGHT OF THE
NORTH ATLANTIC

KNIGHT OF THE NORTH ATLANTIC

Baron Siegfried von Forstner
and the War Patrols of *U-402*, 1941–1943

AARON S HAMILTON

Copyright © Aaron S Hamilton 2022

First published in Great Britain in 2022 by
Seaforth Publishing,
A division of Pen & Sword Books Ltd,
47 Church Street,
Barnsley S70 2AS
www.seaforthpublishing.com

British Library Cataloguing in Publication Data
A catalogue record for this book is available from the British Library

ISBN 978 1 3990 9672 0 (HARDBACK)
ISBN 978 1 3990 9673 7 (EPUB)
ISBN 978 1 3990 9674 4 (KINDLE)

All rights reserved. No part of this publication may be reproduced or transmitted in any form or by any means, electronic or mechanical, including photocopying, recording, or any information storage and retrieval system, without prior permission in writing of both the copyright owner and the above publisher.

The right of Aaron S Hamilton to be identified as the author of this work has been asserted by him in accordance with the Copyright, Designs and Patents Act 1988.

Pen & Sword Books Limited incorporates the imprints of Atlas,
Archaeology, Aviation, Discovery, Family History, Fiction, History, Maritime, Military, Military Classics,
Politics, Select, Transport, True Crime, Air World, Frontline Publishing, Leo Cooper, Remember When,
Seaforth Publishing, The Praetorian Press, Wharncliffe Local History, Wharncliffe Transport,
Wharncliffe True Crime, White Owl and After the Battle

Typeset and designed by Mousemat Design Limited

Printed and bound in Great Britain by CPI Group (UK) Ltd, Croydon, CR0 4YY

For
My grandfather Herbert Schwuchow,
and all those who fought in the Battle of the Atlantic

Contents

Preface   9
Acknowledgements   11
Introduction   13

Chapter 1. The Karlsruhe U-boat   19
    The Captain   19
    The Crew   26
    The Boat   32
    Icebergs and Narwhals   45

Chapter 2. On Holiday   53
    Chance Encounter   54
    Wrong Direction   60
    The Wait is Over   64

Chapter 3. Missing the Beat   79
    Casinos or Broadway?   81
    Chivalry is not Dead   93
    Back to the Outer Banks   104

Chapter 4. Return of the Wolfpacks   113
    Into the Fray   115
    Thrust and Parry   121

Chapter 5. Knight's Cross   131
    Experience and Luck Creates Opportunity   133
    One Man's Determination   140

Chapter 6. Turn of the Tide   155
    Ebb and Flow   158
    Aces Duel   161

Chapter 7. Go Fetch   167
    High Hopes   168
    A Prediction Comes True   175

Chapter 8. Conclusion   181
    On Eternal Patrol   181
    From Submersible to Submarine   183
    Of Wrecks and Sanctuaries   184

Appendix A: Evolution of a U-boat   189
Appendix B: Crew   192
Appendix C: Pompom Life   194
Appendix D: Patrol Summary   197

Notes   198
Select Bibliography   201
Patrol Charts   205
Ship Name Index   223

Preface

As the Second World War recedes further into the past, each year hundreds of new books are published about some aspect of this global conflict. Many offer new insights from recently declassified documents, or the memories of the few veterans that remain. Others look to re-interpret what were thought to be well understood events.

This book is no exception. The history of *U-402*, a German Type VIIC U-boat, is another tile in the mosaic of the war, and more specifically the Battle of the Atlantic. However, its history is personal to me, as my grandfather, Herbert Schwuchow, served on *U-402* during its first four war patrols.

U-402's conning tower was emblazoned with the shield of its sponsoring city of Karlsruhe. Upon that shield was the Latin word '*Fidelitas*' – Fidelity. Baron Siegfried Freiherr von Forstner, the U-boat's captain, embodied that word through his deep sense of loyalty to his profession, country and crew. He remained faithful to his sponsoring city throughout the war, writing letters, visiting and showing homemade films of *U-402*'s early cruises. A strong bond developed between the city's mayor and the U-boat's crew.

Born into an aristocratic military family, with a tradition of U-boat service, von Forstner served without the pretentiousness of title even after winning the Ritterkreuz (Knight's Cross). He fought the war like a knight of old, with a defined code of chivalry, as he duelled with escorts, rushed to the aid of fellow U-boats and rescued his enemy from an often-cruel sea. As the North Atlantic battlefield grew deadlier with each successive patrol, von Forstner remained focused on his duty to sink tonnage while keeping his crew alive. The story of *U-402* parallels the rise and fall of the feared wolfpacks, as Allied intelligence and technology coalesced to doom the surface-bound submersible, which gave rise to the true submarine.

Von Forstner's daring and seamanship captured the respect of Captain US Coast Guard (Ret.) John M. Waters, who was a Watch Officer on board the escort USCGC *Ingham* that fought *U-402* in several convoy battles. After the war, he became the unexpected chronicler of his former enemy, and established an enduring friendship with von Forstner's widow.

Every effort was made to source relevant material regarding the story of *U-402*. The historian's task is made all the more difficult when the participants have passed away, and you are no longer able to ask questions based on new primary sources or observations. Like an archaeologist, you are left with piecing together the crumbled mosaic from the shards of memories, documents and photos, never knowing precisely how the pieces fit. With this in mind, I should note that the worldwide pandemic shuttered many institutions at the time I drafted this manuscript and I was not able to pursue several lines of historical inquiry that developed late in my research. Despite these challenges, I hope those who read this book close the covers with a balanced view of the dramatic events that surrounded *U-402*'s role in the greatest military campaign of the Second World War – the Battle of the Atlantic.

Aaron S Hamilton
Northern Virginia
2021

Acknowledgements

Many individuals assisted in my research over the years. Professor Carl Boyd, one of my graduate advisors at Old Dominion University, initiated my academic research when he put me in contact with the eminent German expert on the Battle of the Atlantic, Professor Jürgen Rohwer, back in 1995. Rohwer offered his historical overview of *U-402*, and in turn, put me in touch with Flottillenadmiral (Ret.) Otto Kretschmer, who was the classmate and friend of *U-402*'s commander von Forstner. I gained unique insights from Kretschmer about von Forstner after an initial exchange of letters with the U-boat ace. Kretschmer offered to put me in touch with von Forstner's widow Frau Annamarie Rapp (who had re-married after the war), but it never happened because shortly after our correspondence, Kretschmer passed away due to an untimely accident.

Also in 1995, I contacted the US Coast Guard Historian's Office in an effort to correspond with US Coast Guard Captain (Ret) John M Waters, Jr. whose vessel, the USCGC *Ingham*, escorted two convoys *U-402* engaged. After the war, he wrote an article 'Stay Tough' for US Naval Institute *Proceedings*, followed by the book *Bloody Winter* about those experiences. Unfortunately, I was too late by two years, as Waters had passed away. It would take almost 15 more years before I was able to contact his son, Dr Stephen J Waters, who willingly shared all his father's remaining research with me in 2013.

In recent years, US Navy Captain (Ret.) Jerry Mason, whose website http://uboatarchive.net/ is the best source of primary documents about both sides of the Battle of Atlantic available on the Internet, put me in touch with Horst Friebolin, the nephew of one of *U-402*'s former crew, Obermaat Walter Friebolin. Uwe Stachelhaus, whose own father was captain of *U-526*, aboard which Friebolin also served, facilitated the exchange of information and photos with the Friebolin family. His efforts were greatly appreciated. These photos, available on Jerry's website, contained images of my grandfather no one in my family ever knew existed, including my grandfather himself. Unfortunately, there was little information about when each photo was taken. There appear to be different cameras, or at least different film and developers used, which made the process of determining an accurate timeline for them even more difficult. While care was exercised to correctly identify each photo's time and place, errors are inevitable under the circumstances. Jerry translated all of *U-402*'s KTBs for me, with the kind assistance of Andi Forster.

Many others contributed in one way or another over the years. Helpful staffs at the Bundesarchiv in Koblenz, Bibliotech fur Zeitgeschite in Stuttgart, Deutsches U-Boot Museum in Cuxhaven, Stadt Archiv of Karlsruhe, US National Archives and Records Administration, College Park Maryland, Naval History and Heritage Command, Washington D.C., US Coast Guard Historian's Office, Anacostia, and The Mariners' Museum, Newport News, all provided documents and photos, some previously unpublished. I also wish to thank those involved in the 2013 *Ashkhabad* Survey, including Joseph Hoyt, William Chadwell, Fred C Engle, Lauren Heesemann, and my dive partner Brandi Carrier. Being able to 'touch' a piece of my grandfather's wartime experience brought home the reality of the war, as well as the hardships all endured.

George Anderson prepared all the maps in the book. These will help the reader visualise the naval actions described across the vastness of the North Atlantic.

As always, I thank my family, who have learned that when I say 'this is the last book I will write', I really mean it as an aspirational goal.

Introduction

This book began its germination 30 years ago after listening to the few stories that my maternal grandfather, Herbert Schwuchow, shared of his time on board *U-402* during the Second World War. Only after writing this book did I truly appreciate his willingness to talk about those events, and pass on the select memories I know he preferred to let fade with time.

It was only after his passing that I sent an inquiry to the Deutsche Dienststelle (WASt) in Berlin and learned more about his wartime career in the Kriegsmarine than he shared. Interestingly, his incomplete record revealed nothing of the time he spent on *U-402*. In fact, a large gap in his service record exists from 1940 to 1944.

I knew my grandfather transferred off *U-402* after its fourth war patrol in the autumn of 1942 to continue his administrative service training once he was promoted to Verwaltungsobergefreiter in July 1942. What he did, and where he served from the end of 1942 through the spring of 1944, remains lost to history. What is known, thanks to his remaining service record, is that from April to October 1944 he was assigned as a member of the Baukompanie (Construction Company) at Deutsche Werke Kiel where he served as a crewman on the *U-492*, a Type XIV U-tanker under construction. During that assignment he was promoted to Verwaltungsmaat in July. *U-492* was never completed as the needs of the war at sea changed. He was then transferred to Narvik in Norway on 20 October 1944 where he served on the staff of the new 14th U-Flotilla through the end of the war. He was discharged from the service in September 1945, and transferred from British to Soviet custody, where he had to prove he was German and not Russian, given his Slavic surname, or be shot as a Russian deserter. Luckily, the British allowed him to keep his paybook (they took everything else), which proved to Soviet officials that the man standing before them was German-born.

U-402 was always of interest to me given my grandfather's wartime service on board. I believe readers will also find it of interest because this U-boat's history reflects the ebb and flow of the Battle of the Atlantic from the early operations in European waters, to Operation 'Paukenschlag' ('Drumbeat') off the US East Coast, to the climatic wolfpack battles of the North Atlantic in 1943. Individual U-boat histories from the period 1939–43 are well represented in

Herbert Schwuchow, July 1942. He is wearing the insignia of a Verwaltungs-obergefreiter, the U-boat Badge awarded after his second patrol on *U-402*, and the ribbon of the Iron Cross 2nd Class. In the lower right is embossed 'MURO, La Rochelle' which means this photo was taken in the famed portrait studio of Abelardo Muro located at 29 Rue Dupaty, La Rochelle. Herbert had the primary duty of cook while he served on *U-402* during its first four war patrols due to his pre-war training as a butcher. He spoke little of the war. When he did, it was often of the sea, which left the greatest impression on him. (Author's collection)

current published literature. Yet few, if any, of these histories, reveal how evolving Allied technology, German countermeasures or cryptographic intelligence impacted an individual patrol, leaving the reader with a myopic view of events derived from the formality of a U-boat's war diary, or an individual captain's recollection. The reader will not find this incomplete historical construct in the following chapters. The traditional 'war diary' view of this U-boat is supplemented through wartime letters from its captain, his wife and the Mayor of Karlsruhe's office, as well as veteran and survivor's testimony alike, to include the few memories of my own grandfather. More importantly, I have endeavoured to place *U-402*'s story within the broader context of the longest campaign in military history.[1]

This story of *U-402* is also very much about its captain, Baron Siegfried Freiherr von Forstner, and how he proved highly capable under the pressures of the ocean's depths, continued technical challenges and naval combat alike. While he is not as well-known as many of his peers, he sunk more merchant ships in less than 24 hours against Convoy SC-118 than any U-boat commander achieved against a convoy during the previous two years of war. What made this combat performance all the more remarkable was that it was achieved in a tactical environment more difficult than that in which earlier U-boat aces achieved their successes. Von Forstner's recorded 41,718 gross register tonnage (GRT) of shipping sunk over the night of 7/8 February 1943 was the product of expert planning and a well-developed understanding of his enemy's tactics that allowed him to exploit the slimmest of openings in the convoy's defences.

Time and again von Forstner correctly guessed the next action of an escort commander, whom he often outmanoeuvred while surfaced. Von Forstner knew that to submerge his U-boat in such a duel was to risk losing contact with the merchant ship or tanker he pursued and expose his boat and crew to the pounding of exploding depth charges. His aggressiveness in battle was noted by those who served under him, but von Forstner was never reckless. His actions were always conducted as that of a highly skilled naval professional and guided through a well-developed personal code of honour, reminiscent of a medieval knight of old. He always put the lives of his crew first and made decisions appropriate to the situation. Von Forstner never hesitated to aid another U-boat in combat, whatever the odds, and even rescued two US Navy sailors from the sea, saving them from almost certain death. He refused to demonise his enemy when ordered to do so by his superiors, and reprimanded the young zealots assigned to his crew in later years.

One can say for certain that von Forstner was no National Socialist ideologue, yet his military professionalism cannot be completely divorced from the regime he served. Von Forstner likely believed, like many of his peers, that a new war with Britain and France was inevitable in the wake of the 'Diktat' Treaty of Versailles. This shared sense of grievance among the officers and enlisted men of the new Reichswehr, which formed under the new Weimar

Republic, was one of Germany's post-Great War experiences that Adolf Hitler drew upon to forge his path to totalitarian power.

The battle for supremacy in the North Atlantic sea lanes and the challenge of the U-boat wolfpacks continues to fascinate many with good reason. The story combines ground-breaking technology, human ingenuity, cryptographic intelligence and tragedy, as well as the power and allure of the sea, in a way that grips readers differently than other campaigns of the Second World War. Routine reminders of the maritime conflict appear in all media forms with the discovery of a new shipwreck or U-boat lost during the war. In many cases, these sites have become protected maritime sanctuaries and dive destinations from North America to Europe.

The merchantmen that sailed from North America to Great Britain in the period 1940–3 faced the dual threat of the unforgiving North Atlantic and the threat of attack by massed U-boats from the ocean's depths. The wolfpack, as it became known, was a uniquely German contribution to maritime warfare which was made possible with the introduction of wireless radio communication in the inter-war period. The wolfpack itself was a counter to the Allied concept of the convoy system, designed to protect merchantmen from attack by single U-boats that previously devastated Allied shipping in the last war.

The wolfpack was a simple tactical concept conceived by the young U-boat commander Karl Dönitz in the early morning of 4 October 1918. His Type UBIII coastal U-boat, *UB-68*, found itself by chance undetected in the centre of a Malta-bound convoy under cover of darkness. While he manoeuvred for an attack his U-boat suffered a catastrophic mechanical failure and was abandoned while under fire of British escorts after an unplanned breach of the surface. As Dönitz bobbed upon the waves hoping for rescue by his enemy, he thought about the evening's events and quickly formed the nucleus of the wolfpack concept he employed with deadly effect several decades later. He realised at that moment 'A U-boat attacking a convoy on the surface and under cover of darkness . . . stood very good prospects of success. The greater the number of U-boats that could be brought simultaneously into the attack, the more favourable would become the opportunities offered to each individual attacker.'[2]

By the start of the Second World War Dönitz's concept was well refined. The intent was to deploy a line of U-boats along a suspected convoy route. Once the convoy was spotted, a single U-boat took the role of spotter and transmitted its position back to Befehlshaber der U-Boote (BdU – Commander of U-boats) ashore. In turn, BdU plotted the convoy route and vectored other U-boats to its position for a nighttime attack. The goal was to sink cargo tonnage, so escort vessels were initially ignored. Their frequent wireless transmissions became a critical vulnerability as the Allies were able to deploy high-frequency direction finding (HF/DF) equipment on board ships that allowed escorts to locate surfaced U-boats. Later, the Kriegsmarine naval cipher known as Enigma was broken, and the Allies were able to read most wireless traffic to and from U-boats under the codename of Ultra.

Despite the view that U-boats coordinated their attacks as a wolfpack, they did not. Individual U-boats did not communicate with each other. Once a convoy battle began U-boat commanders conducted their attacks freely, given the tactical circumstances that presented themselves in the chaotic confusion of a maritime battlefield. Success depended greatly on an individual U-boat commander's ability to exploit the opportunities the tactical situation presented, through their skill and initiative.

An important fact all too often forgotten in modern maritime history is that a U-boat was not a true submarine able to remain submerged indefinitely – at least not at the start of the war. U-boats were submersibles, as were all 'submarines' of the Second World War. They could only stay submerged for 20–30 hours at a time before they had to surface and recharge their batteries, expel noxious gases and refresh the boat's oxygen. They were slow underwater when running on electric motors, and typically spent the majority of their time manoeuvring and attacking on the surface.

Aircraft, not surface escorts, were their main enemy.[3] As RAF Coastal Command aircraft grew in number, U-boats operating off the Western Approaches of Great Britain became more vulnerable. This growing air threat was soon mitigated by the German occupation of France in 1940 that brought naval bases along the Bay of Biscay under Kriegsmarine control. From here, U-boats could deploy even further west into the central North Atlantic. This area was known generally to the Allies as 'The Gap', though it was also referred to as the 'Black Pit'. For several long days and nights merchantmen and escorts sailed without the benefit of air cover that provided overwatch. Aircraft could force a U-boat to dive just by their presence overhead and a submerged U-boat was too slow to maintain contact with a convoy, thus providing the Allies with an opportunity to evade the wolfpack. The lack of air cover left slow-moving convoys highly vulnerable as U-boats used daylight to track them and manoeuvre into position for a night attack. During the first half of 1943 Dönitz's wolfpacks appeared on the verge of a great naval victory. The very lifeline of Great Britain might be severed, forcing it out of the war. In order to bridge 'The Gap' and regain maritime superiority, the Allies introduced long-range aircraft, escort carriers and new airborne radar.

Aircraft equipped with increasingly more effective radar sets were vectored toward expected U-boat locations through HF/DF coordinates triangulated from radio broadcasts or Enigma decrypts. They soon began to decimate surface-bound U-boats until mid-1944 when the Schnorchel (snorkel) was introduced and transformed undersea warfare forever. *U-402*, however, did not survive long enough to take part in the transformation from submersible to something closer to a true submarine. Von Forstner's tactical skill ultimately proved no match for evolving Allied innovations. *U-402* succumbed to the new air-dropped acoustic homing torpedo, known as 'FIDO'. There were no survivors.

CHAPTER 1

The Karlsruhe U-boat

> The commander usually spends the eve of his departure in the circle of his comrades, but it is a solemn moment for him as soon as he sails from his native shore. He becomes responsible for every action which is taken, and for many weeks no orders reach him from his superiors. He is unable to ask anyone's advice, or to consult with his inferiors, as he stands alone in the solitude of his higher rank. Even the common sailor is conscious of the seriousness of the task ahead and of the adventures which may occur below the sea.
>
> Georg-Günther von Forstner, *The Journal of a Submarine Commander* (1916)

The Captain

May 21st 1941 was an important day for Kapitänleutnant Baron Siegfried Freiherr von Forstner. It was the day that his U-boat, *U-402*, was officially commissioned into the Kriegsmarine under a warm sunny sky in the port city of Danzig. Von Forstner certainly

Kapitänleutnant Baron Siegfried Freiherr von Forstner stands at attention on the back of *U-402*'s conning tower facing his crew during the U-boat's commissioning ceremony on 21 May 1941 at the Danziger Werft. (Friebolin collection)

felt the weight of responsibility that came with a wartime command as he stood at attention on the aft section of the conning tower facing his crew during the time-honoured ceremony.

By mid-1941 Britain stood alone against Germany. After the fall of France nearly a year earlier, the burden of the war had shifted to the Luftwaffe, and now to the Kriegsmarine – especially the U-boat arm under the command of Admiral Karl Dönitz. Von Forstner missed much of the early naval action of the war, including the Kriegsmarine's role in the occupation of Norway. As a professional naval officer, he was naturally anxious to see service in defence of his country before the war ended.

Service was expected of von Forstner who was born into an aristocratic family that had served in the Germany military for three generations. His father, Ernst Freiherr von Forstner (1869–1950), was a war hero who began his military service in 1889 and retired as a Generalmajor in 1927. He had been awarded the coveted Prussian Order Pour le Mérite (the Blue Max), having served with distinction as a regimental commander in the First Word War.

Ernst married his first wife, Elsbeth Freiin von Busse, in 1908. Siegfried was born on 19 September 1910 in Hannover, and his younger brother, Wolfgang-Friedrich and twin sister Wolf-Friedrichs, were born in Karlsruhe on 3 October 1916.[4] Von Forstner and his younger brother did not follow their father into army service, but fell under the influence of their uncle and joined the navy. Siegfried joined the fledgling Reichsmarine in 1930 during the Weimar Republic and his brother Wolfgang-Friedrich followed in 1937. Both boys grew up hearing the stories of their uncle Freiherr Georg-Günther von Forstner's exploits as a U-boat commander during the First World War.

Korvettenkapitän Georg-Günther von Forstner was a pioneer in the art and science of submarine warfare and enjoyed the notoriety of being a U-boat ace in the 'Great War'. Born in 1882, Georg-Günther joined the navy at the age of 17. He commanded three U-boats during his time in the Imperial German Navy, which included *U-1* and *U-7* before the outbreak of war, and *U-28*, a Type U 27 boat, during the war. Between August 1914 and June 1916 von Forstner sank twenty-four ships (54,587 GRT), damaged two others (10,511 GRT) and captured two more (3,226 GRT) for a total of 68,324 GRT Allied tons of shipping. He spent 19 years in naval service and was awarded the Iron Cross 1st and 2nd Class, as well as the Friedrich-August Cross (Oldenburg).

When he finished his command of *U-28* he wrote a book about his experiences and U-boat tactics titled *Als U-boots-Kommandant gegen England* (*A submarine commander against England*) which was obtained in England, translated, and published there in an abridged version titled *The Journal of Submarine Commander von Forstner* in 1916. It was read with some interest at the time as it was the first account in English of U-boat operations from the German perspective.

Georg-Günther's book offered some very prescient observations about the strengths and limitations of the 'submersible' that echoed well into the years of the Second World War. He prophetically predicted that the most effective way to ultimately 'kill' a U-boat would be a 'radio-controlled, visibly guided bomb' dropped from an aircraft. As it turned out, it was a self-guided acoustic homing torpedo that found its mark and sunk his oldest nephew's U-boat a quarter of a century later. Georg-Günther passed away on 29 October 1940 before he could witness Siegfried take command of *U-402*.

Siegfried joined the Reichsmarine on 1 April 1930 in the city of Stralsund. He was assigned to the 4th Company/1st Training Battalion of the Schiffsstammdivision der Ostsee (Baltic Naval Headquarter) on the island of Dänholm where he met another cadet, Otto Kretschmer, who later became the top-scoring U-boat ace of the Second World War.

Kretschmer and von Forstner became good friends and shared many experiences over the next several years. After three months at Dänholm they were transferred to the sail training ship *Niobe*. After three months both men earned the rank of Seekadett in October that year and were transferred to the training cruiser SMS *Emden*, which was the third German naval vessel to bear this name. She was the first large Reichsmarine warship built and commissioned after the end of the First World War under the restrictions of the Treaty of Versailles.

Both cadets spent some 15 months serving on board the *Emden*, including a 12-month cruise around the world, with stops in East Asia. While on board von Forstner and Kretschmer passed their next set of exams and earned the rank of Fähnrich zur See in January 1932. They were then transferred back to Dänholm to attend a course to become platoon leaders ashore, which included four weeks at Königsbrück near Dresden in Saxony for army field training.

During this time a world financial crisis occurred, precipitated in part by the commercial banking failure in the United States during 1931–2. Germany was hit particularly hard with millions unemployed, which followed the earlier inflation crisis. Violence broke out in Germany's capital of Berlin between Communists and the rising new party of the National Socialists. The Weimar Republic was collapsing.

Otto Kretschmer, then a Kapitänleutnant, was both a friend and mentor to von Forstner. They enlisted as cadets in the Reichsmarine before the rise of National Socialism. They served together for several years before taking different assignments, Kretschmer to U-boats and von Forstner to surface ships. Von Forstner served as a 3rd Watch Officer under Kretschmer during *U-99*'s seventh war patrol. He absorbed his friend's tactics and employed them with great success during the winter convoy battles of 1942-3. (Author's collection)

In March 1932, von Forstner and Kretschmer's 4.Kompanie was among several units ordered to Berlin, where in field grey uniforms and with loaded rifles, they marched 'against the communists' from the Stettiner Bahnhof to the Dresdner Bahnhof, according to Kretschmer. Four months later, over a third of Germany voted for the Nazi Party, sealing the fate of the country's fledgling democracy.

In April both cadets transferred to the Reichsmarine Naval Academy in Flensburg-Mürwik where they studied 'naval science, history and tactics as well as sports including sailing and riding on horse-back' according to Kretschmer. After a year of academic study, starting in April 1933 they underwent specialised training in gunnery, torpedoes, mines, communications, and sea and air navigation as well as a myriad of other courses. In October 1933 they transferred to the fleet where six months was spent as midshipmen serving on battleships and cruisers. Kretschmer was assigned to the 'pocket battleship' *Deutschland*, while von Forstner went to her sister ship *Admiral Scheer*. As both cadets continued their training, the Reichsmarine was re-named the Kriegsmarine by decree of Adolf Hitler, Germany's new Chancellor. The Nazis were now the sole party as the Weimar Republic was replaced by the Third Reich.

By October 1934 both men had graduated from the Naval Academy at the rank of Oberfähnrich zur See and were sent to different assignments. Kretschmer volunteered for U-boat service in January 1936, but service on U-boats eluded von Forstner for the time-being as he spent the next three years on the cruiser SMS *Nürnberg* as an ordnance officer. In December 1939 he applied for U-boat school while the *Nürnberg* was in port for repairs after she was torpedoed by the British submarine *Salmon*.

With the outbreak of war, von Forstner finally followed in his uncle's wake attending U-boat school in March 1940. While in school, reports of the Battle of the Atlantic begin to filter back. One name began to stand-out, that of his old classmate and friend, Otto Kretschmer. His exploits became well known throughout the Kriegsmarine. Kretschmer sunk over 25,000 GRT of Allied shipping while commanding *U-23*, a Type IIB U-boat, from September 1939 through February 1940.

Upon graduation from U-boat training new officers were typically assigned as a 1st Watch Officer on board a U-boat to learn its operations from an experienced commander before taking over their own boat. However, when von Forstner graduated from U-boat school in September 1940, he was already slotted to take command of his own boat due to both his prior naval experience and seniority as a Kapitänleutnant. To gain the minimum experience necessary to take command, von Forstner was assigned as a '3rd' Watch Officer on board the Type VIIB *U-99* commanded by his old friend Kretschmer, now Germany's top U-boat ace.

The victory over France in June 1940 had a dramatic impact on U-boat operations. New bases were established in the French ports on the Bay of Biscay that allowed U-boats to patrol well into the North Atlantic and operate all around the coast of Great Britain.

When von Forstner arrived in Lorient in early November he had to wait to meet his friend. Kretschmer had just been awarded the Ritterkreuz des Eisernen Kreuzes mit Eichenlaub (the sixth recipient of the Knight's Cross of the Iron Cross with Oak Leaves) on 4 November. After receiving the award and arriving back in port, Kretschmer was ordered to Berlin to meet Großadmiral Erich Raeder and Adolf Hitler at the Reich Chancellery.

Upon his return to Lorient, Kretschmer greeted von Forstner. They only had a short time to catch-up on their careers and the war, as *U-99* was ready to sail back out into the Atlantic four days later. During the thirty days of *U-99*'s seventh war patrol, Kretschmer participated in attacks on Convoys HX-90, OB-251 and OB-252, to the west of Ireland. He sank four vessels totalling 34,291 GRT including one of the largest ships sunk during the war, the armed merchant cruiser HMS *Forfar* (16,402 GRT).

Kretschmer was an aggressive commander who developed a series of standing orders that clearly brought him tactical success. He thoroughly drilled his crew and made them as efficient as possible in crash diving and aircraft spotting. He shadowed convoys in daytime and attacked at night when possible. He preferred to attack from the dark side of the convoy on moonlit nights to silhouette the merchant ships, and from the windward side during storms, as the lookouts on the merchantmen and escorts alike were expected to be less efficient while trying to protect themselves from the elements. He did not submerge his U-boat during night attacks, unless under the direst circumstances, because he correctly believed that his lookouts would see a merchantman before they saw his U-boat. For Kretschmer, the surface offered protection from escorts equipped with active sonar called Anti-Submarine Detection Investigation Committee or ASDIC. Surface radar was not yet common on board escorts and played no role in U-boat detection until well into 1942. Kretschmer also preferred to fire a single torpedo at a target, not a spread, as he viewed this as a waste of resources.

His tactics made a distinct impression on von Forstner. Kretschmer relayed in a 1995 letter to the author that 'obviously he learnt a lot during that mission of mine which ended just before

The Mayor of Karlsruhe, Oberbürgermeister Dr Oskar Hüssy, was excited to offer his city's support to *U-402* as part of the Patenschaftsprogramm (sponsorship). Due to wartime censorship Dr Hüssy was not allowed to know the hull number of the U-boat. He kept up a lively correspondence with von Forstner during the war, providing the boat with several ornate gifts, including a bronze shield of the city of Karlsruhe that was immediately adopted as *U-402*'s unique symbol. (Stadtarchiv Karlsruhe 8/Alben 5/350)

Christmas 1940'. Von Forstner did emulate many of his friend's tactical principles during later convoy battles, except for one. He typically expended two to three torpedoes per Allied vessel, compared to Kretschmer's one, though this could be explained by the series of technical malfunctions encountered early on with his torpedo tubes, and targeting computer. Firing multiple 'eels', as they were known to the crew, offered an increased chance of success.

Although over 1,400 U-boat commanders served during the war, just 33 (2 per cent) accounted for approximately 30 per cent of Allied shipping sunk. A high portion of these sinkings occurred early in the war, by officers who entered service before 1935. Most of these record performances were made in late 1940 during what was called by German propaganda the first 'Happy Time'. Britain was standing alone, the convoy system was still in its infancy, there was a lack of escorts, no surface radar and limited air support. What makes the achievement of von Forstner particularly noteworthy is that out of his total of eighteen Allied vessels sunk or damaged, all but four occurred during the heavy convoy battles of 1942 and early 1943. This was a far more difficult period for U-boats than his contemporaries experienced in 1939 and 1940. Von Forstner demonstrated that a single U-boat commander's skill and tenacity could overcome the advantages of Allied communication intelligence and technology. At least for a time.

The friendship between von Forstner and Kretschmer had been strengthened by the end of the patrol. Von Forstner invited his friend to his upcoming wedding scheduled to take place in the spring of 1941, which Kretschmer accepted. However, fate intervened as *U-99* was scuttled and Kretschmer captured during its next war patrol on 17 March 1941 after being depth-charged by HMS *Walker* (D 27) under the command of Captain Donald Macintyre, the future highest-scoring U-boat killer in the Royal Navy. Von Forstner and Macintyre themselves would meet in the battle of Convoy SC-129.

Von Forstner returned to Kiel where he was initially assigned the Type IIC training boat *U-59* from November 1940 to 16 April 1941. He was ordered to take command of his first operational U-boat, *U-402*, late in its construction. One of the first decisions he made was to find a city to sponsor and christen his U-boat. In early 1941 the Patenschaftsprogramm or 'sponsorship' programme was still very popular. It linked a German city with a U-boat. The city organised gifts and holidays for the crew. Von Forstner quickly contacted the Mayor of Karlsruhe, Oberbürgermeister Dr Oskar Hüssy, a city long associated with his family, in a letter dated 3 May:

Dear Sir,

The number of U-boats currently under construction is well above the number of boats that were constructed during the World War and survived the enemy. Therefore, it is no longer possible to have U-boats sponsored with the same World War number as their original sponsors/patron city, thereby continuing the old traditional relationships, but rather forming new ones.

I am therefore writing you with a very great request, to wit, that the city of Karlsruhe assume sponsorship of a U-boat currently under construction at the Danzig Shipyard. You will certainly understand why the selection of sponsorship fell to Karlsruhe.

My father was the last commander of the 1st Battalion, 109th Baden Guard Grenadier Regiment. Because none of his four sons joined the current 109th Infantry Regiment, it is clear that I am attempting to maintain and deepen the relationship with Karlsruhe, where I also spent 8 years of my childhood.

Dr Hüssy immediately agreed to sponsor the U-boat in a letter von Forstner received five days later. Von Forstner quickly penned a response on the 15th, the day after the final acceptance run was completed, to confirm the details while he conducted the final acceptance cruise with *U-402*. 'Dear Sir,' he began, 'first, I would like to express my very particular thanks for your assurance that the Kreis Karlsruhe is prepared to assume sponsorship of my U-boat.' 'After discussion with my crew,' von Forstner wrote, 'I would be very glad for a gift that will continually remind us of our sponsoring city, a coat of arms or a small picture that can be put in the living quarters.' He also asked for representatives to be present during the boat's commissioning, and reminded the Mayor that due to security concerns, he could not reveal his boat's number. He concluded 'From my crew, I give you and your city hearty greetings, to which I add my own.'

In the short time *U-402* was under his command, von Forstner brought his boat and crew successfully through final construction trials and acceptance into the Kriegsmarine. As he stood there on the back of the conning tower listening to the final proclamations, his new crew of over fifty men stood at attention, just below on the aft deck. Von Forstner knew that forging them into a team that could function under the pressure of the battle and the ocean's depths was his next task.

The crew stands at attention as the officers salute von Forstner from the deck of U-402 during the commissioning ceremony on 21 May 1941. Likely standing in the centre front row is 1st Watch Officer Oberleutnant zur See Adolf-Wilhelm Freiherr von Hammerstein-Equord. To the left is Leitender Ingenieur (Chief Engineer) Oberleutnant Mayer. Likely standing to the right is 2nd Watch Officer Leutnant zur See Otto Hübschen. Note that several other officers came with previous U-boat experience as denoted by their Iron Cross service ribbons usually awarded after several U-boat patrols.
(Friebolin collection)

The Crew

Among the crew standing on the aft deck that morning were two young men – boys really – Walter Friebolin and Herbert Schwuchow. They were typical of many of the new U-boat recruits, drafted primarily from northern and central Germany.[5]

Flotilla Weddigen, named after the First World War U-boat ace Kapitänleutnant Otto Weddigen, was formed in 1935 under the command of then Fregattenkapitän Karl Dönitz, assisted by Fregattenkapitän Leitender Ingenieur (LI) (Chief Engineer Second Class) Otto Thedsen. They established the new training cycle for all U-boat crews with a focus on anti-convoy operations. After the

Walter Friebolin is pictured to the left upon assignment to Kriegsmarine boot camp Schiffsstammabteilung 11 located in Stralsund, September 1940. He spent a full month there before advancing to his next training course.
(Friebolin collection)

Table 1. Walter Friebolin's Training

From	To	Command	Location	Purpose
1 Sep 1940	28 Sep 1940	11.Schiffsstammabteilung	Stralsund	Seamanship and infantry training
29 Sep 1940	10 Oct 1940	1.Unterseebootslehrdivision (ULD)	Pilau	Basic U-boat training
11 Oct 1940	9 Nov 1940	8.(leichte Flak) Lehr Kompanie	Misdroy	Anti-aircraft weapons training
10 Nov 1940	20 Dec 1940	Unterseebootsabwehrschule (UAS)	Gotenhafen	Underwater listening course
21 Dec 1940	28 Mar 1941	1.Unterseebootslehrdivision (ULD)	Pilau	Basic U-boat training
29 Mar 1941	6 Apr 1941	2.Unterseebootsausbildungsabteilung (UAA)	Neustadt	Additional training
7 Apr 1941	21 May 1941	Baubelehrung Kompanie Danziger Werft	Danzig	Pre-commissioning familiarisation

outbreak of war and the growing threat of air attack and mines, all crew training shifted into the Baltic. In Pillau the 1.Unterseebootslehrdivision (ULD) was established along with the 2.Unterseebootslehrdivision in Gotenhafen. Wartime pressures later reduced the training regime to three months, and toward the end of the war to only eight weeks.

Walter was born in Wössingen, just outside the city of Karlsruhe on 16 September 1921. He was 19 years old when he began his military service. Given his close association with the sponsoring city, he clearly stood out to von Forstner who ensured that Karlsruhe's mayor knew one of its own was among the crew. Walter joined the navy in August 1940 and was immediately assigned to the 11.Schiffsstammabteilung (seamanship and infantry training battalion) in Stralsund for four weeks. His Wehrpass (military service record booklet) provides an excellent view of the training regime for new recruits at this stage of the war.

While in Pillau, Walter and his fellow recruits were berthed on the cruise ship SS *Robert Ley* that had been taken over by the Kriegsmarine and assigned to the 1.ULD. At the end of March his training cadre graduated and departed to their initial assignments. Walter was then sent to the U-boat Construction Battalion at Danziger Werft and assigned to *U-402*.

Friebolin is pictured in his cabin on board the *Robert Ley* writing a letter to his girlfriend. This picture was taken around Christmas 1940. On the wall is a picture of a Type II U-boat, as well as several capital ships. Two trainees were assigned per cabin. A pair of bunk beds were on the opposite wall to the right of the table. Friebolin spent three months on the *Robert Ley* before moving on to crew *U-402*. (Friebolin collection)

After six more weeks of training Friebolin was assigned to Unterseebootsabwehrschule (U-boat School) on 10 November 1940 in Gotenhafen for six more weeks. He is pictured holding a life preserver. (Friebolin collection)

Friebolin and his class of cadets were assigned to the 1.Unterseebootslehrdivision (1.ULD – 1st Submarine Training Division) in Pillau at the end of December 1940. They were billeted on board the Kraft Durch Freude (Strength Through Joy) cruise ship *Robert Ley*. The ship was commissioned by the Nazi organisation the German Labour Front in March 1939. She was named after the Nazi politician Robert Ley who oversaw the German Labour Front from 1933 to 1945. She was initially used as a holiday ship for German workers, then she was taken over by the Kriegsmarine and employed first as a hospital ship, then as living quarters for trainees. She was a sister ship of the *Wilhelm Gustloff*. (Friebolin collection)

Trainee inspection on the promenade deck of the *Robert Ley*, winter 1940/41. That winter was particularly cold in the Baltic, and the port of Pillau froze over and prevented U-boat training unless an icebreaker was utilised. (Friebolin collection)

A Type II U-boat is pictured docked next to the SS *Kamerun*, a U-boat tender in the port of Pillau. During U-boat training crews were temporarily berthed on these tenders. This tender was built by Bremer Vulkan Schiffbau & Maschinenfabrik, in Bremen (yard no 753) and launched on 17 May 1938. She was originally delivered to Woermann Linie AG, Hamburg in November that year, then requisitioned by the Kriegsmarine and converted to a repair ship (Werkstattschiff 2). By 1940 she was in service as a repair ship at Pillau, then in 1941 she was transferred to Norway as repair ship for U-boats until the end of the war. (Friebolin collection)

A Type II U-boat returning to dock in Pillau after a training exercise, as viewed by Friebolin from the porthole of his cabin on board the *Robert Ley*, spring 1941. The winter ice was gone, the weather was getting warmer, and Friebolin and his comrades could look forward to graduation and assignment to their first U-boat. (Friebolin collection)

Herbert Schwuchow was born in the provincial town of Schlawe, Pomerania near the Baltic coast on 20 February 1919. He came from a large family, the only son among six daughters. Upon completion of his Gymnasium schooling, Herbert began his training to be a professional butcher. His professional training was interrupted by the war, and he was drafted into the Kriegsmarine at the age of 20. He was assigned to the 10.Schiffsstammabteilung located in Bremerhaven on 1 April 1940, some five months prior

Herbert Schwuchow pictured in Schlawe, Pomerania, during his training as a butcher in the spring of 1940 before he was drafted into the Kriegsmarine. His family had no history of military service. His father was a retired employee of the German railways. (Author's collection)

Schwuchow's enlistment photo as a Gefreiter (Seaman) taken in late 1940. Schwuchow was assigned to the 10.Schiffsstammabteilung located in Bremerhaven for his boot camp. His onward training assignments prior to U-402 are unknown as his Wehrpass was confiscated by the British at the end of the war. (Author's collection)

Pictured are members of *U-402*'s Bauconstruction-Kompanie in Danziger Werft leaning against the 88mm deck gun. *U-402* was the second U-boat built by this shipyard. The construction battalion worked alongside the crew during a four- to six-week period of workups to ensure the crew was familiar with the boat's technical operation and any construction-related issues were resolved. The captain could also request modifications. Both Friebolin and Schwuchow arrived from different training units to join the crew. The two men on the left appear to be wearing the shoulder boards of Bootsmann (Petty Officers 1st Class) as denoted by the diamond at the bottom. (Friebolin collection)

to Friebolin. Herbert thought that he would serve on board one of the large capital ships like the *Scharnhorst* or *Gneisenau* and he was surprised he was selected for U-boat service. He recalled his training was hard, but not without moments of levity, often at others' expense typical of all military service. In one such situation, his instructors asked who knew how to swim, and directed those who raised their hands in the affirmative to jump into the pool and demonstrate their skill. One of the recruits apparently lied and started to struggle in the water. The instructor, with the clear intent of making an example of this recruit, walked over to the edge of the pool and yelled at the 'flailing chicken' in the water 'You swim quite well!' Herbert went on to receive specialised training in supply and cooking under the Verwaltungs career service. Due in part to this training and his prior professional schooling as a butcher, he became the main cook while he served on *U-402*.

Herbert and Walter arrived at the construction company in Danzig in April 1941 where they were assigned to *U-402*. Early in a boat's construction the commander, chief engineer and 1st watch officer spent some six weeks familiarising themselves with their U-boat and its builders, making adjustments as the boat was completed. The crew followed in construction battalions that were assigned to individual U-boats before their build was completed. This gave the crews time to familiarise themselves with the technical characteristics of the U-boat and to make alterations at the direction of their captain.

The bow of *U-402* during what may be its final check-out cruise before its commissioning. Schwuchow is on the left and Friebolin stands in the centre. How well the two men became friends is not known. All three men are wearing their grey leather foul weather jackets, gloves and overseas caps. The German slang for their leathers was 'U-Boot Päckchen'. They were also issued in brown and black. (Friebolin collection)

Each of the men took individual pictures during this check-out cruise. In this picture Schwuchow is now at the stern of *U-402* holding onto the removable deck safety line. Note the raised aft bollards. (Friebolin collection)

The Boat

U-402 was a Type VIIC. It was ordered on 23 September 1939 and its keel laid on 22 April 1940 at Danziger Werft AG, in Danzig (werk 103). It was launched on 28 December 1940. This U-boat type was the most produced during the war, with over 560 being commissioned between 1938 and 1944.

The crew had the opportunity to get to know one another over the last six months of final construction, training and drills. After the official ceremony was over, the crew, von Forstner and his new wife had an opportunity to celebrate the achievement before *U-402* completed its workup in the Baltic.

First, *U-402* was assigned to the UBoot-Abnahme-Kommando (UAK – U-boat Test Commission). During this period the U-boat conducted a number of pressure tests and final installation of torpedo firing controls. Next, came assignment to UBoot-Abnahmegruppe (UAG – Technical Trials Commission) in Gotenhafen, where all equipment and control installations were evaluated during exercises to ensure they were in proper working order. Any issues saw the boat

Table 2. Type VIIC Characteristics

Displacement (tons):	769 (sf)	871 (sm)	1070 (total)
Length (m):	66.5 (oa)	50.5 (ph)	
Beam (m):	6.2 (oa)	4.7 (ph)	
Draught (m):	4.74		
Height (m):	9.6		
Power (hp):	3,200 (sf)	750 (sm)	
Speed: (knots)	17.7 (sf)	7.6 (sm)	
Range: (miles/knots)	8,500/10 (sf)	80/4 (sm)	
Torpedoes:	14	4 bow/1 stern tubes	
Deck Gun:	88mm/35	220 rounds	
AA Gun:	1 x 20mm C30		
Crew:	44–52 men		
Max depth:	ca. 220m (722ft)		

(sm = submerged; sf = surfaced; ph = pressure hull; oa = overall; hp = horsepower)

Chief Engineer Meyer had a vital role during the final checkout cruises. He was in charge of the diesel engines and electric motors, as well as the rest of *U-402*'s technical operation. (Friebolin collection)

The commissioning delegation for *U-402* standing in front of the Danziger Werft. *U-402* is to the right, out of the picture. The building stands there today, a witness to the many U-boats built and commissioned at the facility during the war. The group included family members of the crew, as well as representatives from the boat's sponsoring city of Karlsruhe. Von Forstner is pictured standing second from the right, among the five officers. (Friebolin collection)

sent back to Danzig to have defects fixed. After the technical trials, *U-402* was assigned to a training flotilla for three weeks where navigation was practised, often with trips to the island of Bronholm, and even up to Oslo, in the now occupied Norway. Combat training followed with the Ausbildungsgruppe für Front U-Boote (Combat Training Group), also known as AGRU Front, for two more weeks. Deck gun and torpedo firing practice and anti-convoy manoeuvres were all conducted under the eyes of experienced U-boat officers. Finally, came torpedo loading under the Torpedoversuchsanstalt (TVA – Torpedo Test Section) before it arrived in Kiel for final certification.

The war had changed by the time *U-402* departed Danzig in the late summer and arrived in Kiel during September in preparation for its first patrol. At the time of *U-402*'s commissioning only Britain stood against Germany. Now the Soviet Union had been invaded, and the Heer and Luftwaffe were advancing far into the interior of Russia. Herbert recalled that there was a great deal of anxiety among the crew about what the war's expansion to the east meant for Germany.

Mail was significantly delayed during *U-402*'s final months of training. A package from the Mayor of Karlsruhe finally arrived in early September, much to von Forstner's surprise. In the package was a bronze shield of Karlsruhe's coat of arms bearing the word '*Fidelitas*'. Von Forstner dispatched a letter on 16 September to Dr Hüssy. Von Forstner responded, 'Mr. Mayor, I would like to express my respectful thanks, in the name of the crew as well, for

The entire crew of *U-402* at the time of the boat's commissioning on 21 May 1941. Bottom row left-to-right: (5) unknown Bootsmann who wears the ribbon of the Iron Cross 2nd Class and the Spanish Cross denoting his service for at least three months of service in Spain during the Spanish Civil War in a non-combatant role, (7) possibly Obermaschinist Fischer who wears the Iron Cross 2nd Class, (9) possibly Oberleutnant zur See von Hammerstein-Equord (with rank of Leutnant), (10) Kapitänleutnant von Forstner, (11) Oberleutnant Ing Meyer-Oswald who wears the Iron Cross 2nd Class ribbon, (12) possibly IIWO Leutnant Hübschen who wears the Kriegsmarine Destroyer Badge, (16) Obersteuermann (Navigator) Görtz who appears to wear the Kriegsmarine Battleship and Cruiser Badge, (17) Gefreiter Schwuchow. Top row, left-to-right (5) Matrose Friebolin. The crew looks young in this photo, but they quickly aged under the stress of combat over the next two years. (Friebolin collection)

sending this beautiful coat of arms. It greatly exceeded our expectations, and maybe it works so well because of the clearly recognisable shape in bronze without any paint.' He concluded, 'On the outside on the [conning] tower, we have affixed the coat of arms painted onto a placard. Because the boats are so similar to each other, it has turned out to be very practical to put on some sort of sign, with the coat of arms of sponsoring cities, being accepted particularly willingly.' The shield of Karlsruhe was now adopted by *U-402* as its unique identification. The yellow letters '*Fidelitas*' emblazoned diagonally across the red background optimized von Forstner's professionalism, as well as devotion to his U-boat and crew, to the end.

At the time of commissioning *U-402* adopted the seal of Karlsruhe after receiving a bronze plaque of the city's shield from Mayor Dr Oskar Hüssy. The shield bore the word '*Fidelitas*' – Fidelity – a word that came to embody the spirit of camaraderie that von Forstner established through his professionalism, dedication and genuine love for his crew. (Stadtarchiv Karlsruhe 8/PBS X 570)

The shield, as painted on *U-402*'s conning tower. The shield was believed to later be adorned with two red pompoms that represented those knitted by von Forstner's wife for each crew member to wear upon their service caps as a show of esprit de corps after their highly successful sixth war patrol. This gave the crew and boat some notoriety in port, and *U-402* became known affectionately by the crew as the 'Pompom Boat'. (Author's collection)

Commissioning meant the beginning of training for *U-402* and its crew. Training lasted from May 1941 through October. Von Forstner owned what might be an Agfa Movex 8mm movie camera. This was the first movie camera to use cartridge film, circa 1937. He took great pride in filming the boat's training, and even the first war patrol. The films may still exist, though the author was not able to track down the descendants of Annamarie, who presumably still have them. Note that von Forstner is wearing his black service cap. He stopped wearing this cap once *U-402* departed for its first war patrol. (Friebolin collection)

In early autumn, Dönitz visited Kiel where the crew of *U-402* saw their senior commander in person. Herbert recalled the day vividly, and especially how Dönitz commanded great respect from the crewmen. Herbert did not come from a family with a history of military service. He had little desire to join the military before the outbreak of the war. Nonetheless, he held Dönitz in high regard. Long after the war, he could still recall his commanding presence that day.

U-402 was finally ready to depart Kiel on 26 October, where it was stationed for the last four weeks undergoing final training and preparations as part of the 5th U-Flotilla under the command of Kapitänleutnant Karl-Heinz Moehle. It was clear at the final departure that mechanical problems continued to plague *U-402* as highlighted in their certification titled 'Again, and Again!'. This was a reference to how *U-402* continued to miss its departure deadlines due to technical issues that continued throughout its service history.

Above: A close-up of the *Venus* in Allied camouflage. 'Dazzle' camouflage was originally employed by the Royal Navy in the First World War and continued into the Second. The intention was to obscure the course of the vessel as seen through a U-boat periscope due to the stark contours that broke up the vessel's shape. (Friebolin collection)

Above: The most critical training was practicing torpedo firing in the Baltic. *U-402* lines up for a shot on the target ship SS *Venus*. She was a Norwegian-built vessel requisitioned by the Kriegsmarine after the invasion of Norway in 1940. She was modified in Rostock during the late spring 1941 to be used by the 26th U-Flotilla in Pillau as a target vessel. (Friebolin collection)

Right: Von Forstner is pictured on the forward deck of *U-402* filming torpedo practice. Behind him is the torpedo loader cradle that was stored below deck and used to move the above deck torpedo, stored in the bow, into the forward torpedo room. To the left is the 88mm deck gun. The hatch to the left is the watertight 88mm ammunition storage container. The ceramic insulators to the right were attached to the U-boat's radio aerial wires to reduce static discharge. The thin wire seen running back toward the conning tower was connected to the radio transmitter. The forward radio aerial lines on U-boats that ran to the bow were used for transmitting and those that ran to the stern were used for receiving. (Friebolin collection)

Finally, the 'chains' to port were broken and off it went to sea. Just days before the boat departed for its first patrol, a last package arrived from Karlsruhe. It was a large leather-bound U-boat 'Tradition Book' where the captain could document the boat's experiences during the war.

Below: The following four photographs show the practice removal of the above-deck torpedo in preparation for transfer to the forward torpedo room. It is believed these photos were taken during training and not during a war patrol. The watch is posted for possible air attack during the transfer. The wooden deck is pulled back to expose the torpedo housing container which was raised by the turn wheel just behind the crewman pictured in the foreground. The torpedo loading cradle is being assembled. (Friebolin collection)

Right above: The torpedo loading cradle is now assembled and the pulley is being fitted to retrieve the torpedo. *U-402*'s shield is clearly evident on the conning tower. The crewman on watch, second from the left on the conning tower, may possibly be Schwuchow. (Friebolin collection)

Right middle: The pulley assembly is now mounted to the conning tower and the torpedo is pulled back out of storage. The bands are being secured around the torpedo before lowering it into the bow compartment where it can be loaded into a torpedo tube or stored below the compartment's decking. (Friebolin collection)

The bands are secure and the torpedo is now being positioned to be lowered into the forward torpedo room. The above-deck storage container is being cranked back down into position below the deck. This was a harrowing experience during heavy swells and while under the threat of enemy air attack. (Friebolin collection)

Right: U-boat training also included practice runs from the Baltic to Norway after it was occupied in 1940. *U-402* (on the left) is pictured tied up in Oslo harbour. Directly in front of *U-402* and the second U-boat is the Oslo Town Hall, in the summer of 1941. While in Oslo the crew had an opportunity for sightseeing in the city and surrounding areas. For many of the crew, this was their first time outside of Germany. Curious Norwegians walk past to observe the 'visitors'. (Friebolin collection)

Middle: The crew is pictured taking a meal on the bow of *U-402*. Herbert probably prepared the food being enjoyed by the crew. (Friebolin collection)

Below: A close-up of the meal, showing the variety of china plates and utensils stored on board a typical U-boat. (Friebolin collection)

Levity was an excellent team builder and relief from the stress of training. The crew uses its left-over food crates to build a makeshift 'U-boat'. (Friebolin collection)

Clearly things do not go to well as their comrade ended up in Oslo harbour! (Friebolin collection)

Final readiness certification before U-402's first war patrol took place at Deutsche Werke Kiel under the authority of the 5th U-Flotilla. Von Forstner, now in his white overseas service cap, is preparing U-402 for its check-out cruise. Several other U-boats are tied up along the wharf. U-402 suffered from a series of continuing technical problems that caused it to return to Kiel several times, before it was granted its final certification. (Friebolin collection)

The following two pictures show the magnification power of *U-402*'s search periscope employed in Kiel harbour against a friendly Type VIIC. (Friebolin collection)

The other German submarine is not known for certain, but could possibly be *U-434*, which departed with *U-402* on its first patrol in October. It all depends on the exact date of the photo, which is unfortunately unknown. (Friebolin collection)

U-402's certification certificate reads: 'Again and Again! From 11 October to 26 October 1941. Again and again, but now the last time. Again and again to the shipyard, it was fate. Once again clear to go, and then back from the East, that can disrupt even the calmest nerves. The deadlines are always postponed, always something with the rudder, the tanks and the vessel. But now the time has passed; we want to get out of here and with war luck, again and again. Thanks to the 5th U-boat Flotilla for standing by us in the final struggle to free ourselves from the shipyard.' (Deutsches U-Boot Museum)

Now that *U-402* was certified to join the 3rd U-Flotilla based in France, a final parting celebration occurred in Kiel on board a medium-sized Kriegsmarine vessel, possibly a tender. It was October 1941, and von Forstner's wife, Annamarie, arrived in Kiel for the celebration. They were married in the spring, just before *U-402*'s commissioning. Von Forstner introduces Anamarie to his new 1st Watch Officer, whose name is believed to be Oberleutnant Kiehn. He replaced IWO Oberleutnant zur See von Hammerstein-Equord who departed this month to become IWO on board *U-71*, then later took command of the training boat *U-149*. He later served on the staff of the 14th U-Flotilla in Norway until the end of the war. (Friebolin collection)

Some of the crew surround von Forstner and his wife for this informal celebratory photograph. At the top of the photo with his arm resting over the yardarm is my grandfather Herbert, and to his left (two faces to the right) is Friebolin. (Friebolin collection)

Von Forstner, his wife and the crew of *U-402* in a more formal photograph. Herbert is at the bottom right, sitting in front of von Forstner and the new 1st Watch Officer. Friebolin is directly behind von Forstner. Behind them is the Hamburg-American liner SS *New York*. She was built by Blohm & Voss in 1927 and served as a transatlantic liner until 1939. In 1940 she was commandeered by the Kriegsmarine and used as an accommodation ship for U-boat crews in Kiel. The crew of *U-402* was housed on board her during the U-boat's time in the harbour. The *New York* was bombed and burned out in an air raid on 3 April 1945. She was later towed to England and scrapped. (Friebolin collection)

A final departing gift from Karlsruhe's Mayor was a large leather-bound logbook that could be used by von Forstner to record the history of *U-402*'s patrols. It came in a protective slip case. (Stadtarchiv Karlsruhe 1/H-Reg 902)

The logbook is pictured open to reveal the shield of Karlsruhe and Dr Hüssy's signature. It is dated 15 August 1941, but due to a delay in mail delivery, it only arrived in Kiel in late September. (Stadtarchiv Karlsruhe 1/H-Reg 902)

Icebergs and Narwhals

U-402 pulled away from the Tirpitz Mole in Kiel where it was moored next to the former passenger liner SS *Hamburg* that served as its accommodation ship during the past few weeks. It passed the U-boat Memorial at Möltenort, originally erected in 1930 to the fallen U-boat crews of the Great War, followed by the Marine-Ehrenmal in Laboe dedicated to the loss of German naval crews of the Kaiserliche Marine. These were sombre reminders of the past sacrifices made by the fathers and grandfathers of the men of Dönitz's U-boat fleet who now sailed forth into a new war.

U-402 departed Kiel with *U-434* commanded by Korvettenkapitän Wolfgang Heyda. Both boats were escorted by

U-402 finally departed for its first war patrol on 26 October 1941. This patrol took it out into the North Atlantic, south of Iceland, where it looked for convoys, then to France where it arrived in St Nazaire on 9 December 1941. The crew's enthusiasm, seen in the following pictures, is contagious. This picture shows *U-402*'s bow cutting through relatively calm water during its first patrol. (Friebolin collection)

Von Forstner looking through a pair of standard 7x50 Carl Zeiss U-boat binoculars. There were many different models of binoculars used by the crew. (Friebolin collection)

1st Watch Officer Oberleutnant Kiehn is pictured on the conning tower, and in good spirits, enjoying the sea air. (Friebolin collection)

2nd Watch Officer Hübschen, also enjoying the sea breeze on the conning tower. (Friebolin collection)

Vorpostenboot (Flak boats) or VP-boats from the 16th Vp_Flotilla. Vorpostenboot were equipped with anti-aircraft guns to fight off any surprise air attacks before the U-boats could reach deeper water. The passage to Norway was not without problems as while anchored at Frederikshavn, Denmark before proceeding across the Skagerrak to Norway, the anchor chain became stuck in the down

Pictured is Friebolin, on watch toward the end of the patrol. Behind him it appears the DF Loop is raised. (Friebolin collection)

Unidentified crew on watch in the North Atlantic. The UZO (Unterseeboots Ziel Ortungsgerät – submarine target sight mount) is pictured in the centre. To the left is the attack periscope housing. (Friebolin collection)

Unidentified crewman wearing the characteristic foul-weather U-boat leather jacket, brown-tinted goggles for daytime vision, and a variant of the 7x50 Carl Zeiss binoculars. (Friebolin collection)

position. During work on the deck crewman Neidemann fell overboard while securing a bowline, but was immediately rescued. Some twelve hours later the problem was fixed by the Chief Engineer Oberleutnant Ing. Meyer and Obermaschinst Fischer who both continued to solve technical problems on board *U-402* throughout its service career.

U-402 arrived at Arendal, Norway the morning of 29 October and waited for an escort to return that previously departed with *U-434*. However, von Forstner, impatient with waiting, sent a message to Befehlshaber der Sicherungs der Ostsee (BSO) Admiral Westküste that he would continue on to Kristiansand on his own. Both U-boats were assigned reconnaissance duty. This was the last time von Forstner saw *U-434*, as it was scuttled during the battle with Convoy HG-76 off Gibraltar on 18 December after suffering damage from depth charges.

From Kristiansand *U-402* headed north-west to Egersund on the 30th, and put to sea with two Me 109 fighters as escort on the 31st. Finally, von Forstner and the crew proceeded out to sea and into the war on their first patrol. They passed over the 'Rosengarten' (rose garden) between the Faroe and Shetland Islands, dodging floating mines placed there by the Royal Navy.

Mechanical troubles plagued *U-402*. The Junkers compressor failed on 2 November. The trim pump failed to pump at great depths on the 4th. It was removed, repaired, and re-installed after

Two photos that show Oberleutnant Kiehn aloft on the raised search periscope, high above the conning tower, in order to gain an advantage of several hundred metres over the horizon to spot Allied vessels. Given that the 1st Watch Officer was on the smaller side, his stature made him a perfect candidate for this particular role. (Friebolin collection)

30 hours of work. However, it continued to cause problems for the rest of the patrol. The compressor was a vital component of the U-boat. It generated air for the storage tanks, started the diesels, forced air into the buoyancy tanks and maintained trim. On the 6th, the starboard diesel was out of service because the supercharger could not be disengaged. In this case, the failure was due to improper work at the shipyard as the pivot pins to disengage the supercharger clutch were not properly secured.

During these days the crew drilled in crash diving and loading torpedoes almost daily. These were skills von Forstner knew to be critical based on his cruise with Kretschmer. Herbert recalled his time on watch during the early days of the patrol when the boat was operating in heavy seas and snow squalls south of Iceland. The monotony of watch duty in rough weather was interrupted by the sight of icebergs and a pod of narwhals in the open ocean. This was the first time Herbert saw whales, and this brief interlude of the ocean's beauty made the first of many lasting impressions on him. *U-402*, however, was at war and Herbert, like all the men who rotated on watch, had to keep a sharp eye out for the enemy, whether on the churning sea or in the grey burgeoning sky.

On the morning of the 11th von Forstner received his first set of orders from BdU since departing Norway. They read in part: 'At all costs undetected reconnaissance in these areas. Attack free only against troopships and warships from cruiser upwards. Absolute

Von Forstner is filming with his 8mm camera. These films were later shown during a visit to Karlsruhe in autumn 1942. (Friebolin collection)

radio silence. Messages are to be sent only on demand.' On the 13th the reconnaissance was cancelled. BdU ordered *U-332* and *U-402* to a new operational area noting that 'previous orders invalid . . .'.

What no one on board the U-boat knew was that on this first

U-402's first war patrol took place during the start of Germany's advent season that begins in late November. The inside of the U-boat was decorated accordingly. Here is a wreath with the Star of David in its centre hanging in the area of the captain's cabin. (Friebolin collection)

A Christmas lantern and what appears to be an angel is also hung nearby. (Friebolin collection)

These two photos show members of the crew eating a meal in the forward torpedo room that was likely prepared by my grandfather. Friebolin is pictured centre left in the second photo. (Friebolin collection)

patrol *U-402* was originally assigned reconnaissance in preparation for a 'special operation' of Marine-Gruppe 'Nord. The 'special operation' was the planned breakout of the 'pocket battleship' *Admiral Scheer* from her base in Swinemünde into the Atlantic to conduct commerce raiding. This fact was revealed to the author in a 1994 letter from Professor Dr Jürgen Rohwer. However, this operation was cancelled on 13 November and *U-402* continued with its patrol. Dönitz was not thrilled with having to support this operation and noted in the BdU war diary that 'the U-boat arm has now been spared a considerable dissipation of its strength over an indefinite period'.

For the next month *U-402* found itself patrolling in the middle of the North Atlantic, west of Ireland. After its change of orders, along with *U-332*, both boats extended the line 'Stoertebecker' then operating against Convoy ONS-33. However, *U-402* encountered no Allied merchants. Two weeks later on 26 November, the boat was ordered south along with *U-69* and *U-201* to wait for Convoy OG-79 that the Kriegsmarine

A likely unauthorised photo of the captain's charts in his cabin! These documents were sensitive, but there was no space on a U-boat that was considered private. (Friebolin collection)

December 6th was 2nd Watch Officer Hübschen's birthday. It appears that the crew prepared him a package in celebration, while *U-402* began it return to St Nazaire. (Friebolin collection)

In the package was some sort of plant or flower, likely artificial, that required some assembly. (Friebolin collection

cryptological service, known as Beobachtungsdienst (B-Dienst), determined was inbound to the Mediterranean with 'important supplies'. This order was given despite the knowledge that these U-boats were already low on fuel. After searching for the convoy without success, von Forstner began his transit to the Bay of Biscay on 4 December and was assigned St Nazaire as his home port.

The cryptological war between the Kriegsmarine and the British intelligence services was in full swing. While B-Dienst detected the routing of both convoys, the U-boat line failed to locate them. In August 1942 British intelligence broke the Kriegsmarine three-rotor Enigma cipher and, with some delays, began regularly reading German wireless communications between BdU and U-boats. The Admiralty named this intelligence source 'Dolphin' and the intercepts it generated 'Ultra'. Convoys could now be re-routed around waiting U-boat lines established by Dönitz as required.

U-boat operations shifted to French ports where massive pens were constructed. Operations from these bases allowed the Type VIICs extended operational ranges into the Atlantic and beyond. There was danger here also as the Bay of Biscay soon became a choke point where RAF Coastal Command aircraft focused their resources to find and sink U-boats transiting to and from their pens. On 7 December von Forstner submerged the U-boat for daylight passage and began its return voyage, only proceeding on the surface at night. *U-402* finally pulled into the St Nazaire lock on the morning of the 12th, its six-week patrol completed.

On *U-402*'s first patrol appears to have been a young war correspondent who came equipped with his own camera and notebook (not seen in this picture). Here he poses with the 1st Watch Officer Oberleutnant Kiehn. (Friebolin collection)

This first patrol, while uneventful, was important for von Forstner to establish his command, forge the crew into an effective team, and identify remaining construction-related problems with his U-boat. This became all the more important for von Forstner as the war expanded yet again. On 7 December 1941 the Japanese attacked the US naval base at Pearl Harbor, and four days later Hitler declared war on the United States. The declaration of war shocked many of the crew to include Herbert, who did not understand why they were at now at war with America. However, the US Navy was taking an increasingly active role in escorting convoys mid-way into the Atlantic crossing, as noted by the accidental sinking of the destroyer USS *Reuben James* by Kapitänleutnant Erich Topp on 31 October, during a battle with Convoy HX-156 south of Iceland. Now based in France, *U-402* was ready to start forays into the Atlantic and join in the ongoing battle. Over the course of the next four weeks the boat was overhauled and made ready for its next patrol.

A member of the crew shares a moment of levity during the patrol. The first war patrol of *U-402* was uneventful. No Allied merchant ships were spotted, no aircraft or surface escorts encountered. It was an excellent opportunity to train the crew and work out any final maintenance issues with the U-boat. However, on 7 December 1941 the Japanese attacked Pearl Harbor. Two days after *U-402* arrived in St Nazaire, Germany declared war on the United States, and the Battle of the Atlantic was about to become more difficult. (Friebolin collection)

CHAPTER 2

On Holiday

This is a war, not a holiday trip
Baron Siegfried Freiherr von Forstner in a letter to his wife, 1942

During the autumn of 1941 most U-boat successes were achieved against the north-south convoy route transiting the Mediterranean and North Africa, not the east-west crossing of the North Atlantic. The reason was the intelligence produced through Ultra. The Admiralty also began passing some of this 'special intelligence' to the US Navy, which helped inform their early strategic planning for the North Atlantic and alerted them to the departure of U-boats to the East Coast under the codename Operation 'Paukenschlag' ('Drumbeat') in early 1942.

Simultaneously, German naval intelligence on Allied convoys dried up. This was due in part to the introduction of joint US-Anglo Cypher No 3 that complicated B-Dienst efforts to read merchant-ship communications and identify convoy routing. By December 1941 the U-boat war in the North Atlantic came to a halt. Efforts were made to employ Luftwaffe long-range Focke-Wulf Fw 200 Condor aircraft in a reconnaissance role to locate convoys that U-boat spotters did not. This had some success, but a lack of coordination between the two German services doomed the effort.

For nearly three-quarters of the year no convoy battle occurred north of the Azores. This was arguably the most critical phase in the Battle of the Atlantic as Great Britain and the Royal Navy stood alone against the threat of the U-boat. An estimated 1.5 million to 2 million tons of merchant shipping losses were avoided during this phase of the battle. BdU grew concerned as early as May that the British knew where U-boats were deployed. Evidence mounted that they were re-routing convoys accordingly. By July the north-west Atlantic operational area was temporarily abandoned by BdU. Dönitz needed to know, and he directed his own intelligence assets to learn what they could about Allied intelligence capabilities. The conclusion drawn from that evaluation was that the Enigma cipher system was not compromised. However, out of an abundance of caution a fourth rotor was added to the encryption machine and on 1 February

1942 the intelligence enjoyed by the Admiralty through Ultra dried up. The British named this new German coding system 'Shark'.

At the same time German naval cryptologists realised that the Naval Cypher No 3 worked very similarly to the system utilised by the Royal Navy in 1939–40 and subsequently broke the code. As the game of cat and mouse between Allied and German intelligence services who sought to read the other's traffic played out, it was the lives of the merchantman and sailors alike that bore the success or failure at the end of each intelligence service's balance sheet.

Intelligence, no matter its source, cannot win a battle on its own. It may aid one side or another to varying degrees, if it is timely. Often, intelligence provides little more than a glimpse of what happened, hours, days or weeks earlier. Essentially, it is real-time history. Only when it offers future insight into an adversary's next decision does its true value manifest itself. Yet, knowing what the adversary might do next on the field of battle, or in this case the North Atlantic, does not mean that a favourable outcome is assured. It remained that tactical decisions made by the men on, above, and below the ocean, in varying weather and at all times of day, ensured the final outcome. This was certainly the case in the survival of the *Llangibby Castle*.

Chance Encounter

U-402 departed St Nazaire lock in mid-afternoon on Sunday, 11 January 1942 under a clear but cold blue sky. More food supplies than usual were packed aboard the boat as rumours grew about their destination. Among the crew were several additional 'watch officers' – new officers in training – much like von Forstner had been on board *U-99* with his former classmate and friend Kretschmer years earlier. For the majority of the crew, however,

Pictured below is probably a Sperrbrecher (pathfinder) that escorted *U-402* when it departed St Nazaire in the afternoon of 11 January 1942 in a convoy with *U-581* and two Vorpostenboot (Flak boats) for protection. The Sperrbrecher was typically a converted merchant ship with added hull armour. The purpose was to escort U-boats through friendly minefields and detonate any wayward floating mines. They were also equipped with additional flak guns. (Friebolin collection)

ON HOLIDAY

In the distance to starboard of U-402 is U-581 as they pass the south side of the island of Belle-Île-en-Mer. U-402 and U-581 met again as their fates intertwined among the warm blue waters of the Azores in the coming weeks. (Friebolin collection)

these officers were unwelcome as they took up limited space and food on board the cramped U-boat. The crew gave them the nickname of 'Kakerlaken' (cockroaches), according to Herbert.

Outside the port, U-402 formed into a convoy along with U-581 under command of the 29-year-old Kapitänleutnant Werner Pfeifer who was on his second patrol. The two outbound U-boats were escorted by two VP-Boats. Crossing the Bay of Biscay became more dangerous as the war progressed. By late afternoon both boats were released from the convoy and went off into the Atlantic on their own courses. Fate brought them back together again in the coming weeks.

U-402 was under secret orders to head to the US East Coast. Only von Forstner was aware of the boat's destination when it

On the following day, 12 January, U-402 had just passed the 200m line that marked the Bay of Biscay when another U-boat was spotted abeam to starboard. Von Forstner did not record the specific number or its captain in his logbook. It is believed that Friebolin took two photos of the U-boat as it approached, then departed going in the opposite direction. The only U-boat known to be operating on this day in the Bay of Biscay and heading east-south-east was U-564. Its commander, then Kapitänleutnant Reinhard Suhren, was moving his boat from Lorient to La Rochelle. It is possible these two pictures are of U-564, but this remains unconfirmed. (Friebolin collection)

departed. In the following days the sky grew overcast, but the seas remained relatively calm as von Forstner drilled the crew in crash dive procedures. Every opportunity was taken to reinforce skills that could save the U-boat and its crew.

During the night of the 15th the sea grew rough, with waves averaging some 30–40ft in a storm. *U-402* cruised west, below the turbulence, and approached the surface cautiously on the morning of the 16th. As the winds subsided, the seas began to calm and the sky grew clear. At around 1100hrs in the morning, von Forstner came to periscope depth for a sweep. He raised the search scope from within the control room, slowing turning it around clockwise as he checked the horizon. His sonar man gave no indication of sound contacts, so von Forstner did not expect to see anything except cresting waves on an empty sea. To his surprise, and completely by chance, a large two-stack passenger ship was spotted some 1,000m away. Incredulous, he called to the sonar operator sitting just beyond the watertight door of the control room and asked why he had reported no sound contacts. The response from the sonarman, who like many of the crew was new and lacked operational experience, replied that he 'heard something', but had identified it as a noise from the U-boat, because it was heard coming from the stern section. Either more training was needed on the apparatus, or it was somehow malfunctioning.

The order went out: 'Make tubes ready and set Action Stations!' The crew went to work. Von Forstner made another sweep and identified another similar ship. Growing anxious at the opportunity, he asked if torpedo tubes II and IV were ready. They were not. The initial steamer began to turn and manoeuvre out of range. Now the order was given to prepare a three-fan shot that included tube III. The forward torpedo room quickly confirmed that both tubes II and III were ready, but IV was not, due to a malfunction.

At 1115hrs the order was given 'Fire!' and a two-fan shot from tubes II and III whooshed from the bow. The torpedoes were standard G7e T2s and set to a depth of 3m. The steamer passed to the left of the scope at 1,200m, running at 10 knots. The stop watch ticked away . . . 60 seconds passed, then 70, then 80 . . . would a hit be scored? At 84 seconds two detonations were heard at a range of 1,260m.

As *U-402* dived into the swells it cut under after the shot and the hits were not observed through the periscope. Von Forstner ordered the boat submerged to 14m in order to prevent it from breaching the surface accidently. The periscope was barely protruding above the surface and was awash with waves, making it a difficult visual target. As von Forstner scanned the horizon, he could not see the steamer his torpedo hit, but he did see a small steamer with a curved bow come into view about 300m away. The U-boat dived to 35m and he ordered it to turn in order to prepare for a stern shot. Then he heard the audible sound of machine-gun fire along with the familiar pings of ASDIC. The smaller vessel had opened fire on the awash periscope. 'Fire!' The stern tube released its torpedo, but missed the pursuing vessel, likely due to the heavy swell.

Von Forstner ordered *U-402* to 20m depth, moving higher in the water column. He believed his deeper depth gave away his position through ASDIC and that it would be harder to locate him the closer to the surface the boat was. As the U-boat manoeuvred away from its pursuer, von Forstner consulted his on-board recognition guide and identified the vessel he hit as likely the MV *Llangibby Castle* (11,951 GRT) of the Union Castle line. A large troop-carrying transport was the prize every U-boat commander was after.

After 30 minutes *U-402* surfaced. The tubes were reloaded as von Forstner plotted his next move against the convoy. He received a technical report about tube IV's previous failure. A leak in the safety valve of the ejection cartridge had prevented it from firing. This would be one of many technical problems experienced by *U-402* in the coming years.

By 1225hrs tube III was reloaded. From the surfaced conning tower, the watch spotted a new two stack steamer and a destroyer. The original vessel torpedoed was no longer visible. *U-402* sent a transmission to BdU: 'Convoy in sight square BE 5924, southerly course. Forstner.'

Ten minutes later a crash dive was ordered as a destroyer approached unexpectedly, though it was not known if the U-boat had been spotted. Over the next 40 minutes tube I was reloaded, then *U-402* resurfaced. Von Forstner quickly made his way to the top of the conning tower and through his binoculars saw no destroyer, but did clearly see the second two-funnelled steamer. He ordered a high-speed pursuit.

The radioman received a reply from BdU that was passed to von Forstner. *U-402* was to follow the convoy and provide spotter reports, while three additional boats, *U-581*, *U-85* and *U-87*, were vectored toward the convoy that von Forstner had located by chance. *U-402*'s first cruise to the US East Coast would wait.

The Admiralty was aware of the key role the 'spotter' boat

played in forming a wolfpack. It was paramount to locate it and force the spotter to break contact, thereby ensuring the convoy's escape. This was often accomplished by supporting aircraft.

One of the lookouts heard an aircraft approaching 10 minutes later and the *U-402* crash-dived. It was not clear to the crew if this was an enemy or friendly aircraft, though it was heard over the radio that friendly aircraft had been dispatched to support the attack against the convoy. Two far-off detonations were heard. After a few minutes submerged *U-402* was back on the surface and von Forstner ordered another transmission to BdU: 'Position in Bruno Emil [BE] 5924, pursuing, 5 steamers, 1 destroyer distinguished. South-westerly course.' As soon as his radio message was complete, confirmation of the target came across in clear English on the 600m international distress frequency, which was repeated three times: '*LLANGIBBY CASTLE* torpedoed.'

U-402 dived at 1452hrs for another approaching aircraft, though the spotter noted it had a low wing and retractable undercarriage, suggesting it was indeed a Luftwaffe Fw 200 Condor. Unfortunately for von Forstner the continued crash-diving forced him to lose contact with the convoy. For the next 24 hours *U-402* continued the pursuit, both surfaced and submerged, as von Forstner plotted the expected course of the convoy. He searched for it visually, and also through passive sonar when submerged.

Von Forstner's signal to BdU on the 16th brought aerial reinforcements in the form of a long-range Fw 200 Condor from KG 40 based in Bordeaux-Merignac, France. The Fw 200 was the aircraft that caused *U-402* to crash-dive, making it lose contact with the stricken *Llangibby Castle*. The Fw 200 located the *Llangibby Castle* within three hours of it being torpedoed and dropped two bombs that missed. However, the aircraft's rear machine-gunner raked the deck with fire and killed the vessel's boatswain.[6] The anti-aircraft guns on the troop transport returned fire and reportedly hit the Fw 200 (likely a 200C-3/U2 variant with 13mm MG 131s added in the front and dorsal positions), though the aircraft apparently returned safely as no known Condor of KG 40 was reported shot down that day.

A new message from BdU arrived over the wireless at 1853hrs calling off further pursuit by all U-boats except for *U-402* and *U-581*, if contact was not regained by nightfall. Luftwaffe aerial reconnaissance was also unable to re-locate the convoy. It had escaped.

The ships von Forstner had spotted by pure chance belonged to one of the special fast-moving convoys that carried troops and military equipment. Typically, these convoys were too fast for U-boats to pursue and were lightly escorted. Convoy WS-15 departed the UK on 12 January 1942 en route to Singapore, in the wake of the Japanese attack on Pearl Harbor. It consisted of forty-three vessels that included seventeen escorts and twenty-six large pre-war passenger ships carrying troops as reinforcements. Singapore fell on 15 February, and WS-15 was ultimately routed to Bombay, India where it arrived on 4 March.[7] B-Dienst informed BdU that the possibly Gibraltar-bound convoy was made up of nineteen ships and five destroyers.[8] Clearly, the Admiralty had maintained good secrecy around the size and intent of WS-15.

In this convoy was the intermediate sized Union Castle liner *Llangibby Castle*, Captain R F Bayer in command. At 0815hrs (GMT) on 16 January, a single torpedo struck the vessel's stern and exploded with such force that the rear defensive gun mounted on the poop deck was blown 12ft into the air and overboard, while twenty-six men were killed and four wounded. The rudder was also lost, and the troop transport, carrying over 1,100 soldiers, could no longer be steered.

The Admiralty had a good understanding of the situation thanks to Ultra. The report ending the week of 19 January noted the order to re-direct U-boats that were in the process of manoeuvring against a different convoy to the one *U-402* happened upon by chance.[9] The Admiralty also knew that BdU believed *U-402* had intercepted a Gibraltar-bound convoy heading south-east, which was not the case with WS-15, and this could be the advantage the stricken troop transport needed to make its escape south-west to the Azores. The *Llangibby Castle* proceeded at the relatively slow speed of 9 knots while rudderless toward the port of Horta without escort.

On 16 January von Forstner came to periscope depth and found himself within Allied special Convoy WS-15 en route to Singapore with reinforcements. He fired a two-fan shot from tubes II and III and hit the aft section of the converted Union Castle passenger liner MV *Llangibby Castle* (11,951 GRT). The *Llangibby Castle* lost her rudder, but managed to make her way to Horta in the Azores where she waited for additional escorts to take her to Gibraltar for repairs. *U-402* now spent the rest of this patrol hunting its wounded quarry. (Imperial War Museum/FL005793)

Over the course of the next three days, Captain Bayer showed magnificent navigation and ship-handling skills as he piloted the rudderless troop transport into Horta Bay in the Azores across 700 miles of stormy seas. The Portuguese authorities, who were neutral, gave the *Llangibby Castle* 14 days in port before she was required to depart. The crew and troops were forced to remain on board, though they were allowed the comforts of lights and open portholes during their short respite. It was soon determined that the necessary repairs to the rudder could not be made in Horta. Orders from the Admiralty arrived that the damaged vessel had to make to Gibraltar.

With no ship in sight, BdU ordered *U-402* to patrol half way between the Azores and Gibraltar. *U-402* continued on the surface, crash-diving when an aircraft was spotted. By the 19th, there was still no contact. BdU then ordered two lines established, one north of the Azores called 'Anton' and one to the south called 'Bruno'. *U-402* was ordered to patrol between these lines and toward the east, while it awaited the arrival of *U-581*.

Wrong Direction

U-402 manoeuvred south-east toward the Strait of Gibraltar. At midnight on 21 January the Cape St Vincent lighthouse on the south-eastern tip of Portugal was sighted. On the 22nd von Forstner turned north, remaining submerged due to low-lying clouds preventing early warning of enemy aircraft. Despite being in an active enemy area, each day was filled with training routines, and frequent crash dives to keep the crew prepared.

At 0200hrs on the 23rd, von Forstner took bearings off the lighthouses of Cape St Vincent, St Maria and Vila Real de Santo António. He then turned westward and proceeded surfaced along what he believed was the centre of the line Anton-Bruno. At 1028hrs he ordered a crash dive as an aircraft approached on a north-westerly course that was immediately identified as a Lockheed Hudson due to its 'double empennage, 2 engines, [and] thick fuselage'.

U-402 resurfaced at 1057hrs and cruised north-west. Later that afternoon, just before 1600hrs heavy smoke was spotted on the horizon. Von Forstner adjusted his course and within a few minutes two funnels appeared. Soon, another aircraft was spotted. Von Forstner hesitated to give the order to crash dive as he was hoping that his U-boat might be missed so that he could continue to pursue the steamer. He likely wished he had not taken such immediate action for a friendly aircraft a few days ago, which ultimately caused him to lose sight of the *Llangibby Castle*. However, the aircraft veered off its course and toward *U-402*. 'Dive!' The order was given. As soon as the U-boat reached a depth of 60m two depth charges exploded near the U-boat sending shock waves through its hull. A minute later, two more splashes, two more explosions, and more shock waves.

For many on board, this was their first experience being depth-charged. As the explosions rocked the boat the crew held their collective breath as they braced themselves. After each explosion they glanced with urgency from the pressure hull, to the pipes and valves, looking for any leaks. After the final explosion worrisome looks slowly turned to wry smiles, according to Herbert, as each man realised that their boat could easily withstand the feared depth charges. The report was passed back to the control room, 'no damage'.

U-402 came up to periscope depth at 1700hrs and spotted what was described as a 'V+W Destroyer', approaching the U-boat's position in a zig-zag course approximately 4,000m away. A small 'insignificant steamer', likely no greater than 1,000GRT was spotted as well. Von Forstner ordered a fan of torpedoes prepared. As the crew worked to obey his order, he swivelled the periscope in a 360-degree circle and noticed that the Lockheed Hudson was still present and that all three – destroyer, steamer, and aircraft – were now working together against his U-boat. He caught sight of the destroyer morsing over to the steamer.

At 1723hrs the order to dive deep was given as the aircraft, now vectored in by the destroyer, was fast approaching again. The sonar operator detected three different sound bearings, two turbines related to not one, but two destroyers, and a third piston

U-402 spent the next few weeks in the warm tropical waters around the Azores, at first searching for the *Llangibby Castle*, then once she was located in Horta, waiting for her to depart the neutral Portuguese port in order to deliver the coup de grâce. During this time the crew enjoyed the warmer latitudes. In this picture Friebolin captured a Portuguese Man-Of-War that appeared on one of the protective rails at the back of the conning tower. So much for Portuguese neutrality! (Friebolin collection)

engine, likely the steamer. As von Forstner ordered evasive manoeuvres, several series of depth charges totalling eleven explosions were heard. Several were far off and likely dropped by the second destroyer at a suspected contact some distance away.

U-402 surfaced after dark having successfully broken contact with the destroyers. BdU signalled that an 'English aircraft reported a U-boat in CG 8628 at 1520 hours'. Von Forstner checked the track plot and noted that he was there, though the English time was an hour off.

After midnight on the 24th *U-402* surfaced and found itself in the middle of the north-south independent merchant traffic route between Casablanca and Portugal. The steamers were running lit, and were ignored. At 1122hrs BdU issued a communique: 'To Hirsacker, Forstner, Pfeifer. At 0134 hours Spanish steamer "NAVAMAR" sunk in square CF 9273. Immediately report, on the basis of what observations and situation sinking took place.'

The SS *Navemar* was a British-built steamer now owned by Spain that was cruising toward the Strait of Gibraltar when it was sunk on the 23rd. But by who? This steamer was neutral-flagged and Dönitz wanted to find out if either *U-402*, *U-581* or *U-572*, commanded by Kapitänleutnant Heinz Hirsacker, were responsible. None of them were. The culprit was the *Barbarigo*, an Italian *Marcello*-class submarine commanded by Capitano di Corvetta Enzo Grossi.[10] Grossi encountered the merchantman with its lights on in the same north-south route von Forstner was in, but unlike his German counterparts he decided to sink the vessel without cause and against BdU guidance.

Just before 1300hrs von Forstner received a new message from BdU to move immediately west as B-Dienst confirmed that *Llangibby Castle* had not travelled to Gibraltar but rather arrived at Horta in the Azores. It was also believed that a second transport had been dispatched in order to take off the soldiers on board, though this later proved incorrect. BdU warned von Forstner to observe the territorial waters of Portugal within the Azores but to find and sink the troop transport.

Shortly after midnight on the 25th the night watch officer observed a shadow to port he believed was another submarine on the surface and immediately turned away 90° to port, to avoid a possible collision. Von Forstner was summoned to the bridge and noted that the submarine also made a turn, likely having spotted *U-402*. Von Forstner concluded that '. . . I must accept the possibility that I have a U-boat before me, I decide to exchange recognition signals before attacking. Recognition signal remains

ON HOLIDAY

unanswered. This turn towards represents an act of war and gives me the right to attack without previous determination of nationality.' As he continued to watch the silhouette through his binoculars move closer, he soon realised his mistake. 'The shadow seems too large for a submarine to me . . . .' He ordered torpedo tubes ready to fire as he manoeuvred his boat for a surface shot. He had no plans to submerge during this engagement where von Forstner felt he had the tactical advantage against a still unknown target. At the report of 'Tubes ready!', the silhouette became clear in his binoculars. He was facing a destroyer. A three-fan from tubes I, III and IV was fired, but unfortunately for von Forstner, they all missed and the destroyer turned away from *U-402* and 'ran off at high speed'.

The lack of action during the past days gave the crew some time to enjoy the tropical climate. Dolphins played in the U-boat's wake for the enjoyment and amazement of the crew. Few had a chance to see marine life up close. Von Forstner gave them men an opportunity to take a dip in the ocean, also known as a 'salt water bath'. The crew dried themselves off on deck in the warm sun. It was a break from the monotony of the daily routine. While von Forstner knew this was good for morale, his frustration and desire

The crew was given breaks to jump into the warm water. This 'salt bath' could give a boost to morale and also gave the crew an opportunity to rinse off the daily grime that accumulated from living on board a U-boat. Two crewmen are posted as 'safeties' on the bow to help rescue any of their comrades in the water and to look out for sharks. (Friebolin collection)

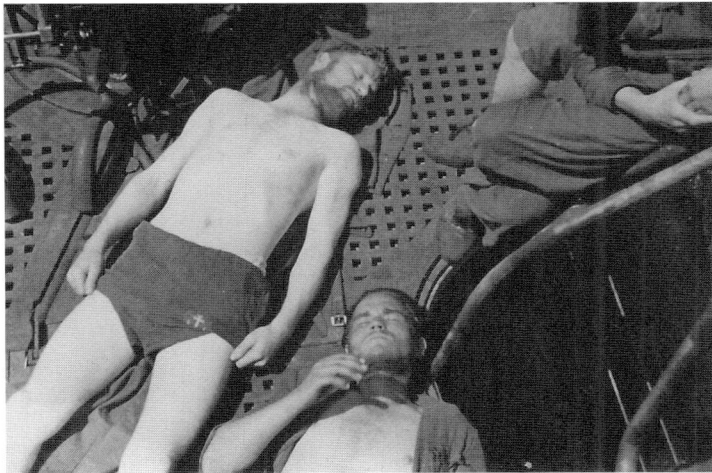

Below left: After a dip into the ocean came time to relax in the sun and dry off as these two crewmen did at the back of the conning tower. (Friebolin collection)

Below right: Von Forstner complained that his second patrol was like a 'pleasure cruise', given all the time the crew had to wait without any combat action. Here crew takes turns sunbathing on the conning tower. There appears little concern about Allied surface vessels or aircraft, though the 20mm anti-aircraft gun appears at the ready just in case. (Friebolin collection)

for action came through in a later letter to his wife about these days: 'This is a war, not a holiday trip. Yet here we sit in an endless expanse of blue water under a smiling sun – no enemy, no nothing – and others have to do all the fighting. It is simply disgusting!'

The Wait is Over

Just before noon on 26 January, Chief Engineer Meyer reported that the Junkers compressor was out of action and under repair. Soon after the report, *U-402* came in sight of Sao Miguel Island where it passed to the north at the limit of visibility. All day *U-402* cruised surfaced north of the island on a direct course that took it just south of Pico Island, to the Faial Channel that opened up to

Navigation fixes were routinely taken to compensate for the imprecise dead-reckoning. Here the navigator, probably Obersteuermann Görtz, is pictured using a sextant produced by C. Plath of Hamburg. The C. Plath company only produced nautical equipment for the German navy and army during the war, producing approximately 10,000 of these devices, each with their own unique serial and marine numbers. The version pictured here is a Kriegsmarine Trommel-Sextant. It would have the Nazi eagle stamped above the letter 'M' (for Marine), with the unit serial numbers stamped below that. It was equipped with Zeiss optics. Note the white adjusting knob made from Bakelite. (Friebolin collection)

Horta, then further west. B-Dienst gave BdU early warning of the *Llangibby Castle*'s departure date, which was relayed to von Forstner that afternoon. 'Departure of the troopship damaged by torpedo hit it is expected in approximately 6 days. There are no reports concerning arrival of transport intended for taking over the troops.'

Von Forstner strictly obeyed the rules of war and BdU's guidance. He noted in his logbook:

> Intention: Do not want to enter territorial waters without a compelling reason. If *Llangibby Castle* or English destroyers lie beyond the territorial waters, which is hardly likely due to water depths, attack immediately. Search waters as far as visibility permits without, however, being seen. If by night without success, continue search during the day submerged. Because in accordance with Radio Message departure is not yet expected, I want to continue to look from the north during the following night and/or during the day.

British naval intelligence was aware that BdU was marshalling several U-boats against the troop transport. A warning was entered accordingly in their weekly summary of U-boat activity on the 26th.[11] Despite the good intelligence on both sides, the *Llangibby Castle*'s fate came down to the training, experience and tactical decisions made by the men on both sides, often assisted by a little luck.

This is likely the unknown Bootsmann (1st row, 5th from l-r) pictured in the crew commissioning photo wearing the Iron Cross 2nd Class Ribbon and the Spanish Cross. Clearly he is on watch, as his binoculars hang from his neck, but he appears relaxed and not concerned about the enemy as he smokes a cigarette in the warm sun. (Friebolin collection)

Meyer relayed the good news to von Forstner that the Junkers compressor was back in service. *U-402* submerged and during the mid-morning entered the southern part of the Faial Channel to look for the troop transport. Von Forstner navigated near Horta, but visibility was reduced due to an overcast sky. He was not able to spot the transport. He did make out two grey-painted funnels, 'well set off from the white pier' but he decided that they were likely those of 'a Portuguese destroyer'. *U-402* headed around Faial Island to the west, then looked for the *Llangibby Castle* from the north, thinking it could be hiding along the coast between Espalhafatos and Ponta da Espalamaca. As *U-402* altered course accordingly at 0400hrs on the 28th, a radio message from Hirsacker to BdU was overheard just before 0900hrs: '0001 hours square CF 7357 troop transport, course west, 16 knots, during attack fired upon by artillery, depth charges.' *U-572* was operating to the south-east of Sao Miguel Island at that time.

This signal altered von Forstner's plan. Now he decided to pass through the Faial Channel submerged and search carefully for the *Llangibby Castle*, believing that the vessel *U-572* identified was likely to be the one that would embark the troops from the stricken troop transport. Von Forstner circled around the island from the west then proceeded south down the Faial Channel submerged in order to intercept the expected inbound troop transport before it entered territorial waters. He believed it could lead him to the *Llangibby Castle*. Von Forstner did not realise that there was no inbound transport. He slowly proceeded south into the channel submerged during the early afternoon of the 28th and finally saw his quarry at 1456hrs as noted in his logbook: 'Abeam the harbour off Horta. The LLANGIBBY CASTLE lies at the mole after all. By her camouflage she differs so little from the background that I could recognise her only later as the previously mentioned destroyer smokestacks . . . . the British merchant flag is easily recognised, no list.'

U-402 exited the channel, then headed east off Pico, before turning west again over the course of the next 24 hours. The U-boat passed through the channel twice more between 30 January and 1 February. Von Forstner also took advantage of the time to prepare the boat for the coming fight. He gave the crew some rest. Then he attempted to transfer the two 'over deck' torpedoes that were stored outside the pressure hull fore and aft of the conning tower into their respective torpedo rooms, but encountered trouble doing so due to the heavy seas.

BdU sent a wireless transmission at 1341hrs on 1 February

that reiterated *Llangibby Castle* would depart the next day and that other transports were expected for the purposes of taking off the soldiers. With this information, von Forstner ordered his boat submerged and back into the southern part of the channel. At 1505hrs the U-boat grounded itself due to either a fault in the charts or navigation. The incident jarred the crew, and von Forstner had the charts rechecked. *U-402* quickly backed off the rocks and continued its observation of Horta, though no changes in routine were seen.

Shortly after midnight on the 2nd, *U-402* spotted *U-581* and they came within hailing distance of each other. Pfeifer communicated that he was surprised to see von Forstner because he thought he was out of torpedoes based on an 'Officer-Only' wireless transmission he had heard on 28 January, but that message it turned out was sent from *U-654* under the command of Hans-Joachim Förster. After the situation was cleared up, von Forstner relayed his plan of attack. *U-402* would head west, then north to the Faial Channel while *U-581* proceeded to the southern entrance. Whoever spotted the outbound convoy first was to transmit the sighting so that the other U-boat could quickly come to its assistance during the attack.

Von Forstner noted in the logbook just past midnight on 2 February that *U-402* came within hailing distance of *U-581*. Von Forstner and Pfeifer coordinated their actions against the *Llangibby Castle*. This photo shows an unidentified U-boat, with its captain (white hat) in the conning tower manoeuvring toward *U-402*. The sailor in the foreground of the picture appears not to be wearing a shirt, suggesting this encounter occurred in the warm waters of the Azores. In addition, the approaching U-boat has expended some fuel because it rides higher in the water, which means it has been on patrol for several weeks. The fact that there appears to be daylight out despite the midnight entry, might suggest the meeting occurred late in the afternoon of the 11th. However, without the U-boat's symbol clearly visible, its identification remains unconfirmed. (Friebolin collection)

HMS *Westcott* (D47) was a Royal Navy 'W'-class destroyer originally launched in February 1918. She displaced 1,100 tons, had an overall length of 312ft, and a beam of 29ft 6in, making her very similar in size to the 'Hunt' class. Her speed and range were both slight greater than the 'Hunt' class at 34 knots, and 3,500nm. She boasted four 4in Mk V guns, one 3in anti-aircraft gun, two quad 2-pounders and six torpedo tubes. In August 1941 her forward 4in gun was removed and replaced by the first prototype Hedgehog forward-firing anti-submarine mortar. This device became a deadly anti-U-boat weapon by the end of the war. (Imperial War Museum/FL22820)

At 0402hrs in the morning *U-402* was surfaced, as it approached the north channel. A British destroyer of the 'V&W' class, it was thought, was immediately spotted. However, this was a misrecognition by von Forstner, as it was actually the Admiralty 'W'-class destroyer HMS *Westcott* (D47). The *Westcott* was the first Allied vessel equipped with the new Hedgehog forward-firing anti-submarine spigot mortar, having participated in prototype testing back in August 1941. It fired a salvo of twenty-four bombs each carrying a 16kg Torpex charge in an arc that was intended to land in a 130ft circular area at a fixed point 590ft directly ahead of the escort. The projectiles sunk at about 23ft per second and detonated on contact.

As it was too bright for a surface attack, *U-402* dived and launched a three-fan shot from tubes I, II and IV, but all missed. Two impacts at 65 and 66 seconds were heard, but no detonations. His boat breached the surface briefly due to the loss of trim after firing the three torpedoes, but the destroyer turned away, and manoeuvred out of sight, likely now aware of the U-boat's presence. *U-402* was low on torpedoes, and for von Forstner there was mounting frustration at the continued misses.

U-402 surfaced again at 0505hrs and manoeuvred close in to the north coast of Faial Island in order to shift the two torpedoes stored outside the pressure hull in the top deck containers, into the forward torpedo room. At the same time, he radioed Pfeifer to warn him about the destroyer that von Forstner believed was heading to the southern channel. At 0645hrs, after completing the torpedo transfer, another destroyer was spotted about 6nm away. *U-402* crash-dived, and came onto an attack course but found the destroyer within Portuguese territorial waters. Von Forstner was not going to launch an attack against orders. It was reported to be a British 'J'-class destroyer that was manoeuvring back and forth at the channel entrance. This could only mean that the *Llangibby Castle*'s departure was imminent. This was another mis-recognition by von Forstner, as it was in fact a Type II 'Hunt'-class destroyer, HMS *Croome* (L62).

Again, *U-402* surfaced, then crash-dived after spotting another destroyer astern of the 'J-class' with distinctive double black rings on its funnel and what looked like a 'L0B' painted on its bow. This third escort was the 'Hunt'-class HMS *Exmoor* (L08). She steered various courses off the opening of the north channel. At 1101hrs von Forstner decided to attack *Exmoor* with only a single bow torpedo so that he could reserve his final two for the *Llangibby Castle*.

He had a reference point of the Ribeirinha Lighthouse to calculate the *Exmoor*'s speed and distance. The firing solution was entered as 18 knots at 600m. The torpedo left the tube at 1159hrs. Von Forstner believed that he had a sure shot. The torpedo depth setting was 2m. However, the actual range of the destroyer proved to be half the distance at 300m, and the keen watch of the *Exmoor* spotted the torpedo as the destroyer reduced speed significantly, allowing the torpedo to pass forward of its bow.

This destroyer, which had already earned a reputation as a U-boat killer after sinking *U-131* in December 1941 off the coast of Portugal, must have been under strict orders not to attack any U-boats and wait for the *Llangibby Castle* to depart. She made no attempt to pursue *U-402*, but instead continued her back-and-forth patrolling off the north entrance.

Early in the afternoon BdU warned that the *Llangibby Castle* was probably putting to sea before the end of the day, under the tow of the Netherland-flagged tug *Thames*. Sure enough, the *Llangibby Castle* finally departed at 1617hrs with the *Westcott* ahead and the *Croome* following. As the *Westcott* passed *U-402* at about 1500m it was identified by von Forstner by its 'L47' marking, a camouflage paint scheme and thick funnel.

The small convoy continued through Portuguese territorial waters at 9 knots as *U-402* pursued. Von Forstner attempted to send a radio message using the rod antenna while submerged, but

A Type II 'Hunt'-class destroyer, HMS *Exmoor* (L08) was the second destroyer to bear that name, as the original was sunk in February 1941 by a German E-boat torpedo. Originally named the *Burton* under the War Emergency Programme, she was renamed *Exmoor* in June 1941 after she was launched in March that year. The original 'Hunt' class was designed in a relatively short period at the end of 1938. The first keels were not laid until 8 June 1939 to conform with international treaties still being observed at that time. Much was asked from this design, given the uncertainties of the expected conflict. Too much was crammed into the hull and by the time the first one was deployed, extensive modifications were made to the next set of keels that included widening the beam, omitting torpedo tubes, lessening the steel strength in some places, removing a 4in gun and more than two-dozen other alterations. Fifty tons of ballast had to be added in order maintain stability in the water because they were top heavy.

Due to the inherent design problems with the Type I, the Type II was modified accordingly, by increasing the beam to 31ft 6in, and modifying and shifting the bridge to increase stability. A third twin 4in gun mount was added and it had ten less depth charges then the earlier class. It boasted six 4in guns, one quad 2-pounder, two single 20mm Mk IIa Oerlikons and sixty depth charges. It was equipped with the Type 290 and 285 radar sets. Other modifications made to the latter Type I were included, and it was found the increased stability of the wider beam and bridge did not require the ballast of the earlier Type Is. Speed and endurance were also slightly modified. She displaced 1,010 tons, was 280ft long and had a beam of 31ft 6in. Her speed was 29 knots and she had a range of 2,500nm. The second *Exmoor* was already a U-boat killer, having sunk *U-131* in December 1941 off Portugal. (Imperial War Museum/FL3708)

A Type II 'Hunt'-class destroyer HMS *Croome* (L62). She was built under the War Emergency Programme and completed on 29 June 1941. Her characteristics were similar to the *Exmoor*. (Imperial War Museum/FL10826)

this effort proved useless as the aerial was defective. He then decided to breach with his bow and attempt to send a signal using the net deflector only, but that also failed. He could not surface as he spotted a 'corvette' zig-zagging from behind, from the north heading on an easterly course. This was probably HMS *Croome*.

U-402 was forced to wait until 1843hrs before it could surface and radio BdU that it was in pursuit of the *Llangibby Castle*. This was a calculated risk as *U-402* was low on torpedoes and fuel. Despite these impediments, Von Forstner pursued his quarry aggressively while being outnumbered by three seasoned U-boat hunters, though he could only guess at the latter fact.

The sea state was mild, with an overcast sky and moderate visibility. At 2038hrs two detonations were heard. Von Forstner believed this was *U-581* hitting the destroyer with torpedoes. He was wrong. *U-581* was positioned in the southern channel between the islands of Pico and Fayal in the early hours of 2 February, as per von Forstner, steering a north-westerly course. The small convoy escorting the *Llangibby Castle* was spotted and Pfeifer ordered a dive followed by a stern shot at the nearest of two destroyers leading the troop transport out of the channel. The shot went wide, and at a depth of 80m (262.47ft) a rivet on the flange of the aft port exhaust pipe gave way and water entered the engine-room compartment. Strenuous efforts were made to control the entry of water, but these were of no avail, because of the pressure at this depth. The flood of water aft made it very difficult to keep trim while submerged, and also threatened to put the electric motors out of action. The crew panicked as the U-boat plunged uncontrollably to a depth of some 160m (524.94ft). Pfeifer had no choice but to order his ballast tanks blown and his U-boat rose quickly to within 20m (65.61ft) of the surface, when the sound of the destroyers' propellers overhead could be distinctly heard. The chief engineer appealed to Pfeifer to dive deep again or run the risk of colliding with one of the destroyers overhead. Pfeifer reluctantly agreed, and after another somewhat uncontrollable descent into the depths, Pfeifer lost his nerve and ordered the U-boat to surface after reaching 150m (492.13ft).

On the surface, *Croome* and *Westcott* picked up a nearby ASDIC contact and manoeuvred to investigate, leaving the *Llangibby Castle* under the temporary protection of *Exmoor*. They soon spotted *U-581* broach the surface at close range. *Westcott*'s commanding officer ordered 'Full speed ahead' and made for the U-boat with the intention of ramming. The initial run missed its mark, due to the U-boat's narrow beam and the fact that the *Westcott* approached from astern. *Westcott* then dropped ten depth charges on this run with shallow settings, while just 9m off the starboard beam. This caused significant damage to *U-581*.

The destroyer turned hard to port in a second attempt to ram. On this second run *Westcott* and *U-581* closed at the rate of about 40 knots on almost opposite courses. *U-581* turned to port as *Westcott* wheeled to starboard, then came about full port. The destroyer's port bow sliced into the U-boat just abaft the conning tower. The shocked crew abandoned the U-boat seconds before impact. As *Westcott* prepared to carry out a second ramming, the bow of *U-581* 'rose clear of the water and she sank by the stern in over 400 fathoms'.[12]

Pfeifer had already issued the order to 'abandon ship' after the first ramming attempt so the entire crew wore lifejackets when they jumped into the water. The two British destroyers rescued forty-one of the forty-six crew from the water. On 8 February BdU received the report that *U-581* had likely been rammed and sunk, and that the survivors were picked up by the British. Only the 2nd Watch Officer escaped capture, swam to shore and later returned to Germany.[13]

None of this was known to von Forstner who continued to pursue the elusive *Llangibby Castle*. *U-402* transmitted to BdU again at 2105hrs that it was pursuing the troop transport which was following a zig-zag course along 120 degrees at 11 knots. Perhaps this transmission was picked up on HF/DF as within minutes the larger destroyer, probably the *Exmoor*, changed course and headed directly toward *U-402* at high speed. This was going to be a direct attack. A crash dive was ordered. The crew ran to the bow where their combined weight provided extra downward momentum that sped the boat's submergence into the depth by a few life-saving seconds. At first von Forstner came to periscope depth but the destroyer was still on its attack approach so the U-boat dived to 120m, then 140m, and finally 168m (554.4ft). The first depth charges were dropped. The sonar man identified not one, but two destroyers now, and a peculiar sound was heard as if pebbles were dropped from the surface and began to strike the pressure hull.

How quickly the hunter became the hunted. The crew kept quiet and a wary eye upward as the distinctive pings of ASDIC bounced off *U-402*'s hull. According to von Forstner,

> sound series of approximately 6 clearly distinguishable single tones, each two closely together in time, little pause, then two again. The first tone of the second double sound was usually louder. Sequence of the tones somewhat like . . . when Morsing. Between each series quite different long pauses, from 13 seconds up to many minutes . . . A total of 41 depth charges, which presumably all detonations above the boat. Concussions very dissimilar. Felt very safe at depth, only slight failures which could be quickly repaired.

They were deep, and being attacked. While he did not know the fate of *U-581*, clearly a broken valve caused by the concussions of depth-charge explosions could easily jeopardise the U-boat. This was the first time the crew experienced a depth charge attack of this severity and the experience was etched deeply in their minds. Herbert recalled 50 years later: 'They exploded for hours, rocking the boat. We were all frightened, but von Forstner kept his cool.' Satisfied they had bought time for the *Llangibby Castle* to continue her evasive manoeuvres, the destroyers withdrew and turned back toward to their escort duties. BdU had received the earlier report and now directed Hirsacker to assist in the pursuit.

U-402 regained sight of its quarry early on 3 February. Von Forstner attacked one of the destroyers at 0730hrs with a shot from tube II, but the shot was a miss at 400m. Both destroyers pursued *U-402* with ASDIC but did not locate the boat. Von Forstner ordered the boat down to 140m. Eleven minutes later a sharp impact was felt against the hull, as the U-boat struck an uncharted rock outcropping. A hull plate was torn loose that rattled even during silent running. The crew was shaken psychologically

U-402 suffered torn plates after grounding on an uncharted rock outcropping at 140m depth during its pursuit of *Llangibby Castle*. After it surfaced, repairs were made to lessen the clanking sound that could be heard during silent running. When technical problems occurred, usually members of the engineering section conducted an inspection and made repairs. In this picture we see who appears to be Oberleutnant Ing Meyer-Oswald (on the right) on the deck of *U-402*, along with another unidentified crewmen (left). They wear leather work gloves and appear to be inspecting something on the deck. The unidentified crewman appears to wear a Luftwaffe Type 10.30 B-2 lifejacket with a solid shoulder panel. The vest did not automatically inflate and a cord had to be pulled releasing the compressed air from the container on the left side of the wait. There was also a mouthpiece for manual inflation that extended up to the neck. (Friebolin collection)

between the depth-charge attack and now hitting rocks while so deep. The navigator poured over the charts and checked his calculations under the glare of the 1st Watch Officer. Von Forstner maintained a calm demeanour during the incident, which again reassured the crew.

Over the next 24 hours von Forstner relentlessly pursued the troop transport. Each time he regained contact, escorting destroyers turned to attack, and *U-402* dived. Again, the U-boat surfaced and gave dogged pursuit. The game of 'cat and mouse' diminished the boat's fuel reserves. Only a single torpedo remained. Von Forstner transmitted the bearing of the *Llangibby Castle* each time it was spotted, believing that his contact reports might help BdU vector another U-boat to the troop transport. Von Forstner believed *U-581* was still operating in the area, along with *U-572*.

However, frequent wireless transmissions were dangerous, because they could be triangulated. BdU finally decided that von Forstner was unnecessarily jeopardising his own U-boat and sent two encrypted messages emphasising that he should 'Send bearing signals only on demand by other boats . . .'. Three more times *U-402* was caught on the surface, dived and was attacked by the destroyers; a final depth-charge attack took place on the afternoon on the 4th.

BdU recognised the *Llangibby Castle* was going to escape regardless of von Forstner's efforts and sent a message to *U-402* in the afternoon to begin its return transit. Seven days later *U-402* returned to St Nazaire receiving an additional admonition against 'superfluous' communications regarding a late report von Forstner

Below left: The following series of pictures depict *U-402*'s return to St Nazaire on 11 February 1942. Friebolin is seen smiling (bottom 2nd-r). Immediately to his left is Leutnant zur See Hübschen, and across from him smiling is Obermachinst Fischer. On the left of the picture is a long wooden flagstaff that flies a thin pennant with a German cross for each successful patrol. The end of the streamer can be seen waving just atop the sky scope. It is better pictured in the following photos. Approaching land can be seen in the background. (Friebolin collection)

Below right: Here the crew, including, Friebolin enjoy cigarettes as they are taken under convoy and approach the St Nazaire lock. The weather was much colder in the northern latitudes then it was around the Azores, just a few weeks earlier. (Friebolin collection)

sent about the action on 25 January because it could be HF/DFed, thereby jeopardising the boat.

This action was important, though unsuccessful, as every Allied vessel sunk had a cumulative impact on the war. Now nicknamed 'Elsie' by the crew, the *Llangibby Castle* made her way under her own power, still rudderless, to Gibraltar on the evening on 8 February. The captain of the *Llangibby Castle*, Ronald F. Bayer, was awarded the Commander of the Most Excellent Order of the British Empire (CBE) for this achievement. The First Officer J Ferguson and the Chief Engineer J Mills, received the OBE and the Lloyd's War Medal for Bravery at Sea donated by Lloyd's of London. There the troop transport remained for 57 days of repair. On 8 November 1942, 'Elsie' took part in the landings in North Africa, bringing troops ashore as well as later reinforcements. She later supported the landings at Anzio, and after transferring back to the Atlantic, she transported the largest contingent of troops to Juno Beach on 5 June 1944 as part of Operation 'Neptune'. How might those operations have been impacted if 'Elsie' had been sunk?

While Captain Bayer received accolades, von Forstner, earned constructive criticism from Dönitz. After reviewing his patrol diary Dönitz did not fault him for letting the troop transport escape, noting 'unfavourable circumstances.' He praised von Forstner's 'consideration and toughness' throughout the action – a characteristic one of his former Watch Officers termed 'Draufgangertum' ('aggressiveness'). However, Dönitz remarked that 'It is wrong to exchange recognition signals at night with an unrecognised shadow'. That decision, he concluded, 'consciously gives up the special strength of the submarine which, by its invisibility, allows it the first surprise attack'. Von Forstner would not make that mistake again.

U-402 is now docked in the St Nazaire lock, pointed toward the basin where the U-boat bunkers were located. Von Forstner is pictured clean-shaven and in good spirits despite the disappointing patrol. Behind him is 1st Watch Officer Oberleutnant Kiehn. The streamer is now clearly displayed with the one of the Iron Crosses denoting its second patrol. (Bundesarchiv, Schwich Bild MW 3686 2A)

Now on deck is 2nd Watch Officer Hübschen. (Bundesarchiv, Schwich Bild MW 3686 4A)

Von Forstner has now left *U-402* and stepped onto the wharf and is talking to officers, likely from the 3rd U-Flotilla. Behind him can be seen the round control room for the northern lock, which is still there today. He is wearing his U-boat leather jacket, a personal scarf, probably knitted by his wife. Directly behind him is the St Nazaire U-boat bunker complex still being built. Pens 9–14 were still under construction and are not visible yet. (Bundesarchiv, Schwich Bild MW 3686 5A)

The crew of *U-402* were housed in the La Roseraie Hotel and the Casino de La Baule located in La Baule, a short bus ride from the U-boat pens of St Nazaire. The hotel is now divided into apartments and the Casino is gone. Friebolin (on the right) and other members of *U-402*'s crew are now cleaned up and enjoying some time ashore after their patrol. On the right side of their overcoats appears to be an embroidered U-boat patch denoting they had completed their second patrol. (Friebolin collection)

One of the many benefits of being ashore was enjoying time with the local girls, as members of the crew are doing here. As the war continued, and the tide turned, these interactions grew far less frequent. (Friebolin collection)

CHAPTER 3

Missing the Beat

> We really should have kept them locked up and all that, but a U-boat is not spacious as you know and they were nice chaps and friendly . . . .
> Baron Siegfried Freiherr von Forstner in a letter to his wife, 1942

After returning to St Nazaire in mid-February, *U-402* spent six weeks at the shipyard for repairs and an overhaul. The U-boat had taken a beating on its last patrol from two accidental groundings and depth-charging by British destroyers. In spite of this pounding, the Type VIIC proved a capable design, though the technical failures suggested that wartime pressures on construction introduced more mechanical defects than might usually be expected.

Von Forstner grew anxious while on shore. Not one for being on the sidelines, he watched his former classmate Kretschmer achieve great success during the winter of 1940/41, while von Forstner was unable to sink a single vessel in two patrols. The escape of the *Llangibby Castle* certainly weighed on him. In addition, stories of easy hunting started to filter back from the captains of U-boats returning from recent patrols to the US East Coast.

Dönitz dispatched six U-boats from France to the East Coast of North America in December on the entry of the United States into the war. It was an opening salvo against what he correctly believed was to be an unprepared defence. The operation was called 'Paukenschlag' or 'Drumbeat'. Phrases like 'Atlantic turkey shoot', 'burning shores', and 'tanker war' have all been used to correctly describe the situation off the US East Coast during the first six months of 1942. Successes along the Eastern Seaboard were desperately needed by BdU.

Allied shipborne HF/DF direction-finding gear and cryptological breaking of the 'Dolphin' code brought the convoy battles in the North Atlantic to an effective end by December 1941 as the Admiralty re-routed convoys around U-boat patrol lines. As early as 19 November, Dönitz documented his concerns in the BdU war diary: '. . . experience shows that individual boats find convoys but that, with one exception, convoys have never been detected by a patrol line, unless there were a previous report on the enemy by an individual boat. The reason for this is not yet clear. Coincidence it cannot be – coincidence cannot always be on one side, and experiences extend over 3 to 4 years.' He expressed the concern that the British '. . . from some source or other, gain knowledge of our concentrated dispositions and deviate thereby encountering perhaps boats proceeding singly'.[14] He believed that based on Allied convoy dispositions provided by B-Dienst his U-boats should have achieved more successes in locating convoys. He was of course correct. Dönitz subsequently ordered B-Dienst to determine what they could about Allied intelligence on his U-boats.

By the end of the year U-boat operations in the Atlantic had all but stopped, while much of their strength was drained off into the Mediterranean and then into the Arctic Circle. Dönitz faced the prospect of a defeat of his wolfpack tactics in the Battle of the Atlantic, but soon a number of factors shifted the odds back to his favour. The entry of the United States into the war solved the problem of sinking tonnage. His U-boats may have struggled to locate convoys in the mid-Atlantic, but dispatching them to the Eastern Seaboard offered the potential for easier hunting. On 10 December, just before Hitler declared war on the United Sates, Dönitz recorded the following about the upcoming operation: 'Their object must be to intercept single vessels and to make use of the enemy's inexperience and the fact that they are not used to operations by U-boats.' As successes mounted in that operational area, he reiterated to his U-boat crews not to attack convoys encountered west of the Bay of Biscay (as von Forstner had done), as noted in the BdU war diary for 19 April. Dönitz wanted his boats to maximise their operational days where prospects for success were all but guaranteed and not waste fuel and food chasing vessels that could easily slip away in the mid-Atlantic.

By 1940 the United States of America was the world's largest exporter of crude oil. Most of this vital wartime commodity was shipped from ports in Texas out of the Gulf of Mexico through the Lesser Antilles and onward up the US East Coast then across to Europe. Hundreds of large oil tankers carried as much as 150,000 barrels of oil each. Early warning by the Admiralty of inbound U-boats did little to ready America's coastal defences. Even their recommendations based on two years of fighting U-boats were also ignored. Blackouts were not ordered for coastal communities for fear of their economic impact, navigation lights and buoys remained in place, new ship routing was not established, and the proven protection of the convoy system was not ordered by US Commander-in-Chief Fleet Admiral Ernest J King. The first three months of 1942 proved devastating along the US East Coast with some sixty-six vessels sunk or damaged, more than half being oil tankers.

As U-boat successes mounted off the American coast, B-Dienst achieved a significant breakthrough during the past few months that offered BdU hope in returning to wolfpack tactics in the North Atlantic. In October 1941 German cryptologists began to draw up a schedule of major convoy sailings that it checked against current intelligence. Starting in February 1942, B-Dienst effectively broke the combined Allied Naval Cypher No 3 and was able to detail the convoy cycles more accurately and rapidly than in the past. As noted in the post-war assessment of B-Dienst activity: 'Step by step details were filled in or adjusted within a more certain framework: details of escort procedure and make up, convoy sections, and convoy regulations and irregularities. By March 1942 B-Dienst was inserting current positions on convoys at sea, thus arriving at the final stage of mastery of the convoy system for operational purposes.'[15] It took some months before this breakthrough manifested itself into an operational shift back to the North Atlantic from the successful operation off the US East Coast.

The success of B-Dienst offered a new offensive advantage to BdU. After an evaluation of how British intelligence were identifying U-boat lines in the mid-Atlantic, it was recommended, purely out of an abundance of caution, to insert a fourth rotor into the three-rotor Enigma machines to better encrypt wireless transmissions between BdU and U-boats. BdU did not believe their encryption was broken, but decided nonetheless to strengthen their signal protection. This became known as 'Shark' to British cryptologists and immediately ended their ability to read any German naval wireless messages. Among Allied cryptologists, this became known as the 'Great Blackout'.

None of this was known to the crew of *U-402* who over the last few weeks had readied their boat for their next patrol. Again, more food and supplies were loaded onto the boat than usual. The rumours began to circulate. 'Are we going to America?' Every available space was packed with cans and dried meat. There was a heightened sense of excitement on board.

Casinos or Broadway?
On 26 March 1942 *U-402* cast off and departed St Nazaire for an evening crossing of the Bay of Biscay. The U-boat headed south-west for the deep water off the continental shelf (known today as the La Rochelle Canyon). On the 28th, at 0342hrs, an urgent

message was received from BdU 'To all boats east of 29°W: Head for BF 6510 at highest speed. English landing at St Nazaire.'

The port of St Nazaire had the Normandie dry dock capable of handling large passenger liners or capital ships. With a length of 350m, a width of 50m and a height of over 15m, it was the only dry dock on the western coast of France capable of servicing large German commerce raiders like *Bismarck* or *Tirpitz*. The *Bismarck* was sunk on 27 May 1941, the day after *U-402* was commissioned, but the *Tirpitz* was still considered a major threat if she sortied out into the Atlantic. The decision was made by the Royal Navy to destroy the dry dock, thereby denying its use to the *Kriegsmarine*.

Under the codename Operation 'Chariot', the obsolete destroyer HMS *Campbeltown* along with 18 other small craft and over 600 British commandos departed from the English coast to cross the Channel on the afternoon of the 26th. Late in the evening of the 27th, RAF bombers conducted a raid over St Nazaire in order to draw German attention away from the seaward approaches. However, the bombers' behaviour, designed to maximise their time over the target, raised suspicions among the defenders that something else might be afoot other than a normal air raid. Despite growing concerns, the British surface flotilla made their way into the Loire Estuary and HMS *Campbeltown*, disguised to look like a German destroyer, rammed the lock. Its bow was packed with 4.5 tons of high explosives set in concrete with a delayed fuse. British commandos stormed ashore to raid a number of port facilities. At noon on the 28th the *Campbeltown*'s explosives detonated, killing over 350 German officers and civilians who were touring the converted British destroyer, and crippling the lock for the remainder of the war. Of the 611 men who undertook the daring raid, 228 returned to Britain, 169 were killed and 215 became prisoners of war.

After receiving the radio message from BdU, von Forstner turned *U-402* around and headed for the new coordinates at three-quarters speed. Four hours later the raid was over and BdU sent the following message 'English attack at St Nazaire by destroyer and fast boats finished, is repulsed.' With the raid over, *U-402* reversed course to continue back toward the west. Von Forstner knew where he was going, though the crew did not. He received an order to proceed to the US East Coast before the boat's departure. More specific guidance on his patrol area was to be sent once he arrived – just like the start of his second patrol. His initial destination was kept classified. The crew knew they were heading west, and began to wonder about their final patrol area. For now,

U-402 was in the North Atlantic south-east of the Flemish Cap during in the early weeks of April. Here it encountered some of the worst surface conditions experienced to date. The U-boat could not make any headway in 30ft waves and had to proceed submerged. In this picture the bow of the *U-402* comes crashing down into the violent sea as water rushes across the deck. (Friebolin collection)

Heavy seas are photographed off *U-402*'s starboard side. The photo was taken from a low position at the rear of the conning tower because Friebolin was likely bracing himself for stability. There are easily 20ft swells. (Friebolin collection)

though, they were in familiar waters just north of the Azores.

The rest of the westbound cruise was uneventful. The monotony of each day was broken up by drills, crash dives and submerged running. On several occasions distant explosions were heard, as well as the sounds of turbine propellers, but nothing was seen through the periscope. Somewhere, just beyond the horizon there was some surface action occurring, a reminder that they were in a war.

On the evening of 2 April, two destroyers were spotted, and *U-402* submerged. Under standing orders, von Forstner did not attack them, but waited to see if a convoy followed. After it was

Serving on watch duty in rough weather meant being cold and wet. Crews usually remained on watch for several hours before a new watch took their place. In rough surface conditions a lifeline secured to a belt around the crewman's waist was clipped onto the conning tower to help prevent them from being swept overboard. Here we see three unidentified crewmen, wet and cold, on watch looking for both potential threats and quarry as they brace themselves next to the attack periscope. (Friebolin collection)

determined that the two destroyers were operating independently of a convoy, he sent a short report and continued on his westward course. Over the next several days the weather continued to worsen and by the 9th, *U-402* could 'barely make way' and von Forstner had to dive the boat 'to proceed submerged'. A sea state of 7 was soon registered with waves 9m (29.5ft) high. *U-402* could average 120nm a day surfaced, but in these conditions it was down to 15nm. Von Forstner decided to continue submerged in calmer water where he could average 50nm a day, though he had to surface periodically to ventilate the boat and recharge its electric batteries. The next evening, the diesel engines gave out, likely due to the strain of the surface weather. *U-402* dived for repairs that took several hours to complete.

The surface conditions grew even worse. The waves now crested at 15m (45.9ft), before the conditions began to slowly improve and *U-402* was able to continue surface cruising. Being on watch offered a break from the damp, noise and noxious smells inside the U-boat, but in a storm like this, being on watch could be dangerous and the men on deck had to lash themselves in to keep from being washed overboard.

In the early evening of the 13th, the watch spotted smoke on the horizon, followed the mast of a steamer heading south-west. Von Forstner ordered a pursuit, but the diesels stalled again, and the

Two photos showing the conditions on watch during rough weather. The officer without any foul-weather gear shows the two stripes of an Oberleutnant zur See and a round patch of an Ingenieuroffizier. This was Chief Engineer Meyer-Oswald taking a break on deck, likely to attempt to smoke a cigarette, which earlier photos showed he enjoyed. (Friebolin collection)

steamer was lost from sight in a rain squall. Its expected course was quickly plotted, the diesels were restarted, and the pursuit began. *U-402* dived and the sonarman was asked for an all-around sweep in order to obtain a correct sound bearing, but nothing was heard. *U-402* resurfaced to locate the target visually, and was rewarded when the steamer burst forth from a rain squall only 4nm away.

The fact that the sonarman did not detect the steamer's propeller disappointed von Forstner as this was not the first time the sonar gear – or its operator – had failed. An investigation revealed that there had been a repairable malfunction, possibly caused by the harsh North Atlantic weather that often played havoc with sensitive gear. As *U-402* had been forced to spend so much time submerged over the previous week, this could easily have generated high condensation and humidity within the boat that damaged the on-board electronics.

Now that the steamer was so close, von Forstner ordered a crash dive for a torpedo shot, but the steamer zig-zagged, so he decided on a two-fan shot. He was able to get a better profile view of his target, 'Normal freight steamer, 2 masts, 1 smokestack, armament astern, no markings or flag, estimated at 5000 GRT'. Fire! Two torpedoes were launched from tubes I and III at 30 knots and set to a depth of 4m. The target was only 800m away with its port side fully exposed to *U-402*'s bow. The seconds ticked by . . .53, 54, 55, 56 . . . then a loud thud . . .a faint metallic 'crack' but no explosion. At least one of the torpedoes struck the vessel, but the contact pistol failed. The steamer, possibly not knowing what just happened, came to a complete stop, and blew off steam from her funnel.

The German G7e T2 torpedoes were notoriously unreliable as both their contact and magnetic pistols often failed to ignite the explosive charge. It was not until mid-1942 that these torpedoes were replaced with the upgraded T3 version that redesigned the entire exploding mechanism. It is not known what version *U-402* was equipped on this patrol, but they were almost certainly the earlier T2s.

Von Forstner decided to fire another torpedo and deliver the 'coup de grâce', as he wrote in his war diary, but determined there was a mechanical defect in the periscope's direction compass. There was a 13-degree difference between the fire-control computer and the boat-fixed setting circle on the periscope. In order to compensate for the discrepancy, he decided to zero out the lead angle and fire at 0 degrees. The third torpedo was fired almost 45 minutes after the first two, but the torpedo from tube II missed the stationary target completely.

Frustrated, von Forstner asked the Torpedo Control Officer to quickly investigate and it was determined that the 'boat-fixed setting circle was not screwed down' and 'while moving the retaining ring, the setting circle unintentionally turned'. What this meant in practice was that any course of a target spotted from the periscope was incorrect. Now that the problem was understood, von Forstner quickly ordered a fourth torpedo fired from tube IV at 0024hrs on the 14th that struck near the aft mast and detonated. Water began to rush on board the stricken vessel. It settled quickly astern, as the bow 'rises almost vertically into the air, after 7 minutes a boiler explosion, 7½ minutes after the hit the steamer is sunk'.

The explosion killed the vessel's master, seven crew and four gunners, but thirty-two crewmen and six other gunners successfully abandoned the stricken vessel in lifeboats. As per standing orders, von Forstner surfaced and steered among the lifeboats to question survivors and determine what vessel he had sunk. Von Forstner learned that it was the *Empire Progress* (5,249 GRT). He did not obtain any further information from the crew.

The *Empire Progress* was one of twenty-seven merchant vessels and ten escorts travelling in the westbound Convoy ON-80. She was the only vessel in the convoy that straggled for an unknown reason, and found herself in the path of *U-402*. The crew's reaction to the sinking of their first merchant was initially one of excitement, but their mood soon turned sombre. Seeing survivors bobbing in the life rafts for the first time brought home the reality of war, as it could be the *U-402*'s crew bobbing in the open sea next time. The survivors were later rescued by the Norwegian-flagged merchant *Olaf Fostenes* and landed at Halifax.

After putting some distance between his U-boat and the *Empire Progress*, von Forstner radioed the sinking to BdU who did

The British-flagged SS *Empire Progress* (5,249 GRT) was hit by her first torpedo from *U-402* at 2226hrs on 13 April 1942, 151nm south-west of the Grand Banks of Newfoundland (40° 29'N, 52° 35'W – Grid CC 2855). Only one torpedo of the first two hit the straggler from Convoy ON-80. A third torpedo launched at the stopped vessel missed, because a malfunction between the attack periscope and fire-control computer was causing a 13-degree difference. Once the problem was recognised a fourth and final torpedo struck the vessel at 0024hrs near the aft mast and the vessel went under 7½ minutes later. The first true sinking of an Allied merchantmen left the crew sombre as they watched the crew abandon their vessel and bob on the open ocean in life rafts. (Author's collection)

not acknowledge the report, but recorded the success in its own war diary that day. For the next five days *U-402* continued its westward approach to the US East Coast, spotting a neutral Swiss vessel along the way that was ignored. The rumours about *U-402*'s final destination grew among the crew given they had now passed far beyond the area where U-boats typically deployed for wolfpack operations. *U-402* was 340nm south-east of New York. They were heading toward the American coast, a fact that could not be hidden from the crew any longer. Some joked that they would soon visit the casinos of Atlantic City, New Jersey. Others suggested they might cruise up the Hudson River and see New York.

On the evening of the 17th von Forstner radioed BdU to confirm the correct radio circuit he needed to operate. He received a response the following morning confirming the switch, with the note that it should have been done almost 12 days earlier. Von Forstner checked with the radioman and confirmed that the request to switch over to the 'Greenland' circuit was broadcast, but the 'To' was decrypted as 'Forster' and not 'Forstner'. It was believed BdU had been referring to Oberleutnant Ludwig Forster in *U-654* who was also headed to the US East Coast. This was neither the first nor the last time that communication from BdU was interpreted incorrectly by the radioman.

With the confusion resolved, BdU issued *U-402* its final operational area. At 1240hrs on 18 April, von Forstner received the following message: '*U-402* free to manoeuvre on traffic in operations area naval square CA 98 and 99 and south there from in accordance with referenced "Schuch" situation report.' The report referenced by BdU came from Korvettenkapitän Heinrich Schuch who was in command of *U-105* operating off Cape

Hatteras, North Carolina when on 30 March he reported 'crossroads of medium sometimes heavy shipping traffic proceeding in SW-NE and SE-NW directions'. This meant that *U-402* was to move to an area some 280nm west of Cape Hatteras, well off the coast to look for merchant traffic.

As *U-402* cruised on the surface toward its new destination, the watch on the bridge spotted an aircraft and the U-boat crash-dived. The aircraft was identified as a floatplane, and noted in the log as a possible Vought-Sikorsky OS2U-1. If the visual identification was accurate, this was a ship-launched seaplane that suggested a large warship was in the vicinity, so caution was advised.

From 19 to 25 April *U-402* cruised on station without finding a single merchant vessel. On the 20th three lifeboats with sails were spotted at a distance of 4nm, and were left alone.[16] Light air cover continued to be observed, possibly looking for the lifeboats, as well as an aircraft identified as a B-25 Mitchell. If it was a B-25, it was likely from the 17th Bombardment Group that had recently transferred from Pearl Harbor to the US East Coast in order to bolster anti-U-boat operations.

Frustration grew as *U-402* sat out in the ocean without any targets. While his peers had sunk scores of Allied vessels along the unprepared coast in the preceding months, von Forstner appeared to have arrived too late to reap the harvest of tankers and merchantmen as American defences improved. Von Forstner's own inexperience and strong sense correct procedure was showing. He interpreted the 'freedom of manoeuvre' to mean within the two grid squares he was given; however, this was incorrect. He noted his mistake in the war diary, owning the error that cost his U-boat a week of fuel and fruitless searching:

> Following receipt of radio message that boats should operate under the coast due to the fuel situation, the radio message directed to me on 18 April was checked concerning attack area and it is determined that if after the sentence: '*U-402* free to manoeuvre:' a period was placed, there arises a completely different meaning than I had taken from the radio message. I would have had freedom to manoeuvre without limitations, the second sentence: 'on traffic in CA98 and 99' . . . was only a traffic advisory.

After he clarified his misunderstanding with BdU, he received a mild admonishment at 1128hrs on the 26th: 'To Forstner. In accordance with Radio Message you had freedom to manoeuvre from 18 April. Traffic note means no obligation. Do not think too rigidly. 20 cbm [cubic meters] without provisions intended as supply. Lost 8 days are very disappointing, especially as now the bright nights arrive; but nevertheless, some time can still be spent with an additional 20 cbm.'

BdU certainly played a central role in the coordination of U-boat attacks on convoys. But it did not have the resources to direct every U-boat's actions and it relied on the independence of its commanders to make the most of the tactical situation as aggressively as possible.

The loss of eight days was critical, especially off the Eastern Seaboard in April where U-boats were finding numerous unescorted merchantmen and oil tankers moving north-south along the coast. Von Forstner noted his intention: 'Head for the coast at Cape Fear, then on [north east] course to Hatteras to detect traffic in Onslow and Raleigh Bays. If favourable, remain there, otherwise continue north at Hatteras or Wimble Shoals to operate on traffic there.' *U-402* sped along on the surface toward the North Carolina coast.

In the early hours of the 29th von Forstner spotted a small fishing boat and a small 'U-boat hunter' of the US Navy's PC-450 class within sight of the Flying Pan Shoals, which he evaded to maintain surprise. As the sun rose, *U-402* submerged as it was within visual range of the coast. At periscope depth it proceeded northeast in Onslow Bay with only 30m of depth below its keel. The boat surfaced at 2040hrs to ventilate, and as von Forstner conducted an all-round sweep he noticed what he believed was another patrol boat 10 minutes later and dived again. He set course for Cape Lookout with the lights of the sea town of Beaufort clearly visible to port.

At 2200hrs von Forstner spotted vessels on the horizon, first two freighters, then a large tanker of the 'North Atlantic' class estimated at 10,000 GRT. This convoy was escorted by a destroyer that he noted was of the 'Barney' class. The small convoy had air cover from a B-25 circling overhead. He was unable to set up a torpedo shot due to the shallow depth, and changed position in the hope of catching another convoy. Otherwise von Forstner planned on attacking patrol vessels, a sure sign his frustration had reached its peak over a lack of merchant targets. Less than an hour later a British tanker came into view, just as a Martin PBM Mariner flying boat was spotted overhead. Again, von Forstner was unable to line up a shot as the tanker headed north-east out of the area. Shortly after midnight (around 1900hrs local) on the 30th, von Forstner's patience gave out and he launched a torpedo from tube IV at a small patrol boat which malfunctioned and struck the sandy bottom after 15 seconds. The sonarman confirmed the dull thud of a soft impact. The patrol vessel never noticed the torpedo attack and continued on her way.

As the sun set, *U-402* surfaced. The sea was flat and a bright moon glowed. A shadow appeared heading north, and as von Forstner manoeuvred his boat to take a shot, he was spotted by alert lookouts and his radioman reported hearing the transmission 'S.S.S.S. Cape Lookout'. The vessel fired a shot from one of its deck guns at *U-402* that fell wide. Von Forstner made the tactical decision to move the U-boat closer to the coast so that he was on the dark side of the horizon, and not silhouetted.

Some 30 minutes later a new shadow appeared out of the darkness. Von Forstner wanted to make a submerged attack but could not due to the shallow water depth of about 17–19m (56.1–62.7 feet). A second shadow appeared and von Forstner believed that one of the two was an escort. He found himself in between both shadows, with the starboard one taking the shape of a freighter with two masts, one funnel, four cargo hatches and a large superstructure clearly visible in the moonlight. The port shadow was indeed that of an armed escort. At 2036hrs (2036hrs local time) a single shot from the reloaded tube II was fired. He recorded the result: 'After 1 minute 33 seconds = 1400m a hit at the after mast, high explosion column, stern settles quickly deeper, in 4 minutes disappeared up to the smoke stack. Boiler explosion, freighter lies with stern on the bottom at 19 meters.'

Tension was running high among the crew given the situation. Von Forstner continued on the attack course of the torpedo track for another minute because he believed it presented a sharp, and thus limited, silhouette to the escort. The freighter was heard transmitting the distress signal 'SS Kapelnos'. Von Forstner thought that this was the name of the vessel, but in actuality it was Russian for 'sinking'.

The vessel hit was the Russian-flagged steam merchant SS *Ashkhabad* (5,284 GRT). She was under escort by HMS *Lady Elsa* (FY 124), which fired a single 4in shell at the surfaced *U-402* and may have also dropped depth charges to scare off the U-boat, as detonations were heard aboard *U-402*. In any case *Lady Elsa* proceeded to pick up all forty-seven members of *Ashkhabad*'s crew who were brought to Morehead City.

Von Forstner wanted to use his deck gun to finish off the vessel, but realised this was not tactically possible and believed she

The Soviet-flagged SS *Ashkhabad* (5,284 GRT) was hit by a torpedo from *U-402* at 0336hrs on 30 April 1942, 31nm south-east of the brightly-lit Cape Lookout lighthouse (34° 19'N, 76° 31'W – Grid DC 1221). *U-402* had to escape north after it was identified surfaced at night by Lieutenant (jg) Robert A Proctor in his PBY-5A that was equipped with the new ASE airborne radar system. This was the first time a PBY identified a surfaced U-boat by radar. (The Mariners' Museum P0001.003-01–PB6252_MM)

was a total loss anyway. Clearly, the escort did not spot the surfaced U-boat as it manoeuvred out to deeper water at three-quarters speed. A few hours before midnight *U-402* crash-dived as an approaching twin-engined land-based aircraft flew out of the darkness and dropped several bombs delivering 'slight damage'. *U-402* was only in 20m (66.6ft) of water, running with only 10m below its keel. *U-402* remained submerged for an hour, then surfaced at 2208hrs.

The lookouts were sharp that night to spot the approaching aircraft. This incident marked one of the turning points against the U-boats operating along the Eastern Seaboard. Squadron VP-84 had arrived from California to be rebased in Norfolk under the Eastern Sea Frontier command in mid-April. During the evening Lieutenant (jg) Robert A Proctor in BuNo 7277 went aloft after receiving a report about the torpedoing off Cape Lookout. His PBY-5A was equipped with the new ASE airborne radar system and Proctor was able to identify the surfaced *U-402* in the darkness. This was the first time a PBY located and attacked a U-boat by radar. As the use of airborne radar increased throughout the war, aircraft became the number one destroyer of U-boats.

The master of the *Ashkhabad*, Captain Alexey Pavlovitch, was taken back out to his vessel on 30 April. Upon arriving he found that crew from the armed trawler HMS *Hertfordshire* (FY 176) had boarded the vessel and removed sensitive equipment from the bridge. *Hertfordshire* was in command of all British trawlers at Morehead City. As the *Ashkhabad* appeared to be salvageable, arrangements were made for a tug to tow the ship to port for repairs. Once the British were informed that the vessel was to be salvaged and was not abandoned, they returned all the items to the Russian captain. This exchange was not entirely friendly as later events suggest. During the next several days the *Ashkhabad* remained in its position.

It was not widely known that the stricken merchant was to be salvaged, and on 3 May, the destroyer USS *Semmes* (AG 24) fired three rounds from its 3in gun at the *Ashkhabad* and set the superstructure on fire, based on standing orders to sink all derelicts in the shipping lane. Then HMS *St Zeno* (FY 280) arrived, drawn by the smoke on the horizon, and fired a final shot into the burning vessel to ensure it sank after authorisation was given by the captain of HMS *Hertfordshire*.

When the captain of HMS *Hertfordshire* was asked why he authorised the sinking, despite his knowledge of the *Ashkhabad*'s pending salvage, he justified the action by stating that he hoped to 'put out the flames' by sinking the vessel, which he viewed as a hazard to an approaching convoy. A US Navy relief tug arrived soon after the incident to tow her to port for repairs, but it was too late and the vessel was no longer salvageable.

The *Ashkhabad*'s stern came to rest in about 60ft of water and she was salvageable. However, before a salvage tug could arrived to take the vessel in tow, the ship was spotted by the US destroyer USS *Semmes* (AG 24) on 3 May, which fired three rounds from her 3in gun into the *Ashkhabad* based on standing orders to sink all derelicts in the shipping lane. The shells set the superstructure on fire. Drawn by the smoke, HMS *St Zeno* (FY 280) arrived and fired the final shot, sending the *Ashkhabad* to the bottom. (Courtesy of Dale Hansen)

Herbert was one of the first crew up on deck for watch duty the following morning as the sun rose in the east. He saw the distant glow of the Cape Hatteras lighthouse in the west, as the sun caught the looming structure. He was in awe of its magnificent size. Lighthouses in Germany were not that large, and this was the largest structure Herbert ever saw with his own eyes. It was a serene moment, he recalled fondly long after the war.

U-402 continued its northward course, and with the rising sun, it submerged. Off in the distance an airship was spotted heading south-west. Shortly after noon three very distant explosions could be heard, probably depth charges being dropped on a suspected submerged target. From the airship's height, visibility off the Outer Banks could be as much as 20m deep, making submerged U-boats easily recognisable as lurking dark shadows below the surface.

Just before 1300hrs a sound bearing was heard, one of the first from the sonar room during the last three war patrols. Von Forstner peered through the periscope and spotted the airship even closer overhead, and below it were three freighters and one destroyer. He manoeuvred into position for a shot. They were far off, some 1,800m away, but they began to overlap and offered a tempting target. He fired a torpedo from tube III at 1335hrs. The shot passed aft of the targets and missed. Nearly an hour later yet another freighter came into view, another torpedo fired, and another miss. This torpedo sounded like a 'bottom runner', having struck the bottom without detonation while the propeller churned the water until its battery ran out. Frustration grew anew.

In the morning of 1 May, von Forstner sent a situation report to BdU radioing his previous sinking of the 'Kapelnos', not knowing it was actually the *Ashkhabad*. He decided 'With these failures with submerged attacks in shallow water I decide during the bright nights to proceed on the [north-west] approach to Cape Hatteras and Cape Lookout and to operate in the slightly more favourable nights again on the identified route close off the coast.' It was expected that *U-402* and other returning U-boats from the US East Coast would refuel in mid-ocean. This would allow the U-boat to remain off the Eastern Seaboard longer. However, BdU confirmed later that day to von Forstner and Kapitänleutnant Adalbert Schnee operating in *U-201* that 'Contrary to previous commitment no fuel supplement. Time delay of 10 days for U-tanker is not supportable.'

Chivalry is not Dead
Faced with an extremely limited fuel supply, von Forstner decided to remain in the area near the coast for one more day. A few hours before midnight on 1 May the lookouts detected a shadow to the north-west, heading in a southerly direction at a distance of 4nm. *U-402* turned to match its course and speed, and manoeuvred ahead for a shot. Von Forstner could tell this was a 'warship silhouette', but could not distinguish further details because it was dark and the target was still far away.

After manoeuvring for nearly two hours, von Forstner ordered his boat submerged for an attack. As he peered through the search periscope in the control room, he found it difficult to re-locate the target, and realised it was smaller than originally thought. After another 30 minutes he ordered a three-fan shot from tubes I, II, and IV as he did not want to miss the target given the previous torpedo problems experienced off the coast. The target was 2,000m away and the torpedoes ran long. Two torpedoes ran deep, with the first passing directly under the bow and the second passing under the stern. The third ran true. At 2 minutes and 9 seconds a detonation was heard and through the periscope von Forstner observed a '. . . high black explosion column amidships, shortly thereafter various smaller detonations, probably depth charges. . . . The bow rises high out of the water briefly, 1 minute after detonation with the dissipation of the smoke it is no longer seen.' The secondary detonations were in fact the ship's depth charges exploding as the stern sank.

Von Forstner ordered *U-402* to surface and head toward the

USS *Cythera* (PY 26) (602 GRT) was sunk by *U-402* at 0644hrs on 2 May 1942, 98nm southeast off Cape Lookout (33° 15'N, 75° 26'W – Grid DC 1591). She was originally the steel-hulled yacht *Agawa*, which was converted into a Patrol Yacht U-boat hunter in 1918. She was returned to her owners but reacquired by the US Navy for $1 in 1941. She was converted back into a patrol yacht at the Philadelphia Naval Yard. This photo shows her before her conversion in December 1941. (US National Archives Records Administration)

debris in order to confirm the identity of the target. As the watch turned on a spotlight and swept the sea upon which a large oil slick appeared, they spotted two survivors. As von Forstner noted in his war diary, 'a raft with 2 men whom we get aboard. It is unlikely that many more survivors exist.'

The vessel was the steel-hulled 212ft, 602-ton USS *Cythera* (PY-26). The patrol yacht, under command of Commander Charles Rudderow, had just departed Norfolk, Virginia en route to Pearl Harbor via the Panama Canal where it was expected to join the fight against Japanese submarines in the Pacific.

The two men were covered in oil and clinging to the dingy as *U-402* came alongside. Both men were brought onto the deck forward of the 88mm deck gun. Soon a small crowd surrounded these unexpected 'guests'. They were US Navy Pharmacist Mate First Class Charles Harold Carter and Seaman Second Class James Brown, III – the first US Navy personnel captured by Germany during the war.

Carter and Brown were topside on watch duty that night. Brown was posted as forward lookout, while Carter was on the bridge standing next to Commander Rudderow. After the war Brown provided testimony to the US Navy about the sinking:

> At approximately 0045, 2 May 1942, the *Cythera* was struck by a torpedo. Just previous to that time I was standing watch as a trainer on the forward gun mount. I was looking out to starboard and saw two flashes of

The *Cythera* was armed with one bow-mounted 3in deck gun, possibly four .50cal machine guns, and two stern racks that could hold fifty depth charges. This photo shows her stern at the Philadelphia Naval Yard on 2 March 1942 after her conversion. As the stern sank, depth charges went off killing most of the crew who managed to survive the initial torpedo hit. Two survivors, however, were rescued and brought on board *U-402*. (US National Archives Records Administration)

white on the water. The full moon was off the port quarter at that time. It was a very clear night and the sea was calm. As soon as I saw the flashes, I gave the warnings to the man on the telephone just aft of the gun mount. Immediately after giving the warning, I saw a torpedo wake passing under the bow. I then saw another wake directly approaching the ship. A couple of seconds late the ship was struck about amidships and there was a terrific explosion. I was thrown in the air and landed on my knees on the gun mount. I couldn't see the stern but in my opinion the ship broke in two immediately, just aft of the bridge.

Brown watched the forward part of the ship heel over to port and sink. He watched several others jump overboard, then heard two of the depth charges explode and jumped into the water. As soon as he surfaced, two waves broke over him.

After the waves passed, I looked around and saw the last part of the ship, the bow-sprit, sink from sight. A minute or so later I saw Carter, PHM1/c, USN, sitting in a life raft about fifty feet away from me. I shouted to him and when he answered, I started to swim towards him and on the way picked up a life ring which was floating in the water. When I reached the raft, Carter was sitting on part of a hatch cover he had laid across the raft. With Carter's aid, I climbed partially into the raft and then we looked around in the water to see if we could see any other survivors. We could see none, and only a very small amount of debris. After a couple of minutes, we heard the submarine surface. We saw it slowly circle around toward us. We attempted to hide in the water but the moon gave away our position and the submarine closed and picked us up. While on the conning tower, Carter and I again looked around for other survivors before we were taken below. The German submarine personnel later told us that they had seen no other survivors or bodies.[17]

No one else from the *Cythera* survived the sinking. Most of the crew were below in their bunks sleeping when she was torpedoed.

The appearance of US sailors on the U-boat's main deck caused quite a stir among the crew. Von Forstner asked them their names, ranks and what vessel he had sunk. Obermaschinst Fischer spoke perfect English and conducted the questioning of the two men. Brown spoke fluent German. After obtaining the necessary information, von Forstner gave Brown his sweater, both men some brandy, then ordered them to be taken below and cleaned up.

Von Forstner's order caused confusion, if not consternation, to both Carter and Brown. Both men requested to be returned to their dingy and left adrift where they were found, to be hopefully picked up later by a rescue vessel.[18] Brown recalled that von Forstner replied 'No, boys, the war is over for you.' According to Herbert, von Forstner knew that no S.O.S. had been broadcast from *Cythera* before she went down and that they were outside the commercial shipping lane. There was little hope that the two US Navy sailors would be found and rescued. The only choice for von Forstner was to take Carter and Brown on board as 'prisoners' on their return trip to France.

Resigned to their fate, Brown asked von Forstner one more question before they were brought below. 'Why didn't you machine-gun us at sea?' This question shocked von Forstner and the crew members on deck. They stated their disbelief that the two US sailors would even consider such a thing possible. As a professional naval officer, this question offended von Forstner, though he understood that this belief was a result of Allied propaganda. Out of thousands of U-boat patrols and Allied vessels sunk, only a single U-boat commander, Heinz Eck of *U-852*, admitted that he machine-gunned survivors of a torpedo attack. He was tried, convicted and hanged for his crimes after the war. Wartime propaganda painted U-boat crews as bloodthirsty 'wolves' of the sea who mercilessly 'hunted' defenceless Allied ships and machine-gunned any survivors found in the water. Decades of historical research by both professional and avocational historians has proven there to be no systematic 'machine-gunning' of survivors by German U-boat crews. While isolated cases of wartime brutality can never be ruled out, German U-boat crews behaved no different than their Allied submarine counterparts at that time, all of whom shared a common enemy – the sea.

USCG Captain (Ret.) Waters, a veteran of the Battle of the Atlantic, penned as much in his conclusion to *Bloody Winter* published in 1967:

> In the aftermath of war, the men of the U-boat arm were painted as the blackest of villains, guilty of the wanton killing of thousands of defenceless merchant seamen. Undeniably, they, like our own submariners, inflicted great destruction and much human misery, but the death from a torpedo is more grievous or stealthy than a bomb dropped from the sky at night is no more supportable than the contention that a convoy of armed merchantmen screened by warships is a defenceless target.[19]

Bringing Carter and Brown on board the U-boat boosted morale as their presence broke the monotony of the already six-week long patrol. Herbert recalled that at that time, the crew viewed Britain as their main enemy, and harboured no ill feelings toward the two US Navy men now on board. Most of the German crew, like their American counterparts, were young, in their early twenties, and came from rural communities. Few had ever left Germany before, let alone met an American.

Submariners quickly learn everything there is to know about each other, as they have to live and work together in extremely close quarters. The crews were genuinely excited to talk to their new guests during the more than two-week journey back to St Nazaire. No armed guard was posted to watch them. As there was no place to lock up both men, Carter and Brown shared the same sleeping berths in the bow as the crew, and ate their meals with them. The crew learned that Carter was aboard the USS *Oklahoma* when the Japanese attacked Pearl Harbor on 7 December 1941.

U-402 (on the right) photographed on the morning of 29 May, is passing Belle-Île-en-Mer Island on its way into St Nazaire lock. The U-boat to the left is *U-136*, commanded by Kapitänleutnant Heinrich Zimmermann, also returning from a successful patrol of the US East Coast, having hit a total of four vessels (21,662 GRT). Note that both U-boats have some form of camouflage. While hard to see, *U-402* has what appears to be black/dark grey swatches on the bow, and just visible on the aft section. *U-136* wears bold angular stripes on the conning tower and along the lower hull. (Bundesarchiv, Bild_MW_6414_19 Kramer)

His story of survival certainly resonated with the crew.

According to Brown, he and Carter '. . . were treated well. They were given cigarettes every day and allowed to go topside for fresh air every day.' Brown specifically recalled that 'von Forstner was a compassionate man who was not signed on to Nazi ideology. He was a professional sailor who came from a family of military background. He was not enthusiastic about war, but he did his job well as a German officer.'[20]

The cruise back to France was briefly interrupted on 9 May when in calm seas a shadow travelling eastward was spotted making a zig-zag course. Von Forstner had nothing to lose and fired a torpedo from tube III at 0914hrs that missed. He turned for a stern shot as there were no other tubes ready, and the second shot also missed. He noted the following in his war diary: 'Under the existing conditions, the breaking dawn and the armament of the steamer as well as elimination of the element of surprise that I foresaw with the use of artillery, because I had no more tubes ready and my fuel oil inventory prevented manoeuvring ahead during the day, I had to let him go.'

Carter and Brown had their first and only view of the war through enemy eyes as they watched the efficiency of von Forstner's crew in their response to his orders. One might imagine the crew felt awkward, carrying out their wartime duties with two US Navy personnel on board. Everyone realised that the world was on fire

In this somewhat overexposed photo, *U-402* is seen making its way toward St Nazaire. The crew is on deck raising the bollards. (Bibliothek für Zeitgeschichte 1-52-0180-a)

U-136 pulls alongside *U-402*'s starboard side, flying its four victory pennants as both U-boats make their way into the St Nazaire lock. *U-402* was given the privilege of docking alongside the wharf as it was carrying the first two US Navy prisoners of war taken by the Kriegsmarine. (Friebolin collection)

Just before *U-402* pulled into the lock, Propaganda-Kompanie Kriegsberichter (war reporter) Kramer came aboard to interview the crew and the prisoners of war, and take photos of the two 'guests'. Here Kramer interviews Seaman Second Class James Brown, III and Pharmacist Mate First Class Charles Harold Carter. Brown is on the right speaking with Kramer as he was fluent in German. The biscuit tin contained going away gifts from the crew. (Friebolin collection)

around them and that they were all playing a small part in a far larger conflict.

Many of the German crewmen were very interested in America, having heard stories about its natural beauties and big cities. Discussions about each other's homeland continued long into the night. Soon a bond was formed between the German crew and their guests. By the time *U-402* reached St Nazaire both men invited the German crew to visit them in America after the war, a fact confirmed in both Brown's post-war interview and Herbert's recollection. Brown was from New York City, and Carter was from Corsicana, Texas. Both locations were of great interest to the crew, who listened intently to their guest's stories of skyscrapers, Broadway, as well as Cowboys and Indians.

The arrival of *U-402* at St Nazaire on 20 May was met with much fanfare due to the arrival of the first US Naval prisoners-of-war. A Propaganda-Kompanie (PK) photographer was present along with a full Kriegsmarine band and high-ranking officers from the 3rd U-Flotilla. The surviving photographs of *U-402*'s arrival show both Carter and Brown smiling on the conning tower as they smoke a pipe and cigarette given to them by the crew, as they share a final

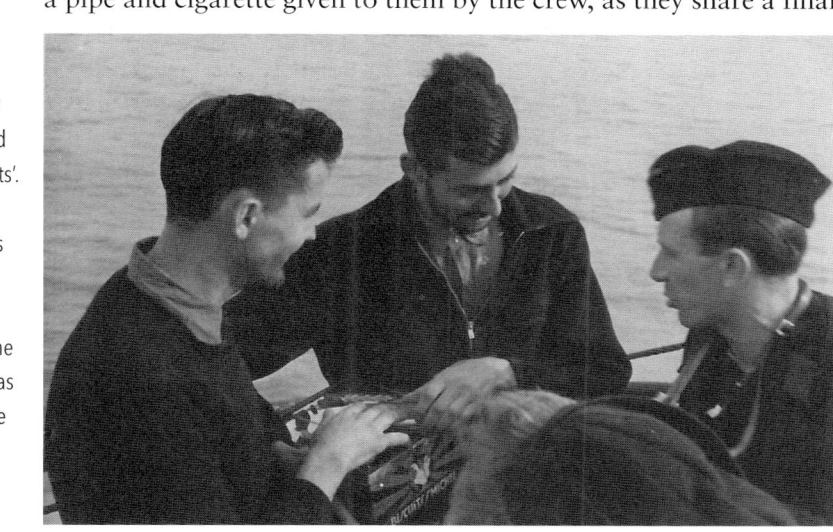

U-402 has pulled into the lock and docked along the St Nazaire wharf. Friebolin took a quick snapshot from the main deck looking up at both Brown (l) and Carter (r). To the far right is the 1st Watch Officer. The other crewman to the far left is unknown. (Friebolin collection)

Von Forstner with a full beard and wearing his binoculars with an 'M' marking and serial number 2173. He knew this was an important return that would attract more than the usual officials and PK men so he dressed to look the part of a returning U-boat captain. (Bundesarchiv, Bild_MW_6414_21 Kramer)

moment of levity with their new found friends. Both men were provided a package that contained biscuits as well as cigarettes and a few mementos. It was in fact a care package the crew prepared in secret and presented to them for their onward journey to a prisoner-of-war camp. As the proceedings continued the seemingly jovial mood was about to abruptly end as the reality of the war finally caught up with these German and American sailors.

As Carter and Brown walked off the U-boat they were turned over to the German Military Police – the 'Chain Dogs' as my grandfather referred to them because of the gorget that hung around their neck on a chain. The Military Police, however, had no bond with the two Americans. Carter and Brown represented the new American enemy that Germany faced and would be treated as such. The German MPs immediately took their care package away from them while still in sight of *U-402*'s crew as they shoved Carter and Brown roughly toward the waiting truck that would take them away.

The crew of *U-402* were not going to accept the rough treatment they just witnessed. They poured onto the wharf yelling at the 'Chain Dogs'. In an instant the crew and military police were standing toe-to-toe shouting curses and threats at each other in front of shocked senior naval officers and PK photographers.

Herbert was below deck going through the normal routine of a U-boat's arrival back to port, but managed to get up on deck to see the commotion. Pushing and shoving began between the two groups of men. Had punches been thrown, the situation could have escalated into a real mess for the crew of *U-402*. Von Forstner and other Kriegsmarine officers quickly intervened and stopped any

On the right is Obermaschinst Fischer, while the other man is our unknown Bootmann pictured on watch in the previous chapter. He wears a bowtie for the occasion. Fischer could speak perfect English and was responsible for communicating with the two US Navy guests on board *U-402*. (Bundesarchiv, Bild_MW_6414_25 Kramer)

actual fight from breaking out. Brown corroborated this story when he was interviewed by his nephew, Mike McCarthy, after the war who wrote that there was '. . . consternation between the U-boat crew and the German soldiers, who may have manhandled the POWs'. I suspect that without Brown's own recollection, some might not believe the account of how a German U-boat crew risked punishment to protect the two US Navy servicemen they had befriended at sea. This was the last the crew of *U-402* ever heard of Carter or Brown, both of whom survived their time as prisoners of war.

Both men were initially interned at the Marlag und Milag Nord Prisoner-of-War Camp for British Merchant Navy and Royal Navy personnel, as there was no such camp dedicated to US military personnel at this time. The arrival of the first US Navy sailors was even mentioned in the national German language newspaper *Deutsche Zeitung in Den Niederlanden* based in Amsterdam. The paper ran a story announcing how two American sailors "Charles and James" were brought back from American coastal waters. The good news was that this allowed their families

Brown (R) and Carter (l) on the conning tower of *U-402* as it pulls into St Nazaire. Both men were treated well. They kept their rings and watches, and whatever they managed to carry when the *Cythera* went down. The biscuit tins contained some food and cigarettes for their journey into a prisoner-of-war camp. The crew had befriended the two men, and a natural bond formed. The crew did not react well to the military police who treated the two men roughly when they were taken into custody and put onto trucks for their onward movement. The crew spilled onto the wharf and stood toe-to-toe with the military police. Blows were almost landed right in front of the PK cameras, but cooler heads prevailed as officers defused the situation. (Bundesarchiv, Bild_MW_6414_27 Kramer)

Fischer talks to Brown as all three share a smoke. (Bundesarchiv, Bild_MW_6414_30 Kramer)

A delegation from the 3rd U-Flotilla was waiting for the arrival of *U-402* and *U-136*. A band was ready and many people came to see the two US Navy prisoners, including French civilians. Note the damage caused to the buildings from the British commando raid that took place on 28 March 1942, when *U-402* departed. (Bundesarchiv, Bild_MW_6414_32 Kramer)

to learn they were alive. Letters soon began to exchange with family back home.

Von Forstner summed up the situation in a letter to his wife he wrote at the end of the cruise:

> We really should have kept them locked up and all that, but a U-boat is not spacious as you know and they were nice chaps and friendly – they joined us in our meals, and we brought them home in our own way, and nobody the worse for it. At our arrival, they were met by an escort and taken away in the usual manner thought fit for prisoners of war, much to the consternation of my crew, whom they had invited to come and see them back home in the States after the war.

Von Forstner filed a separate report at the end of his patrol that contained details of his conversations with the two men.

The reality of the arrival appears to finally resonate with U-402's two guests. They now realise that the show on the wharf is to celebrate their capture. The 1st Watch Officer looks on as announcements are made. (Bundesarchiv, Bild_MW_6414_34 Kramer)

Carter's conversations proved the most fruitful, as was noted in his report that 'The statements were all derived from Carter'. Brown, it appeared, while friendly, preferred not to discuss the current war situation. The statement offers insight into the news 'from the other side of the hill' that certainly generated interesting talk on board the U-boat during its return trip. Carter gave an accurate depiction of the Japanese attack on Pearl Harbor, as he was indeed an eyewitness to those events, though he gave away little information not already available in the press. Interestingly, he stated that there were no 'suicide attacks' by Japanese pilots, some two years before such attacks occurred. He also noted that Japanese submarines had problematic 'depth keeping', perhaps referring to the five Type A midget subs that participated in the attack. He offered an exaggerated assessment of US East Coast defences, the new US battleships and cruisers being launched, and the numbers of US

Carter (l) and Brown (r) on the conning tower of U-402. Friebolin is standing behind Brown next to the UZO mount for the attack binoculars. Behind Carter is likely Obermaschinst Heinrich Prause, but this remains unconfirmed. Centre rear is the control room for the northern lock. Note that it now has sandbags placed on top, likely after the raid. Just to the right, rear of the photo is the St Nazaire U-boat bunker complex that is still under construction, though the final pens (14 and 13) are complete. (Bundesarchiv, Bild_MW_6414_38 Kramer)

Right: Crewmen from *U-402* begin to assemble on deck after Carter and Brown had left the U-boat. The U-boat next to them is *U-136* whose crew is also assembling. (Friebolin collection)

Another photo of *U-136* taken by Friebolin from the conning tower of *U-402*. The two crews are already exchanging stories of their patrols off the US East Coast. The officer standing to the far left might be the 1st Watch Officer Oberleutnant Paul-Friedrich Otto. (Friebolin collection)

soldiers amassing in England awaiting a cross-Channel invasion. One accurate statement he did make was that '29 German U-boat men were put ashore from a steamer' on 18 April 1942 and sent to a 'prison Camp for Officers that was a hotel in West Virginia'. This was the surviving crew of *U-85* sunk by the destroyer USS *Roper* on 14 April 1942 off Kill Devil Hills, Outer Banks.

The date that *U-402* pulled into its pen at St Nazaire was 20 May 1942. The U-boat and crew had been at sea for 56 days, their longest patrol yet. The overhaul by dock workers quickly began. While ashore the crew was likely housed at Casino de La Baule and the La Roseraie Hotel in the seaside town of La Baule, a short bus ride from St Nazaire. Here they could relax and forget about the cramped, damp and odorous conditions of their U-boat for a short while. There was no time for extended leave, however, as the plan was to get the boat ready and back out to sea quickly. Personnel transfers also occurred, and the young Walter Friebolin was among them. Now considered an experienced crewman, he was assigned to the larger Type IXC/40 *U-526* and the 10th U-Flotilla.

Back to the Outer Banks
The Battle for the Atlantic continued. Based in part on von Forstner's report off Cape Lookout, Dönitz recorded in the BdU war diary on 30 April that:

When sinking declined after 21 April, this at first gave the impression that traffic conditions on the American coast had changed and that the constant stream of independently-routed ships and ships in convoy had ceased. This impression was confirmed by the decline in the numbers of SSS and attack reports received from the B-Dienst Service. But during the last days more frequent reports from boats, which had lain right under the coast despite bright full-moon nights, have shown this view to be false.

On 6 May it was determined that B-Dienst was again proving effective at identifying convoy routing. Dönitz now gave consideration to shifting U-boats back to the North Atlantic from the Eastern Seaboard, but he had to make sure the intelligence reports he received were accurate. He recorded his thinking in the BdU war diary:

> Radio intelligence reports of the last months show that the convoys proceed mainly along the great circle between the Northern Channel and Newfoundland. So far, these convoys have not been attacked, because operation in the American area was more worthwhile. As at present 8 boats have sailed within 5 days, of which 3 C.O.'s are experienced in convoy operation, it is intended to rake the North American convoy route with these boats, in patrol line from AK 60 to BB 90. If this yields no results, it is intended to supply the boats in CB from *U-116* and operate them in the American area. Boats will be ordered to keep radio silence north of 49⁰ N.

'Raking', which was in practice a reconnaissance in force, occurred even in the final months of the war. U-boats formed a line heading west and looked for convoys they might happen across in their approach to the North American coast. Stragglers were attacked, and confirmation of any convoy radioed back to BdU. On 14 May Dönitz recorded his decision to deploy U-boats off the US East Coast just a little longer, as he still saw that area of operation as fruitful. 'As at present on the one hand there is doubt as to shipping routes on the North American coast but on the other traffic must go to the large ports, *U-593* has been stationed off New York, *U-455* off Delaware Bay and *U-107* off Chesapeake Bay.' Again, this was a tactic BdU still used in the last months of the war.[21]

U-402 departed St Nazaire with *U-576*, commanded by Kapitänleutnant Hans-Dieter Heinicke, in the evening of 16 June. *U-402* reached the 200m line with four VP-Boats providing protection instead of the usual two. This was in response to increasing Allied air attacks in the Bay of Biscay. Due to the clouds, which prevented early spotting, von Forstner travelled submerged for the next 16 hours to reach his first ordered patrol location in the middle of the North Atlantic. It was not clear where his patrol area was planned to be as a full resumption of convoy attacks had not occurred. On the 18th both von Forstner and Heinicke received their orders to proceed to CA 50, and back to the area off the Delaware Capes and Cape May, New Jersey. The word went out among the crew that finally they were going to see the casinos and boardwalk of the famed Atlantic City.

The westbound cruise continued in calm seas for the next four days when BdU changed *U-402*'s objective. A signal arrived at 1030hrs on the 22nd: 'Radio Message to Forstner and Heinicke: Continue transit via square BE 67. Forstner 2 days in square 60 left half, Heinicke square 50 right half operate on traffic reported by von Schäfer economical fuel consumption.' Given where *U-402* was positioned already, von Forstner thought it was an incorrect cipher translation as his area of patrol was currently in BD. A request for re-transmission confirmed this, and BdU retransmitted 'BD' nearly seven hours later.

The change had come from a report sent by the U-tanker *U-460*, a large Type XIV supply and replenishment boat known colloquially by German U-boat men as a 'Milch Cow' (Milk Cow). *U-460* had observed a stream of merchantmen in Square BD while resupplying westbound U-boats.

Von Forstner reached the ordered square the following day and began a back-and-forth sweep looking for any vessels. Nothing was spotted and he resumed his westward course at economical speed, perhaps thinking he might receive a further update to his orders. The next morning, he did. *U-402* and *U-576* were ordered to re-supply from *U-460*. On his re-supply approach von Forstner received another message on the 28th re-directing *U-402* and *U-576* away from the Delaware Capes to Cape Hatteras. There was disappointment among the crew. Atlantic City would have to wait.

On his way to the rendezvous point, on the afternoon of the 29th, the watch officer reported a steamer about 11nm away. Von Forstner gave chase, but gave up after being unable to get into a good firing position seven hours later as a rain squall reduced visibility down to 1nm.

On 1 July von Forstner manoeuvred *U-402* in heavy seas alongside the U-tanker *U-460* in order to take on fuel and supplies. In this amazing photo taken from *U-460*, we see a member of the 'Milch Cow's' crew being ferried in a rubber dingy over to *U-402* and the fuel hoses are connected between the two boats. All the crews are wearing their flotation devices in the heavy seas as the swells wash over the deck. Von Forstner was only able to secure 34cbm of fuel and no other supplies due to the conditions before he decided to break off further refuelling and continue toward the US East Coast. (Courtesy of Axel Urbanke)

At 0115hrs on 1 July von Forstner arrived at the location to find *U-460* supplying *U-173* abeam. *U-402* attempted to link its fuel lines, but worsening weather prevented it that evening. Eleven hours later, and in worsening seas, *U-402* was able to hook up the towing rig and transfer 34cbm of fuel oil, before the rig was lost due to the weather. It was not possible to transfer additional provisions, and von Forstner decided to continue on to his assigned patrol area without waiting any longer for surface conditions to improve. Kapitänleutnant Ebe Schnoor, commander of *U-460*, noted in his war diary the circumstances surrounding the transfer: 'It is not possible, even with the utmost nautical caution, to recover the equipment in the weather.' After *U-402*'s departure the transfer gear was severely damaged, and some lost overboard.

On 5 July BdU sent out a radio message that the Portuguese-flagged SS *Serpa Pinto* 'with Germans on board' was expected to be in square CC 40 by midnight. 'Do not attack.' The Portuguese-flagged vessel had left Lisbon for Casablanca and was en route to Philadelphia. It had hundreds of refugees on board, including Germans, some of whom were Jewish. It remains unclear why this particular order was issued by BdU.

The following afternoon a steamer was spotted in almost the exact grid square BdU had warned that the *Serpa Pinto* was sailing, but the former had two masts, while the latter had only one. Von Forstner decided that this was not the Portuguese vessel and gave chase, but lost sight of it in overcast and rainy seas. Then later the same day another Portuguese-flagged vessel, the *S. Thome* from Lisbon, was spotted. Von Forstner wanted to stop this vessel 'for examination' but was unable because his diesels gave out. He decided that given she was heading back toward Europe, he did not want to waste fuel unnecessarily, so he radioed BdU for further instructions. The response came back almost two hours later: 'To *U-402*: do not attack.'

As *U-402* got closer to the coast, two more vessels were

spotted on the 10th, but quickly lost. Von Forstner estimated one to be a single-stacked passenger steamer and the other a patrol vessel. Later, on the 12th he identified a destroyer and a passenger steamer, which may have been the same two vessels he previously identified, heading west on a zig-zag course north east.

U-402 was now about 330nm north-east of the Outer Banks, when a PBY Catalina was spotted flying north, astern of the U-boat. A crash dive was immediately ordered. With aircraft this far out, it was clear that the United States' defences against U-boats were more organised than several months earlier. The following day, at 2015hrs on the 13th, a '4-engine fast land-based Boeing' aircraft dropped three bombs on *U-402* that was at a depth of 22m. This was a B-17E piloted by Captain A H Tuttle of the 2nd Bombardment Group out of Langley Field, Virginia. He identified a surfaced U-boat both visually and by radar, dropping six depth charges with little effect, other than oil leakage.[22] 'No damage' was recorded, but it was clear that *U-402*'s presence off the North Carolina coast was now known. Tuttle remained in the area for over five hours, never spotting *U-402* again, even though the U-boat surfaced and dived five more times as it observed 'the same aircraft type' each time. *U-402* finally headed further south away from Cape Hatteras as it had drained its electric batteries during the encounter.

At 1200hrs on the 14th, *U-402* surfaced, which was indeed dangerous given the increased defences. Von Forstner recorded his thinking in the war diary:

> Remained on the surface after beginning of brightness with completely clear visibility, because experience shows that getting into attack position submerged with [ships] coming in sight in the periscope or sound bearings is no longer possible. Manoeuvring ahead with aircraft escort in this area is hardly possible. Proceeding on the surface gives me more chance to detect traffic. Besides, I want to be positioned under the coast with a full battery, because I was detected by aircraft which held me submerged, as yesterday shows, I must expect search groups.

Four hours later a PBY Catalina was spotted to starboard heading in the opposite direction and

A photo of the *U-402*'s oil slick as seen by Captain A H Tuttle who had just completed an attack run with his B-17E and dropped a series of depth charges on the U-boat in the late afternoon of 13 July. The attack occurred some 100nm due east of Diamond Shoals and did not result in any significant damage according to von Forstner. However, the U-boat was attacked again on the 14th, 35nm south-south-east of Diamond Shoals by a PBY Catalina, then later by two land-based aircraft that seriously damaged the U-boat. *U-402* began a harrowing 10 hours submerged as the boat struggled to surface, and was even stuck on the bottom at one point. The crew did not think they would make it back to the surface alive, but they did, departing the area and heading back to France early. (US Airforce Historical Research Agency 109A)

U-402 submerged. More than 90 minutes later *U-402* resurfaced and manoeuvred close in to the coast where von Forstner wanted to reach the 40m line. It was 1745hrs (1245hrs local time).

Manoeuvring so close to the coast in broad daylight with little cloud cover was risky. *U-402* was only 34nm due west of Cape Lookout and 25nm south-east of the southern tip of Ocracoke Island. At 2038hrs (1538hrs local time) look outs on watch spotted two single-engined land-based aircraft approaching from the starboard side. *U-402* slipped beneath the surface in shallow water and had reached a depth of approximately 13–14m when six well-placed depth charges exploded around the U-boat, causing severe damage. Gauges popped, lights went out, pipes burst, and the U-boat went bow down, stopping only when it hit hard against the sandy bottom, throwing everything loose onto the deck.

The assessment was bleak:

> Both periscopes, compass installation, compressor, negative buoyancy tanks, main drain pump, battery 2 heavily damaged. In addition, quickly eliminated and minor damage such as all water level and depth gages, except for the dampfmanometer [presumably the Papenburg depth gauge], nearly all electrical installations by breakage of fuses, leakage at pressure hull through fittings and air installation. Port outer exhaust valve, depth sounder rectifier and stern torpedo tube out of service, ventilation air intake shaft torn, diesel clutches jammed, leakage at fuel oil tank 2 (internal) and all outer fuel oil tanks, main ballast tank 2 starboard torn twice, heavy damage to sound gear.

U-402 came to rest on the bottom at a depth of only 55m (181ft). Von Forstner had to wait nearly an hour for the electric motors to be repaired, then proceed by sounding for deeper water, as he expected a surface search group to arrive. Seventy-minutes later the sounds of an approaching patrol boat coming from the west was heard. He noted in the war diary, 'Because I cannot shake off the patrol boat in spite of silent running and changes of course, probably due to the very strong rattling sounds in the upper deck and grinding clutches, boat put on the bottom at depth of 120m [396 feet]. No further depth charges. Sounds slowly got more distant.'

At 0100hrs (2000hrs local time) on the 15th, von Forstner attempted to move the boat after he heard the surface vessel move off. The bilges were pumped out by hand, and compressed air fed into the regulating tanks. However, the boat settled back into deeper water at a depth 140m (462ft). *U-402* sat on the bottom for nearly five more hours as the crew tried to free the boat. Herbert recalled how von Forstner ordered the crew to run side-to-side in the boat to shake it free of the bottom. Von Forstner wrote in the war diary '. . . after new pumping the boat was made bow down with the crew and freed from the bottom with reverse thrust'. At 0625hrs *U-402* finally surfaced after on the bottom for some ten hours. 'Everything went to shit' that day, Herbert recalled years after the war. The crew thought that 'it was all over, and that no one was getting home alive'.

Their troubles were not over. The already-damaged batteries exploded after blowing the ballast tanks as two blue tongues of flame shot up from the intake and exhaust air grills, bending the battery deck upwards. It was a 'complete failure of the battery'. Von Forstner decided to remain submerged by day in order to effect repairs, given that he had lost the ability to crash dive. By the afternoon repairs were being made, and he took a moment to note in his logbook that the behaviour of the crew under these trying circumstances 'was good'. 'Especially distinguished' was engineer Oberleutnant Kiehn who 'through calmness and deliberateness, as well as clear and expedient instructions, . . . showed great ability'.[23] Additionally, 'as he has already shown by repeatedly correcting malfunctions, Ob.Masch. [Eugen] Fischer clearly distinguished himself by his special talent and indefatigable zeal'.

Despite its damage, *U-402* was directed to report on traffic north-west of Bermuda, which it did from the 17th to the 20th. Von Forstner was still keen to hunt for merchantmen, but received increasingly concerning reports from his engineer about *U-402*'s operational readiness. On the 20th he knew he could no longer operate the boat effectively without unnecessarily jeopardising the crew. His battery banks had completely failed, preventing *U-402* from utilising its number one asset, invisibility. *U-402* could not dive. Von Forstner sent his status to BdU. Six hours later he was authorised to return to France.

Eleven days later *U-402* approached the Bay of Biscay, but could not transit submerged during the day given its damaged state. After repairs about 13 hours of battery charge was achieved, and the boat was given the authorisation by BdU for a partially-submerged crossing at night. He was also informed that an Arado 196 floatplane would provide air cover. As *U-402* began its crossing at high speed it had to crash dive twice due to approaching aircraft that were unrecognised. After two harrowing days, *U-402*

On the way back to France Obermaschinst Fischer (right), 2nd Watch Officer Hübschen (left) and an unknown crewman (centre) inspect the damage from the aerial depth charges. *U-402* was directed to shift its home port to La Pallice, just outside La Rochelle. (Deutsches U-boot Museum).

was greeted by a Ju 88, and then passed onto an Arado. After meeting up with two surface escorts, *U-402* was ordered to rendezvous point Paula 1, then to proceed to La Pallice.

U-402 pulled into port, heavily damaged, on 5 August 1942 after a 51-day patrol that netted von Forstner no enemy ships sunk. He had missed his opportunity to profit from the early days of 'Drumbeat', when America's defences were unprepared for the threat that arrived on its shores. His experience off Cape Hatteras, along with other U-boats in the area, informed Dönitz's decision of 27 July to all but cease operations off the North American coast. The BdU war diary reflected this thinking: 'In the sea area off Hatteras successes have dropped considerably. This is due to a drop in the traffic (formation of convoys) and increased defence measures.' The recent loss of *U-701* and *U-215* and the near-fatal damage to *U-402* and *U-576* did not justify the limited opportunities to attack merchantmen. U-boat operations off the North American coast were to be halted, with the exception of 'occasional operations by single boats and minelaying operations in harbour entrances, areas along the east coast of America will come under consideration as before'.

The damage to *U-402* was extensive and it required just short of two months of repairs in drydock, while the crew enjoyed the late summer days relaxing in the French seaside establishments, much like their fathers and uncles who were U-boat sailors in the First World War did in Bruges, Belgium. Lothar-Günther Buchheim's anti-war novel *Das Boot*, turned into a German television programme, and later a feature-length movie, portrayed off-duty U-boatmen as fatalistic debauchers. Such a depiction was false. Jochen Frintrop, a cadet watch officer on *U-402*, was critical of Buchheim's portrayal. He recalled after the war that 'as a Leutnant zur See on *U-402*, I was at that time stationed in La Pallice, which is where the programme "*Das Boot*" takes place. The manner of debauchery conducted by the U-boat men [in the film] is simply not true.' He went on to criticise Buchheim 'as a war correspondent' who 'goes along one time on a patrol (which would, in any event, not be looked on kindly by the crew)', and leaves behind a 'realistic book' that has a tendency 'to treat its subject in a way that it was not'. 'On my Boat,' Frintrop recalled, 'during the trip against the enemy, there was joint singing every evening, musical request programmes that we put together ourselves, and there was an on board newspaper, which included news from Radio London, because it gave us a more up-to-date picture. The very fact that the crew turned on an "enemy broadcaster" clearly is the best illustration of the "Nazi-free" air in the Navy and how much we were a conspiratorial community.'[24]

Frintrop was clearly no fan of Buchheim's fictional, and somewhat salacious, account of a U-boat crew at war. However, *Das Boot* resonated with post-war German readers because it offered a dramatic view of the war from their perspective, as seen through the eyes of men who were seemingly 'sacrificed' on the altar of Nazi aggression. It was compared to Erich Remarque's *All Quiet on the Western Front*, though such a comparison has its limitations. Its 'realism' was taken for granted, and many U-boat veterans were not necessarily pleased with their portrayal or, in some quarters, the anti-Dönitz undertones.[25] The actual commander of *U-96*, Kapitänleutnant Heinrich Lehmann-Willenbrock, upon whom Buchheim based his fictional 'Old Man', wrote to his former propaganda officer in 1973 and stated of the book 'Today's reader will find out and see for himself what kind of men the submariners were, and what their fortitude and "heroism" were really about. Certainly there will be a lot of criticism from our ranks, because it is unpleasant to take that gently-dusted, gold-framed picture under the magnifying glass again. And the Dönitz myth is spoken with such reverence.'[26] Nearly 50 years after its publication, *Das Boot* remains the dominant portrayal of the Battle of the Atlantic from the German perspective in popular literature.

Personnel transfers took place. Herbert received the Iron Cross after his fourth patrol, then departed to pursue further administration training. His time on *U-402* was now behind him, but never forgotten.

Von Forstner's last four patrols were not notable. The circumstances of each patrol had not offered him an opportunity to fully showcase his tactical leadership or his crew's capabilities, though a strong bond of trust and respect formed between commander and crew. He expressed some frustration to his wife: 'You know it is far easier to limp back successful, though somewhat the worse for wear, than to return to port safe and sound after a completely uneventful war patrol – and yet under such adverse conditions, maintain discipline, or rather establish it [as the inexperienced young commander you are] in a crew still waiting to be welded together by action and built up to a high level of morale.' The opportunity to 'weld' his crew together in the crucible of battle would come on his next patrol.

CHAPTER 4

Return of the Wolfpacks

Each man in the crew holds a responsible position and knows that the slightest neglect endangers the welfare of the whole boat. The commander must be certain that everything is completed according to the highest standard.

Georg-Günther von Forstner, *The Journal of a Submarine Commander* (1916)

U-402 underwent an extensive overhaul to repair the damage suffered during its last patrol off the Eastern Seaboard. However, the boat was never the same mechanically as its diesel engines were plagued with problems for the remainder of its service.

During the summer of 1942 the Kriegsmarine became aware that British aircraft were now equipped with radar operating at the 1.5cm wavelength. A downed Wellington bomber equipped with the Air to Surface Vessel (ASV) Mk I radar was captured in North Africa in the summer of 1941. This provided the first indication

U-402 (right) and probably *U-132* (left) photographed inside one of the bunkers in La Pallice. Repairs were made from the almost fatal air attack off the US East Coast in July. This is clearly a morning photograph as the autumn sun is shining brightly at the bunker entrance. Only three of the ten bunkers in this complex were designed for two U-boats, and of those, only two were allotted extra room for maintenance and repairs. This means this was Bunker 2. Note the floodlight system along the left wall that allowed repairs to continue through the night. (Bundesarchiv, Bild 101II-MW-6853-08 Tiemer)

U-402 on a trial run in the Pertuis d'Antioche straight after its extensive repairs. Behind the U-boat is the nearly 3,000m-long Pont de Ré bridge. The U-boat is now painted in a uniform dark grey, with the lower hull and saddle tanks perhaps even darker. Now that *U-402* was heading out to participate in the convoy battles of the North Atlantic, where U-boats typically operated surfaced at night, the dark hull colour offered some camouflage. (Bundesarchiv, Bild 101II-MW-6853-38 Tiemer)

that aircraft equipped with radar could be used to detect surfaced U-boats at night or in bad weather. All 110 aircraft of RAF Coastal Command had been equipped with radar by the end of 1941 and losses of U-boats crossing the Bay of Biscay increased. Night-time crossings of the Bay of Biscay once thought safe were now interrupted by aircraft that seemingly swooped of the darkness to

U-402 (right) and *U-132* (left), under the command of Kapitänleutnant Ernst Vogelsang, are pictured in the La Pallice lock preparing for their departures. The U-boat bunker is clearly visible behind the U-boats, as the lock gate is open. *U-402* will depart first on 4 October, followed by *U-132* on 6 October. Von Forstner can be seen in the white cap on the conning tower of *U-402*. *U-132* still requires to take on more fuel as it rides higher out of the water than *U-402*. Note the darker grey of the lower hull. Both U-boats will take part in the battle of SC-107, except that only one will return. *U-132* was believed lost in the massive explosion of the British ammunition ship SS *Hatimura* that it torpedoed on 4 November. It is believed the U-boat was too close when the vessel exploded and was caught in the blast. (Bundesarchiv, Bild 101II-MW-6853-19 Tiemer)

turn a spotlight on the unaware boat, followed by depth charges and strafing.[27]

Over the next year a detector was created in order to provide U-boats with early warning of radar-equipped aircraft. This was the FuMB 1 Metox 600A receiver with the FuMB Ant. 2 antenna mounted on the U-boat conning tower. Also known as the 'Biscay Cross' this wooden-framed device alerted U-boats to emissions with wavelengths of 130–260cm. It was imperfect, often picking up friendly Luftwaffe radar signals as well. By August all U-boats making the crossing from French ports to the North Atlantic were equipped with this device and sinkings of them dropped sharply. *U-402* received this new detector during its overhaul and employed it for the first time on its next patrol.

Into the Fray

U-402 left La Pallice in the late evening of 4 October 1942. As per standing orders, the boat dived to proceed by day across the Bay of Biscay, and cruised surfaced at night. It surfaced in the evening of the 5th and began to employ the new radar detector. In the early morning of the 6th, a steady tone was heard in the sound room from the new FuMB receiver and von Forstner ordered the boat to dive. After almost 50 minutes submerged, *U-402* resurfaced. Forty minutes later another tone was detected and again *U-402* submerged for another hour before it surfaced and continued uninterrupted into the North Atlantic.

U-402 now casts off at low tide out of the La Pallice lock on 4 October with a send-off from Kriegsmarine officers, nurses and other well-wishers at the port. The crew waves back, as von Forstner is observing the activity (right most figure on the conning tower). Von Forstner's first foray into the convoy battles of the North Atlantic allowed him to successfully showcase his tactical ability and that of his well-trained crew. (Bundesarchiv Bild 101II-MW-6855-35 Tiemer)

Action was developing east of the Newfoundland Banks with the return of the wolfpacks. An eastbound SC convoy was spotted, but not attacked, by a group of U-boats that formed the patrol line 'Luchs'. Heavy seas, strong gales and flying boats out of Greenland prevented the U-boats from getting into a position ahead of the convoy to conduct an effective attack. The convoy slipped away from the U-boats without a single loss. Two U-boats were sunk and one was damaged for the effort.

In the afternoon of the 7th BdU ordered *U-71*, *U-89*, *U-132*, *U-402*, *U-571*, *U-609*, *U-658* and *U-704* to head to square AK 93. *U-89*, *U-402* and *U-571* were then directed to lengthen the southern end of the patrol line of the new group 'Panther' on the 10th. BdU believed their best chances were to form their patrol lines as close to the originating point of the convoy as tactically feasible in order to ensure it was encountered. *U-402* reached the position on the 12th, where it began moving back and forth seeking targets. A new convoy was expected in the area on the 14th, so BdU gave full warning to all U-boats. On the 16th, *U-704* reported that a convoy had been spotted on a westerly course, doing 12 knots. In response, BdU directed the southern portion of 'Puma' as well as patrol lines 'Leopard' and 'Wotan' to converge on the convoy.

As *U-402* began to manoeuvre toward the convoy it lost its starboard diesel and had to replace two fuel nozzles. It took a day to repair, but the engine continued to cause problems for von Forstner. At 1650hrs he noted that 'while simultaneously carrying out propulsion inspection, [it was] determined that a guide shaft bearing of the starboard diesel is damaged and loose. Without immediate repair, breakage of the guide shaft can be expected.' The new chief engineer, Oberleutnant Ing. Hermann Hartke, who had replaced Meyer-Oswald back in June, determined that no repair work could continue while surfaced due to the heavy seas that averaged over 10m (30ft). Von Forstner ordered the boat to dive, and by the morning of the 18th the starboard diesel was repaired after nearly eight hours of work while submerged.

Being submerged meant that the *U-402* made little headway and could not keep up with the convoy. The heavy seas and overcast weather also complicated the U-boat's ability to spot Allied merchantmen. Von Forstner noted that 'because there is no other indication for the location of the convoy, continued search to the [south-west], particularly as I cannot make up for lost ground again in the bad weather'. The heavy seas continued to cause technical havoc with *U-402* and by the evening large quantities of water were observed entering the boat through the diesel air intake that the drain pump was unable to handle. U-boat operations against the convoy, which was SC-104, resulted in eight vessels sunk for the loss of two U-boats.

Meanwhile, a transmission regarding the date and time of an upcoming SC convoy was transmitted from the Convoy and Routing Section of Commander-in-Chief, US Fleet (COMINCH) to their British counterparts concerning SC-107 departing on the 24th. This encrypted message was intercepted by B-Dienst and handed over to BdU. Based on the already well-understood convoy cycle, BdU concluded the intelligence was accurate and began to deploy his U-boats accordingly.

On the afternoon of the 21st, twenty-eight Allied masters and commanding officers gathered in a conference room to receive their brief on the upcoming crossing. No one in the room knew that there were already fifteen U-boats sitting in a patrol line in the fog south of Greenland and the Newfoundland Banks waiting for them. The young navy officer concluded his brief, as he had numerous times before, with a warning.

'Don't dump refuse; it could give away the fact that the convoy has passed that spot. Try to keep your smoke at a minimum during daylight; it's a sure giveaway to any U-boat within 25 miles. Be sure that no lights are showing at night, and that includes the captain's cigarette. Above all, gentlemen, maintain a proper station within the convoy. I know it is crowded, but collisions are second only to the Jerries as a cause of ship losses. If you are inclined to chuck it all, and romp or straggle where you have more room, don't! It is a very likely way to buy the farm. Good luck and smooth sailing.'[28]

An aerial photo of a convoy that formed off Nova Scotia in October 1942. This could be SC-107, though the specific convoy photographed has not been confirmed. The convoy's departure and routing were known to Kriegsmarine intelligence through B-Dienst decrypts. The U-boats were waiting south of Greenland, just off the Newfoundland Banks. (Naval History and Heritage Command 80-G-405261)

This warning was not unjustified. One-quarter of all merchant ships lost during the war were due to collisions in convoys, foundering and marine causes not related to U-boats.

SC-107 consisted of forty-five merchants and twenty-two escorts. As the Liverpool-bound convoy departed New York Harbor on 24 October, and sailed along the coast toward Newfoundland, it was joined by vessels from the ports of Halifax and St John. The coastal escort was relieved by the mid-Atlantic escort responsible for the crossing to England. The merchantmen were commanded by Vice Admiral B C Watson CB, DSO (RET) who sailed on board the British-flagged cargo liner *Jeypore*. While the commodore was responsible for the management of the convoy, he had to follow the orders of the escort commander of TF 24.1.14, Lieutenant Commander Desmond W Piers (RCN), his junior, who was responsible for the overall safety of the merchantmen crossing the Atlantic.

Convoy attacks in the North Atlantic had dropped off significantly during the first half of 1942 with the start of Operation 'Paukenschlag'. That trend was now reversed as attacks in August and September increased with the return of the U-boats after the operation off the Eastern Seaboard was concluded.

At the southern end of the search line, *U-402*'s watch reported no surface vessels as it headed south-west over the next several days, despite the numerus reports of ship sightings from other U-boats. BdU continued to hope that the 'Panther' line would locate the convoy, but by the 20th the line was dissolved. 'Veilchen' was ordered formed that consisted of *U-71*, *U-438*, *U-84*, *U-89*, *U-704*, *U-381*, *U-658*, *U-402*, *U-571*, *U-454* and *U-132*, spaced some 15nm apart.

On 24 October *U-132* reported numerous ship sound bearings, and on the 25th *U-704* spotted a seaplane inside its patrol area. However, the continuous heavy fog over the last several days reduced visibility to only 200m. No merchantmen were spotted. On 27 October two more U-boats, *U-442* and *U-437* joined 'Veilchen' and occupied positions that extended the patrol line to the south.

U-402 still required parts for its broken starboard Junker's compressor as the boat limped along in its assigned position. Luckily, at 1150hrs on the 27th a lookout spotted *U-658* at a bearing of 330 degrees at 8nm distance in calm seas and a clear sky. Von Forstner made a recognition signal and the U-boats rendezvoused. Von Forstner acquired a spare piston ring from *U-658* and had it installed, then dived to test his sound gear. Coincidental meetings at sea were not uncommon among U-boats, and could prove beneficial, as in this case.

In the afternoon of 29 October *U-437* sighted a convoy at the southern end of the patrol line and was granted permission to pursue. The rest of 'Veilchen' was ordered 40 miles to the southeast to established a new line. Von Forstner took the opportunity to drill the crew in crash diving on 30 October. This was a skill that captains always tried to improve upon because it could be crucial in saving the boat. Even a second or two could make the difference between life and death. In this case, the dive itself almost proved fatal. 'By a combination of different circumstances, malfunctions and mistakes, went to depth [230] meters' as von Forstner noted in his logbook. A depth of 230m (759ft) was exceptional – in fact dangerous, given that the expected 'crush depth' of a Type VIIC was between 250–295m (820–968ft).

At 1624hrs *U-522* sighted a convoy and sent out a spotting report. *U-522* was not part of group 'Veilchen' and was operating alone south of the Newfoundland Banks when it had its chance encounter. The convoy was in fact SC-107 passing south of Cape Race. The patrol line tightened its formation and moved toward the direction of the reported convoy, which had benefited from the dense fog over the course of the last six days.

Now the shadowing U-boat, *U-552* took over the role of following the convoy and transmitted its position back to BdU headquarters in Paris. BdU then realigned the U-boat patrol line to ensure they converged on the eastbound convoy. These radio transmissions were picked by the 'C'-class destroyer HMCS *Restigouche* (ex-*Comet* [H00]) and shore-based HF/DF stations. They knew a U-boat had spotted the convoy and the commodore on *Jeypore* was notified.

Fuel was getting low for many U-boats in the patrol line, but on the 31st BdU ordered them to remain in position as contact with SC-107 was expected shortly. With anticipation building, von Forstner ordered maintenance on the torpedo tubes to ensure they were serviceable. This work lasted almost 24 hours, and was completed with test firing of all tubes.

The following day SC-107 entered the 'black pit' south of Greenland where it had no air cover. Only five escorts were present to fend off an unknown number of U-boats. The convoy's best defence was not to be located, but B-Dienst and *U-552* had already done that. Now all the escort commander could do was to keep the U-boats at bay, and force them to break contact as individual destroyers made large sweeps at the rear of the convoy to locate ASDIC and HF/DF contacts.

At 1454hrs hours on 1 November, *U-381* was the first of the

U-boat line to spot the merchantmen in good visibility to the north of *U-402*'s position. *U-552*, which was still shadowing, reported some twenty 'steamers' with the clearing weather. B-Dienst informed BdU that there were twenty-seven ships in the convoy. There were actually forty-five merchants. BdU did not want to lose contact before nightfall and ordered *U-522* not to 'hunt independents', though he should take advantage of 'shooting opportunities'. He had to stay with the convoy.

Von Forstner crossed-checked the spotting reports on his charts and noted his agreement with the convoy's estimated course. His war log entry clearly shows he was working out the situation in his own mind, tactically visualising the convoy's actions, and planning his upcoming attack. The convoy was only 60nm to his north, and *U-402* turned and headed on an intercept course. With luck, von Forstner might be able to engage the convoy that evening. Less than four hours later, *U-704* transmitted a destroyer sighting report that was located north of *U-402*, and confirmed von Forstner's course.

At 1940hrs *U-402*'s watch spotted a two-masted steamer heading north-west in mild seas and an overcast sky, followed by a destroyer 15 minutes later. This was indeed Convoy SC-107 that they were after. At 2027hrs von Forstner sent a short report to BdU with the vessels he spotted. A minute later three more merchantmen were sighted.

BdU knew the time to strike was now and at 2147hrs transmitted: 'To Veilchen. 1.) Take advantage of weather situation and element of surprise in the first night . . . Forstner send bearing signals.' *U-402* now became the contact keeper. A destroyer was spotted and *U-402* kept its distance. The U-boats began to align as it grew dark and an overcast sky developed. An hour later von Forstner radioed BdU 'Forced off by destroyer, contact lost. Last position, convoy AJ 8867. Forstner.'

U-402 dived in order to use its hydrophones to detect the convoy, but nothing was heard except for other U-boats' diesels. After surfacing, a U-boat was spotted to starboard. Von Forstner needed to maintain contact with the convoy if he had any hope for success, and he ordered course 30 degrees at four-fifths full speed. Again, von Forstner spotted a destroyer, and manoeuvred away from it, noting at ten minutes past midnight on the 2nd that 'I believe that I am in the vicinity of the convoy, continued to search on northerly course'.

Thrust and Parry

Just before 0100hrs on 2 November von Forstner spotted the convoy's starboard side, just ahead. Within minutes star shells went up to port. At 0144hrs he sent a short report with the convoy's course and speed. He immediately turned to port to make his attack but spotted a destroyer three minutes later and turned away from the convoy. This was the *Restigouche* pursing an ASDIC contact, though not *U-402*, which she passed without detecting. There was only one escort left on this side, the 'Flower'-class corvette HMCS *Arvida*, and her radar was broken. A surfaced U-boat could now only be detected visually, and this was not an easy task at night given the low silhouette of its conning tower. Von Forstner manoeuvred past her stern and thus past the escort screen, and was now in the middle of the convoy. Eight minutes later he returned to his attack course and was met by two large freighters in his field of vision.

He ordered a shot from tube I, but an electronic failure prevented the signal from the conning tower from reaching the torpedo room. Tube II was ordered fired at one of the freighters now only 500m distant. The torpedo ran at a depth of 3m, but

The first vessel torpedoed by *U-402* was the British steam merchant SS *Empire Sunrise* (7,459 GRT) carrying steel and timber. She was later finished off by *U-84*. After the initial torpedo hit by *U-402*, an escort, probably HMCS *Restigouche* (ex-*Comet* [H00]) pictured above, pulled out from the other side of the stricken merchant and forced *U-402* to dive, dropping depth charges that did no damage. Originally commissioned as the RN *Comet* in 1932, this 'C'-class destroyer was transferred to the Royal Canadian Navy in June 1938 and re-commissioned as *Restigouche*. The destroyer's exact armament configuration at the time of SC-107 are not precisely known, but at a minimum the 329ft, 1,375 GRT destroyer had multiple 4.7in guns, a 3in and multiple 2-pounder AA guns, and depth-charge racks. She was likely equipped with the early Type 271 surface-search radar. (Nova Scotia Archives 1992-304/ 43.1.4 38)

clearly missed the intended target as it ran erratically and later exploded without a hit on the other side of the convoy, two minutes and 20 seconds (2,150m) later.

At 0205hrs a shot from tube III was ordered, as the range to the target had reduced to 350m. 'Hit after 23 seconds (355 meters). High explosion column. Steamer shoots 2 red rockets, 1 high, 1 in our direction. Hole can be seen. Steamer quickly takes on a list to starboard. Turned to port. Out of the steamer line ahead a destroyer comes with sharp target angle on enemy course 700m away – evasion on the surface is no longer possible.' The explosion rained debris down on the U-boat's conning tower, as they were that close to their target. White flares went up. The British-flagged SS *Empire Sunrise* (7,459 GRT) was hit, the first of the battle. 'The torpedo hit amidships, blasting a gaping hole in the side, sending the mainmast crashing to the deck and wrecking the starboard lifeboat. Ship control and main engines were disabled.'[29] The stern settled into the water for the next two hours and the crew had to abandon ship, but were quickly picked up by the rescue vessel *Stockport*. The *Empire Sunrise* was later finished off by *U-84*.

As star shells started to light up the night sky, a destroyer, possibly the *Restigouche*, immediately pulled out of the convoy line and was spotted bearing down on the conning tower's silhouette. Von Forstner issued the order 'Dive!' as he could not outmanoeuvre her on the surface. *U-402* quickly slipped below the waves. 'Poorly placed depth charges' were dropped, and the sounds of turbine-powered propellers could be heard crossing over *U-402* several times. Von Forstner displayed cool nerves and was not concerned by the escort. He immediately resurfaced to continue the attack, now that he knew he was in a perfect position.

Once back on the surface, *U-402* continued on a northerly course, and attempted to get to the dark side of the convoy, so that the merchantmen were silhouetted by the rising moon. He watched two destroyers signalling each other but was not able to fully make out what they were saying. He avoided them. He evaded another destroyer that dropped depth charges in *U-402*'s wake, not realising he was still surfaced and outmanoeuvring his pursuer in the darkness.

Von Forstner's persistence was rewarded. He noted in his logbook: 'Destroyer out of sight. Convoy now easily distinguished, 21 steamers counted, possibly there still 2 columns beyond. Closed on the port side of the convoy, again looked for a spot where the largest steamers are together.'

Von Forstner was confident and at 0342hrs sent BdU his first success report and a brief spotting report. At 0404hrs *U-402* was on its next attack course. The U-boat was in the middle of the convoy at night, approaching from the dark side, just as Otto Kretschmer had done two years earlier when von Forstner was on board *U-99*. Six minutes later tube I was working again and fired. 'After 62 seconds (960 meters) hit amidships, about 20-meter-high explosion column. Followed by a heavy detonation, probably munitions. After the hit, shot some white rocket to starboard. A following small steamer was not attacked.' The ship hit was the Greek SS *Rinos* (4,649 GRT) which after five minutes rolled over and sank. A minute later tube III launched. 'Target is a loaded freighter about 6000 GRT. Type not recognised. After 55 seconds (855 meters) hit with 30-meter-high explosion column, nearly amidships. Steamer shoots red rockets to port and settles burning astern.' This was the British SS *Dalcroy* (4,558 GRT) and she began to burn brightly.

What happened next becomes confused as *U-552* joined the attack from the starboard side of the convoy, and *U-84* from the port side. *U-402*'s tube II was reloaded by the efficient crew who had no time to dwell on the hits. Thirty-two seconds later tube II fired again, but the torpedo missed a target 850m away. The target zig-zagged as white rockets went up, and underwater explosions could be heard from the previously-hit ships now sinking. Two minutes later at 0413hrs von Forstner made a quick calculation and launched another torpedo from tube IV. He recorded that 'after

Von Forstner sank five merchant ships during the battle of Convoy SC-107. The second was the British SS *Dalcroy* (4,558 GRT) carrying steel and timber which was sunk at 0413hrs on 2 November (52° 30'N, 45° 30'W - Grid AJ 8674). (Bibliothek für Zeitgeschichte BZ00000002-a)

52 seconds (800 meters) hit forward edge of the bridge, high explosion column. Steamer breaks apart and sinks about 1 minute later. Turned for stern shot tube V: depth 3 meters, bow left, target angle 70°, enemy speed 8 knots. Shot does not go, electric firing did not work, order failure, order did not get through.' Ten minutes later, while the forward torpedo tubes were being reloaded, the aft torpedo tube was made ready and fired. 'Missed, electric firing failed, fired too late by hand.' The vessel reportedly hit remains a mystery, as none was listed as hit at the time. The next hit scored was by *U-552*, close enough to this incident that perhaps what von Forstner witnessed was another U-boat's hit.

Von Forstner attempted to manoeuvre ahead of the convoy to be in a good firing position for his next attack. The 'Flower'-class corvette HMCS *Amherst* (K-148) now came out of the darkness from behind a steamer, zig-zagging toward his U-boat. The corvette closed the distance and opened fire on the conning tower with her machine gun that raked *U-402*'s bridge. At the same time the deck gun of the steamer opened fire and a shell went through the diesel air intake trunking. The order rang out loudly: 'Dive!' *U-402* went under. For the next hour *U-402* manoeuvred to avoid the depth charges from the surface, most of which were poorly placed. Twice von Forstner tried to surface, but the destroyers kept him down and he dived the boat to 120m, which was generally below the depth-charge settings, to wait for his pursuers to tire and move on.

Help was requested by the Task Force commander after two separate U-boat attacks. Reinforcements came from Convoy HX-217 and Iceland, with HMS *Vanessa* (D29) USCGC *Bibb* (WPG-31), USCGC *Ingham* (WPG-35) and USS *Schenck* (DD-159) dispatched, but they would not arrive for another 24 hours.

At 0615hrs *U-402* surfaced in a relatively calm sea. Despite the cloud cover, the Northern Lights could still be made out, making this a particularly surreal naval battlefield. Forty-five minutes later the convoy was spotted again. Von Forstner knew there were only a few hours of darkness left he could use. *U-402* radioed BdU at 0741hrs to report the results of its previous night's attack. While inaccurate due to the fog of war, claiming four steamers hit, his performance that night was tactically impressive. He was not done with the convoy either.

Nearly 25 minutes later he launched an attack on two large steamers, leaving the two smaller ones spotted between them, alone. The shot from tube II found its mark 'Hit after 80 seconds (1250 meters) amidships with high explosion column. Immediately

The fourth vessel sunk was the British-flagged SS *Empire Leopard* (5,676 GRT) carrying zinc concentrates for manufacturing ammunition. She was torpedoed at 0803hrs on 2 November (52° 26'N, 45° 22'W – Grid AJ 8658). (The Mariners' Museum P0001.003-01–PB7340)

The fifth and final vessel sunk by *U-402* during the battle of SC-107 was the British SS *Empire Antelope* (4,945 GRT) carrying general cargo and steel. The vessel was torpedoed at the exact same time as *Empire Leopard* on 2 November (52° 26'N, 45° 22'W – Grid AJ 8658). (The Mariners' Museum P0001.003-01–PB7259)

after the hit the steamer shoots red rockets to port.' A minute later tube IV fired. 'After 69 seconds (1050 meters) hit forward 10 meters.' The British SS *Empire Leopard* (5,676 GRT) was struck and sank with all but three of her crew. The British SS *Empire Antelope* (4,945 GRT) was on fire and fell astern of the convoy. Her crew safely abandoned ship before she sank an hour later.

A destroyer roared into view from port, and *U-402* dived. ASDIC pings. More poorly-placed depth charges. 'Up to 0849hrs continuous detonations heard. Sinking sounds from a steamer are clearly distinguished . . .' While he was submerged and being hunted, von Forstner took the time to order his bow torpedo tubes reloaded.

U-402 surfaced and von Forstner manoeuvred toward the larger steamer he previously hit. He 'recognised that the steamer torpedoed by me is down by the bow. Because of the presence of the destroyer, went to the other side for a coup de grâce.' As he manoeuvred toward the steamer, U-402 passed through numerous small white lights, coming from life jackets, rafts and cutters. At 0936hrs, the steamer began to sink on her own. 'However,' von Forstner recorded 'he doesn't want to have a second torpedo. The steamer suddenly settles up to the bridge, rears up steeply, stern high out of the water and sinks. Large areas rise to the surface of the water, because of the proximity of the destroyer and the beginning of twilight I can no longer stay to see if it is cargo.'

The pursuit continued during the course of the 2nd with U-402 looking for stragglers. At 1321hrs BdU sent this acknowledgement 'Forstner and Schneider well done'. This was Kapitänleutnant Herbert Schneider's first command and patrol with U-522. Schneider was previously IWO under the now famous Kapitänleutnant Reinhard Hardegen who proved so successful in the opening stage of Operation 'Paukenschlag'. U-522 sank three ships and damaged one from the convoy.

Von Forstner, however, was not done. At 1008hrs after some manoeuvring, he managed to regain contact with the convoy and attempted a dangerous daylight attack. He realised his plan was unworkable and tried to manoeuvre ahead and be in a position for a submerged attack. For several hours he dodged escorts, dived, withstood depth charges, surfaced and kept up his pursuit. At 1520hrs he recorded:

> Came to periscope depth, by sound bearings steamers must still be passing to port, the other weak sound bearing is astern. On this bearing an escort is positioned about 800m off. Cannon on the stern easily distinguished, a steamer passes my port side at about 700m with target angle 80°, setting ordered, periscope again turned on the escort, received artillery fire, no longer have time to take the shot, Asdic sounds, went deep. Sound pursuit, depth charges. Failures: both diesels initially out of service, with starboard diesel the discharge block is torn and its mounting bolt broken, with the port diesel the lubricating oil filter is heavily damaged. Port diesel was initially made ready by exchange of the filters, want to have a diesel ready as soon as possible to be able to surface and pursue.

Eight minutes later he recorded: 'Steamer with piston engine passes to starboard. 10 minutes after the last steamer passes to starboard there are absolutely no sound bearings in the gear, convoy is then about 1nm away!'

With another destroyer spotted, von Forstner ran off at 1617hrs at half speed to commence repairs on the diesels. His battle with SC-107 was already over, although he refused to yield to the situation and continued repairs. On the afternoon of the 3rd *U-402* was surprised by an approaching destroyer, and overrun. *U-402* dived as 'well placed depth charges' exploded around the boat. He ordered silent running, and made subtle course changes to throw off his pursuer. Von Forstner decided to wait until twilight before he resurfaced. Damage was light: 'Except for slight glass and fuse damage the gyro compass and main drain pump in parallel switching temporarily out of service, damage can be repaired with on board means.' At 2240hrs *U-402* surfaced and continued pursuit on one diesel engine.

In the early morning hour of the 4th BdU urged 'Veilchen' to 'utilise every opportunity, also to attack submerged by day. The weather and defence situation is favourable, the screen from a westbound convoy may join.' Von Forstner required no order to do his duty. He attempted to pursue, despite the continued mechanical failures of his U-boat. At 1810hrs his port diesel gave out. At 0015hrs on the 5th the starboard diesel was put back into service, and von Forstner again continued his pursuit.

Later that morning he finally gave up the pursuit. Given the current convoy's course projection, von Forstner concluded 'from plotting the convoy is now located in AK 1827, this is 34nm away of me, can no longer get there in the dark, manoeuvring ahead during the day cannot be accomplished with my fuel oil inventory of 13 cbm'. He headed toward the mid-ocean rendezvous point to refuel from the Type XB *U-117*.

On 6 November, 'Veilchen' was dissolved. On the 11th *U-117* supplied *U-402* and *U-381* with fuel for their return cruise and *U-454* for further operations. Von Forstner recorded 'Supply is completed as first boat, 20 cbm taken over, tow line not utilised, because the hose was too short, proceeded in sharp echelon.' 'On the instruction of the tanker I should not report supply . . .'

By the 15th *U-402* was approaching the Bay of Biscay. Von Forstner noted the new FuMB antenna was broken again due to a 'shitty' sea 'after repeated repairs' and that there was 'a risk that it will fail completely'. *U-402*'s port electric motor was out of service because the diesel clutch could not be disengaged. Not wanting to

U-402 returned from its fifth patrol to a hero's welcome given the sinking of 27,287 tons of merchant vessels in a six-hour period. As a celebration for their success, von Forstner arranged with Dr Hüssy to visit Karlsruhe with some thirty members of the crew on 26–27 November, 1942. This photograph and associated news article ran in the *Frankfurter Zeitung*, *Der Führer*, *Völkischer Beobachter*, *Badische Presse* and *Durlacher Tagblatt Nr. 323* newspapers on 27 November. The U-boat crew arrived in Karlsruhe on Thursday and was welcomed in the reception room of the city hall by Mayor Hüssy in the presence 'of a number of honoured guests, including Oberst Schröer and Kreisleiter Worch'. A series of short films made by von Forstner with his 8mm camera were shown. Von Forstner is pictured above in the centre holding flowers, surrounded by members of the crew, Administration Director Supper, SS Obersturmführer Huber and a delegation from the Bund Deutscher Mädel (BDM) as the Schloßhotel, where they lodged for the night. (Stadtarchiv Karlsruhe 1/H-Reg 902)

risk a run on the surface, he dived to proceeded submerged due to the poor visibility. *U-402* surfaced and after reinforcing the FuMB antenna, he continued the crossing only to crash dive for aircraft that flew low, 200m from the U-boat's stern on a southerly course.

On 20 November *U-402* entered La Pallice flying its first set of pennants. Dönitz recorded in *U-402*'s logbook 'A good, successful and fortunate patrol. The commander finally had a chance to showcase his skills. The success was tenaciously and resolutely fought against changeable weather conditions and multiple strong enemy defences.'

Fifteen ships in the convoy were sunk and four damaged for the loss of a single U-boat, *U-132*. *U-402* claimed more than a third of them, with four sunk and one damaged for a total of 27,287 GRT. The survivors of the torpedoed vessels landed at Reykjavik, Iceland on 8 and 10 November. All ship's masters and officers were interviewed. Their criticisms of the convoy action were logged and shared with the US Tenth Fleet and the Royal Navy. The list was long: lack of escorts; excessive use of snowflake flares and rockets which illuminated the night sky for long minutes and gave away their position; escort vessels failed to attack; convoy failed to manoeuvre evasively; and the U-boat attacks all came as a surprise.[30] Task Force 24.1.14 also was criticised for a lack of effective coordination, despite the 'extreme difficulties' of the situation. SC-107 was attacked eight times over a 48-hour period. It was a reopening of the battle for the North Atlantic for which the Western Allies were not fully prepared. In the final assessment from US Navy Captain Hewlett Thebaud, Commander TF 24.7, that was sent to Commander-in-Chief, Western Approaches on 25 November he stated that '. . . the scale of enemy attack [was] as heavy as any that has yet been made on an escorted convoy . . .'.[31]

A guest list signed by all the crew members of *U-402* that participated in the visit to Karlsruhe from 26 to 27 November. (Stadtarchiv Karlsruhe 1/H-Reg 902)

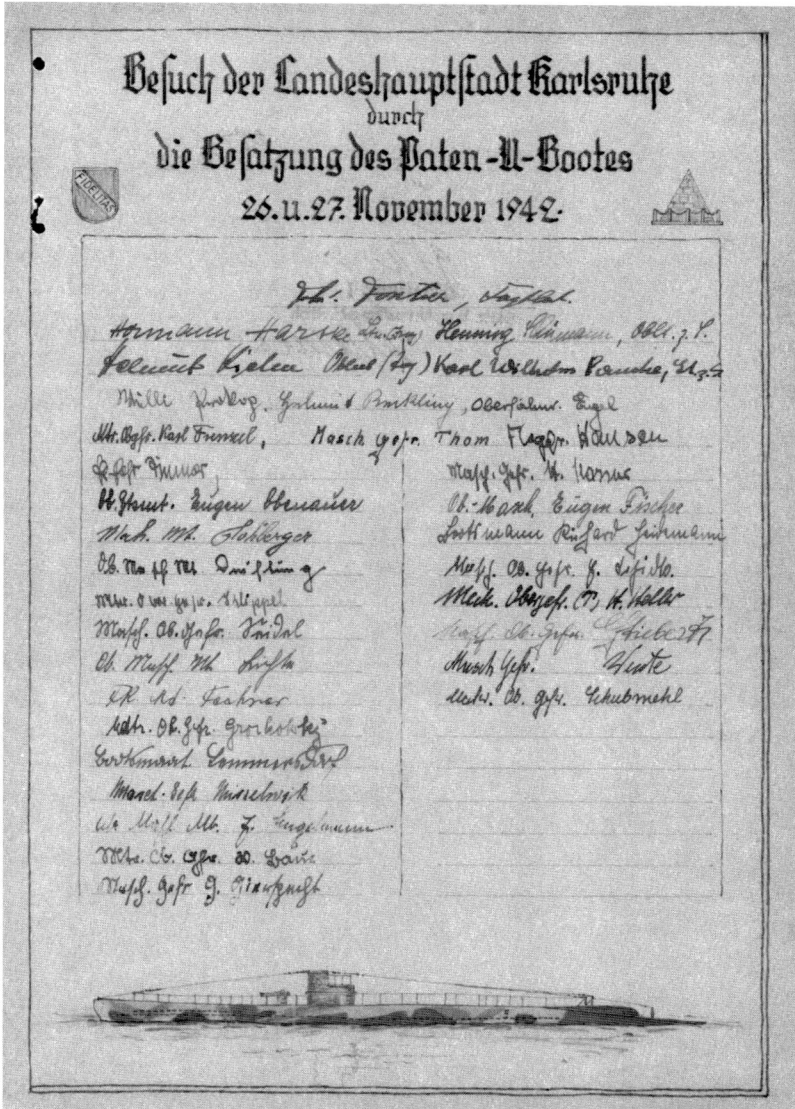

Despite the destruction of SC-107, a major event took place, Operation 'Torch', the Allied landings in North Africa beginning on 8 November 1942. Due to the battle of SC-107, and the simultaneous attack on SL-125 en route from Sierra Leone to the United Kingdom, all U-boats around the Azores and Gibraltar were drawn off to the North Atlantic. The invasion fleet was not detected by B-Dienst, but even if it had been, no U-boats were in a position to attack. The cost to establish the foothold in North Africa was high, however, as thirty-eight Allied vessels were sunk or damaged for only three U-boats lost or damaged.

As *U-402* began its overhaul, von Forstner made his way with approximately thirty members of his crew to Karlsruhe. They had achieved great success in the battle with Convoy SC-107, and it was now time to share that victory and its accolades with *U-402*'s sponsoring city. Von Forstner and the crew arrived by train on 26 November and returned the following evening. Their visit ran in the *Frankfurter Zeitung* and other news outlets. Due to reasons of operational security, the name of von Forstner and the designation *U-402* was kept out of the press by the military censors.

Von Forstner brought with him a series of films he made during his early war patrols that 'gave those assembled an interesting glimpse into the special world of the outgoing U-boat and its crew. Test trips, diving manoeuvres, details of the deck equipment, the tense watchfulness of the bridge watch, signals, as well as the occasional comradely joke that shortens the long approach path for the crew, which had become a unit in the meantime, were reproduced here in a living way.' The article concluded '. . . . One can clearly see that all these men are bound by an obvious hearty comradeship that has been grown and steeped on long trips against the enemy. The population of Karlsruhe is proud to have these men in their city.' Though he followed in his uncle's footsteps, von Forstner finally came into his own as a skilled U-boat commander. He could allow himself a moment of pride in both his tactical judgement and the skilled crew of professional sailors he commanded.

CHAPTER 5

Knight's Cross

> Except for Forstner, the week-long battle around SC-118 would have been an overwhelming victory for the escorts. One determined individual had proven that, in a struggle increasingly dependent on sophisticated weapons systems, the human could still prevail.
>
> Waters, 'Stay Tough'

U-402 spent another two months going through its normal overhaul and maintenance schedule in La Pallice before it departed on 14 January 1943 on its sixth war patrol. The crew had no idea of the larger strategic debate then occurring within BdU about future U-boat deployments.

After the successful Allied landings in North Africa, BdU debated whether to deploy U-boats to the Mediterranean instead of the North Atlantic. This debated lasted through November and December 1942. The best prospects for sinking tonnage were always going to be in the North Atlantic, but some argued more U-boats were required in the Mediterranean where ongoing naval logistic support was required by the Allies in the aftermath of the landings. Dönitz had noted in the BdU war diary on 19 December that the Mediterranean offered little hope in winning the 'tonnage' war. U-boats, he concluded, were to deploy to the North Atlantic, even if that meant missed opportunities elsewhere.

The intelligence war also continued. The Allies began re-cyphering their merchant signal traffic, which increased B-Dienst decryption time by as much as seven days during the second half of December. Simultaneously, the frequency of Allied Ultra intercepts increased and convoys were being successfully routed around waiting U-boat lines based on this intelligence. The post-war assessment of German special intelligence concluded of this time that 'there was no determining when it was reliable and when not. The most correct operational decision could lead to failure, mere chance to success. A convoy could pass unharmed or be decimated, its fate influenced decisively by the relative success at the moment of the two opposing decrypts.'[32] In addition, U-boats might attack a convoy they thought they knew, only to find out it was a different one altogether, as in the cases of SC-111 and HX-217.

B-Dienst realised toward the end of January 1943 that the cycle plots of Allied convoys had shifted from an eight-day to a ten-day schedule, and that the Allies were re-routing them based on the deployment of U-boat lines. BdU now viewed previous B-Dienst intelligence on convoy routes 'not as an absolute guide, but as a point of departure for outguessing the Allies in their attempt to route convoys around waiting U-boats'.[33]

Such guesswork resulted in success for Dönitz when a line of U-boats codenamed 'Pfeil' encountered the eastbound convoy SC-118. His assessment of the tactical situation based on B-Dienst intelligence was recorded on 1 February:

> It is expected that the SC convoy will take approximately the same route as the HX reported by *U-456*; as soon as he notices U-boats shadowing the convoy, the enemy will assume, with some justification, that the convoy route astern of the convoy is free of U-boats. A new patrol line is therefore being formed in this area with the former 'Landsknecht' boats proceeding west. Order: *U-594, 413, 267, 187, 465, 402, 609, 262, 454* and *89* to form Group 'Pfeil' and form a patrol line at maximum speed from [Grid Squares] AK 8421 to BD 2316.

A delay in the decryption of Ultra intercepts prevented Allied intelligence from reading the order to form 'Pfeil' until after contact was made and by then it was too late to re-route the convoy.[34] On 4 February, Convoy SC-118 was discovered where BdU expected and attacked by twenty-five U-boats. In the fog of war, the U-boats claimed fourteen ships sunk, but the actual losses were only twelve sunk and one damaged. *U-402* was responsible for more than half of the convoy losses.

The convoy originally departed New York on 24 January with forty-two merchantmen and tankers. Once it reached Newfoundland it was handed over from Western Local Escort to British Escort Group B2, under the command of acting Commander F B Proudfoot RN in HMS *Vanessa*. They were then joined by another nineteen merchantmen from Halifax and St John's. Eight escorts now accompanied the 61-vessel convoy. This was a strong escort force for this stage of the war, with the British 'V & W'-class destroyer HMS *Vimy* (D33), the 'V'-class destroyer HMS *Vanesa* (D29), the former US Navy *Clemson*-class destroyer HMS *Beverly* (H64), three British 'Flower'-class corvettes HMS *Campanula* (K18), HMS *Mignonette* (K38) and HMS *Abelia* (K184), the Free French corvette *Lobelia* (K05) and the temporarily assigned US Coast Guard Cutter *Bibb*. Only the *Bibb* and the rescue vessel *Toward* were equipped with HF/DF gear. None of the three services had worked together in the past, and their tactical procedures were relatively unknown to each other. The usual commander of B2, Royal Navy Captain and experienced U-boat killer Donald Macintyre, was absent while his flagship HMS *Hesperus* was undergoing repairs after ramming and sinking *U-357* several weeks earlier. As the Royal Navy's most experienced U-boat hunter, his presence was to be sorely missed on this crossing.

Back in Europe, crossing the Bay of Biscay grew more difficult with the increase of Coastal Command patrols with radar-equipped aircraft. *U-402* departed La Pallice in the evening of 14 January at 1755hrs and encountered aircraft only three hours later. The convoy was overflown at 800m but not attacked, likely due to the effective anti-aircraft fire of the Flak vessels and *U-402*'s crew. Twice more over the next few days *U-402* dived due to air detection.

Experience and Luck Creates Opportunity
On 18 January 1943 BdU issued orders for *U-402* to head to Grid Square AJ 90 and form Group 'Landsknecht' along with eighteen other U-boats that were to wait for Convoy HX-224. The patrol line ran from square AL 4447 to BE 2136, as a south-west-bound convoy was expected from noon on 24 January. The U-boats were ordered to remain submerged by day on the 22nd and 23rd to avoid possible detection by Allied air reconnaissance.

As the U-boats waited for the convoy the North Atlantic was unsettled with winter storms that brought heavy seas, snow, hail, thick fog and overcast skies. On the 30th BdU broadcast out that Großadmiral Dönitz had been promoted to Oberbefehlshaber der Kriegsmarine, replacing Erich Raeder as overall commander of the German Navy. This was welcome news to the U-boat crews.

With new intelligence from B-Dienst in hand, Dönitz ordered the formation of Group 'Pfeil' on 1 February, detaching eleven boats from the 'Landsknecht' line. He correctly assessed that the stormy seas did not offer an effective opportunity to continue the attack on HX-224 and allowed only a handful of U-boats to continue operations against it during the next few days.

U-402 reached its assigned position in the patrol line at 0900hrs on the 2nd and began its back-and-forth sweep, operating on electric motors. The North Atlantic had calmed considerably and visibility was good. At 1600hrs von Forstner corrected his position in the reconnaissance line after recognising the difference between dead reckoning and his actual position during a noon navigation fix. U-boats were to maximise their ability to spot a convoy by keeping some 15nm apart, but errors in navigation often caused an accordion effect in the line. For example, shortly after midnight on the 3rd, *U-402* had to reposition itself, as it came within signalling distance of *U-262*, then *U-609*. Being so close to each other only opened up gaps in the line that might let a tightly-grouped convoy slip through, regardless of how effective B-Dienst intelligence was.

On the morning of the 4th, *U-402*'s watch sighted a bright light on the horizon that lasted for one minute. *U-402* initially steered away under the incorrect assumption that this was a destroyer and they were spotted, then realised it was much further along on the horizon and came back to its original course. Then the radio room picked up a short signal from *U-187*: 'Enemy in sight . . . .' Von Forstner quickly plotted an intercept course on the map in the control room and issued the order to proceed at the highest possible speed.

Another report from *U-187* came in at 1130hrs that read: 'Very large convoy, broad formation, NE course, 8-10 knots.' Based on the report, BdU ordered all of Group 'Pfeil' to attack the convoy. Von Forstner needed no prodding as *U-402* was already on an intercept course at high speed when at 1210hrs smoke clouds were spotted on the horizon. *U-402* manoeuvred ahead to get into attack position for the evening. His radio man worked to put out a short report but enciphered it incorrectly and had to re-compose the signal. Timely sighting reports could make a significant difference during a convoy battle.

With the convoy in sight, *U-402*'s starboard diesel gave out and it could not continue pursuit. A frustrated von Forstner sent a short report out stating this fact to BdU and providing the convoy's last known position and course. As work began on the diesel, depth charges were heard as well as that of a torpedo detonation by the hydrophone operator. The battle for Convoy SC-118 had begun.

An hour later Chief Engineer Hartke got the starboard diesel back in service, just as the convoy changed course and smoke was again visible on the horizon. Von Forstner immediately headed toward the smoke. Twenty minutes later he sent out another short message to BdU with the convoy's position and course. Within minutes the *Vimy* was spotted heading north-west across *U-402*'s bow in the distance toward the growing smoke plumes on the horizon. *U-402* quickly changed course to avoid the destroyer, but von Forstner did not submerge. He had no intention of losing contact unless forced to.

As a naval tactician, von Forstner showed a well-developed sense of when an escort had detected his U-boat and how much time he had before it closed the range and attacked. He rarely submerged when a destroyer was spotted and often outmanoeuvred it while surfaced, only slipping below the waves when he believed he had no other option.

Off to starboard two other U-boats were identified by the watch, also bearing down on the smoke plumes. Anticipation was building among the crew as a transmission from BdU was received in the radio room '. . . Convoy is probably destined for Murmansk. Go! Operate ruthlessly to relieve the Eastern Front.' As thirteen U-boats from Group 'Pfiel' closed in on the convoy, BdU directed another ten from Group 'Haudegen' to join if they had enough fuel, as they had been on station since 19 January. The Battle of Stalingrad had just concluded and the Red Army was driving westward at that time. This disastrous situation on the Eastern Front was certainly behind BdU's broadcast.

As *U-402* drew closer, von Forstner took evasive action as an approaching escort, probably the USCGC *Bibb*, drew near. *U-402* came back to its northerly course, and an hour later was again driven off by an escort. Contact reports continued to come in from *U-402*, *U-608*, *U-267* and *U-609* as each were driven off by destroyers. BdU assumed this was due to ASDIC, but the reality was that ship-based HF/DF and radar was providing rough estimates of U-boat bearings as signals were being sent. The destroyers kept manoeuvring down on those signals to force the U-boats to break contact and allow the convoy to get away.

SC-118 was going to be hard pressed to escape the U-boats arrayed around it given the excellent intelligence BdU had received. Of note was the fact that *U-632*, commanded by then Kapitänleutnant Hans Karpf, sank the British-flagged tanker *Cordelia* south of Iceland on 3 February, which was an unescorted straggler from Convoy HX-224. The sole survivor, Chief Engineer I C Bingham, was rescued and brought aboard the U-boat. During questioning he revealed that a large eastbound convoy was following. This information was reported to BdU. Bingham's statement confirmed what was already known, and did little to alter the course of the upcoming battle.

Von Forstner continued to correctly estimate the convoy's position and bearing through the night. This was evident as destroyers continued to attempt to drive him off five more times, each attempt occurring after von Forstner sent a short report to BdU. The last attempt was probably conducted by the *Bibb* that spotted a U-boat on the surface and tried to drive it off with depth charges. The depth charges landed off von Forstner's portside. In a bold, if not dangerous move, *U-402* remained surfaced and did not dive, despite it only being twilight.

Von Forstner's tenacity was rewarded when he spotted two masts on the horizon. This was confirmation he was back on the convoy. Suddenly, a larger destroyer, probably HMS *Beverly*, was spotted off the U-boat's stern 300–500m away, and closing. 'Dive!' von Forstner yelled. The watch and officers on the bridge slid down the ladder and closed the watertight hatch. 'Seemed to have detected us with radar, yet still not sighted us,' von Forstner noted of this incident. Then the depth charges dropped. The first was when *U-402* was at 20m. The U-boat descended deeper in the water column. At 160m more exploded nearby. The explosions were getting closer, though at this depth U-boats were generally operating below their normal setting. Half an hour after diving, at 2306hrs the drain pump was turned on to handle the water entering the U-boat from minor leaks. Two more series of depth charges were dropped over the next two hours. But by 0130hrs on the 5th, *U-402* resurfaced to regain contact with the convoy.

Just past midnight the convoy turned. However, the left (port) three columns failed to get the signal and wandered off for 15 miles. This section was followed by the U-boats, while the other nine columns slipped past them. Reports came in from *U-609*, and *U-267*, who were both then driven off by destroyers. Between 0218hrs and 0255hrs Von Forstner kept working out the suspected position of the convoy in the control room. Then *U-187* reported seeing star shells at 0317hrs, confirming the new easterly course of the merchantmen.

What they saw was a star shell fired accidentally by a careless crewman on board the Norwegian-flagged transport *Annik*. It could be seen 20 miles away. Pursuit continued for the next 11 hours. Some confusion occurred when *U-402*'s radioman incorrectly took the reciprocal bearing of the convoy from the spotter's report, which interpreted the convoy as having turned around in a westerly direction. Von Forstner corrected him, and the new course was set.

U-402 drove hard along the northerly course to regain contact and get into an attack position. Then at 1112hrs the chief

Two sequenced photos of USCGC *Ingham* (WPG-35) taken from her sister ship USCGC *Bibb* (WPG-31) during a North Atlantic crossing, date unknown. She is clearly escorting a convoy as shown by the steam merchantmen visible in the second photograph. These pictures accurately depict the harsh conditions of the North Atlantic often faced by friend and foe alike. The *Ingham* was a 2,700-ton 'Treasury'-class Coast Guard cutter commissioned in 1936. She was 327ft long, had a range of 8,270nm and a top speed of 21 knots. In this configuration she appears to be armed with two 5in/51 (fore and aft) and four 3in/50 guns, two mounted fore and aft. A depth-charge rack was mounted aft. There were likely to be as many as eight .50-cal machine guns as well. She was only equipped with an early radar set that could not easily distinguish a conning tower from heavy seas. Both the *Ingham* and *Bibb* encountered *U-402* during the battles of Convoys SC-107 and SC-118 during the war. They both rescued survivors from the USS *Henry R. Mallory*, SS *Kalliopi* and *Newton Ash*, all sunk during the convoy battle by *U-402*. (US Naval History and Heritage Command, 26-G 04-02-43 and, 26-G 04-07-43)

engineer reported that the port thrust bearing was running hot and that the diesel engine had to be stopped. Further inspection revealed that the bearing was worn out, and the thrust disc damaged. It had to be replaced and that the duration of repairs would be approximately 24 hours. Von Forstner thought about the recommendation and quickly made up his mind. He ordered repairs to be made, but he was not going to stop his pursuit. 'Because I must initially give up search for the convoy, intend to pursue with highest possible speed on one diesel on general course of the convoy without operating on individual contact keeper reports.' He was going to continue on his own with only one operable diesel engine. For the next 14 hours *U-402* headed north-east following a course based on von Forstner's tactical intuition.

With the convoy now under attack, reinforcements were called in by the convoy commander. The USCGC *Ingham* was dispatched from Iceland to assist. At 0420hrs on the 6th, BdU sent out words of encouragement to Group 'Pfeil' who were still chasing down SC-118: 'With all means attempt to gain contact. Convoy may not be lost any more. Favourable weather conditions. The defence is powerless with the weather. Surface and submerged detection strongly hindered.' The message concluded with 'Be tough and ruthless in operations. Think of the Eastern Front.'

The sea state was moderate with thick cloud cover. Surface radar was impacted as the waves interfered with the detection of the low silhouette of the U-boats, when it was even operable. The rough seas played havoc with the sensitive electronics, as in the case of the *Ingham* whose radar dome was cracked and took on water causing it to cease operation when it flooded. Her radar was also of the older SC-1 surface-search radar that had trouble distinguishing a surfaced U-boat's conning tower among the waves in heavy seas. Her sister ship, the *Bibb*, was equipped with the more modern SG on the 10cm wavelength and could often distinguish between a conning tower and wavetop, which allowed her to often bear down on the surfaced *U-402* during the battle.

By 0800hrs new bearings were installed in *U-402*'s diesels. This required von Forstner to stop the boat and throw the engines into reverse several times to get the new fittings in place. He noted his situation at 0917hrs: 'Repairs to the thrust bearing ended, however, it must be broken in slowly. If I take no account of it, and it stops, I have absolutely no chance of getting to the convoy. I decide to shorten the required time for breaking in such that I can still get in contact in the next night, have luck that the bearing holds out.'

At 1230hrs *U-624* came along side *U-402* to check its current position. After a few minutes of coordinating, both U-boats continued on their easterly course of 90 degrees. Almost three hours later, a land-based aircraft came out of the clouds. *U-402* dived, and the sounds of six detonations were off in the direction of *U-624*. *U-402* came to the surface and spotted the aircraft circling over the area of *U-624*'s last position. *U-402* then dived again as von Forstner did not want to be spotted. More distant detonations were heard. He then ordered a rare sonic transmission to confirm if *U-624* was OK. U-boats could attempt to communicate submerged through this underwater communication technique. A 2 x 2 transmitter and 2 x 2 receiver were located on the port and starboard side, near main ballast tank 5, under the waterline. It had a frequency of 3.5kc per second and a range of 10 miles. Incoming sound waves were passed from the receivers through the amplifier to the headphones of the sonar operator. There was no recorded response. *U-624* reportedly survived this devastating air attack, but was sunk by a British-crewed Boeing B-17 that attacked it with depth charges the following day.[35]

Over the next several hours aircraft from Iceland flew out over the convoy driving U-boats, including *U-402*, back underwater. They needed to break U-boat contact and force them to use up fuel before nightfall, when the convoy might be able to escape in the darkness.

At 2009hrs von Forstner sent a signal requesting an updated convoy bearing. Just eight minutes later his watch observed a 'flying boat' dead-ahead at 5,000m lining up for an attack. *U-402* dived as 'poorly placed' bombs were dropped 17 minutes after diving. Von Forstner noted in his war diary 'oil trace?', suggesting that he was leaking oil, which gave away his position. The reality was that radio direction-finding, coupled with airborne radar, assisted aircraft in vectoring in on surfaced U-boats. What von Forstner and other commanders began to instinctively realise was that not long after they sent wireless transmissions, they were often attacked. As the war continued, experienced U-boat commanders began to refrain from excessive radio communications as a result. By the time the new snorkel device was retrofitted into the U-boat fleet a year later, wireless transmissions from boats on patrol had dropped off sharply.

Over the next several hours depth charges were heard being dropped as the escorts again worked to break U-boat contacts before another night arrived. Multiple times *U-402* was forced to dive due to approaching land-based aircraft or surface escorts. At 2155hrs star shells went up, again giving away the convoy's position, and soon the Greek-flagged SS *Polyktor* was hit and sunk by *U-266*. But the escorts continued their work as more depth charges were dropped and surface gunfire erupted at targets. The convoy appeared to be slipping away again as U-boats were forced away, as in the case of the heavily damaged *U-267*.

Von Forstner heard the spotting reports as they came in late into the evening. Again, he tried to work out the convoy's position. He believed that the reports put the convoy too far south, but even so, the convoy was still to starboard of *U-402*, so he steered for a southerly intercept course. The seas were calm with an overcast sky. While surface radar might pick him up, there was no moonlight. He calculated that while conditions were not perfect for a night surface attack, they were not unfavourable either. He dived *U-402* in an unsuccessful attempt to get sound bearings from the propellers and turbines of the convoy, then resurfaced.

At 0135hrs *U-402* dived as the watch thought they were

detected by a destroyer. No sound bearings were heard, and once resurfaced 10 minutes later, the FuMB was turned on in order to get early warning on any radar in use. The seas were calm, but the there was heavy cloud cover limiting the ability of the watch to give an early warning of approaching aircraft. Twenty minutes later the watch spotted silhouettes off in the distance along the horizon to the south. The sighting was followed by the sound of torpedo detonations over the hydrophone, confirmation that they found the main convoy. These explosions were runners fired by *U-262* that missed their targets.

U-402 manoeuvred toward a large freighter at 0217hrs. Just before he fired a torpedo, von Forstner sent a short signal to BdU that probably gave away his position, as during the next 45 minutes the steamer conducted a series of evasive manoeuvres, finally turning toward *U-402*, before turning away north-east. Just as the steamer turned, an escort emerged from behind the vessel. The time was 0302hrs and the escort raced directly towards the surfaced *U-402* at a sharp angle, in an attempt to drive it off. A crash dive was ordered. Nine minutes later *U-402* resurfaced, as von Forstner was not going to miss his opportunity. He had made it past the escort screen. 'Am positioned on the starboard side of the convoy, that drives in a long formation at very irregular distances. Exact course determined by passing the wakes of steamers.'

One Man's Determination
The surface conditions were ideal and von Forstner had an excellent view of the situation. Two large steamers were proceeding on an easterly heading, one close behind the other 'seemingly in the wake; forward a tanker, behind a freighter'. His initial plan was a single torpedo on the tanker, then one on the freighter – always trying to target the largest vessel he could. He quickly changed the plan, because as *U-402* manoeuvred in for the shot, the tanker passed by so close to the U-boat that its wake splashed the binoculars of the torpedo officer and fogged them up so that he could not make the correct calculation. Due to the acute firing angle on the tanker, von Forstner quickly reversed his plan to fire 'first on the freighter, while then turning back on tanker' to fire the second shot.

'Fire!' At 0347hrs the first torpedo was launched from tube I. 'Target is an about 6,000 GRT large freighter, type not recognised, did not fit in the binoculars at the shot.' The freighter was closer than anyone on the bridge of the U-boat realised as they had calculated the initial torpedo range at 1,000m. 'Range greatly under

The American-flagged steam tanker *Robert E. Hopkins* (6,625 GRT) was the second vessel sunk by *U-402* during the battle with SC-118. The tanker was carrying 68,000 barrels of fuel oil when at 0352hrs on 7 February, a stern torpedo shot from *U-402* on the starboard side forward of the #1 tank in the dry cargo hold. The explosion buckled the forward decks as well as the 3in gun. The tanker came to a full stop, but remained afloat. At 0402hrs a coup de grâce shot was fired and hit the tanker's engine room on the starboard side. After flooding, the boilers exploded and tore away large portions of the hull that caused the tanker to sink within three minutes (55° 13'N, 26° 22'W – Grid AK 6668). (The Mariners' Museum P0001.003-01–PB9637)

estimated, after 135 seconds 2,075m a hit amidships. Freighter starts to burn, shoots rockets, crew abandons ship passing showers, 0400hrs sunk.' What von Forstner thought was a large freighter was actually the British-flagged steamer *Toward* (1,571 GRT) that served as the convoy's rescue ship. Her loss contributed to the unfortunate loss of life among the sailors whose vessels were torpedoed later. But arguably more importantly at the time, she was one of only two vessels that had HF/DF gear on board that could vector in the escorts to U-boats sending radio transmissions. Later that day the convoy commander sent a transmission to the CINC Western Approaches that read in part 'If available in the vicinity suggest assistance HF/DF ship to replace *Toward*.' None would come.

Two minutes later two more torpedoes left the boat from tube II and tube III. 'Target is about 10,000 GRT large tanker, type: W.B. WALKER (10,468 GRT).' The first shot missed, as 'tanker probably zig zagged after the hit on the freighter, had a different course on the next attack. Also turned out that did not drive ahead of the freighter, but still [manoeuvred] farther away at 2,075 meters.' The shot from tube III 'was a tube runner' that never left the U-boat. 'After repeated cocking of the ejection mechanism the torpedo left the tube.' Von Forstner manoeuvred for a shot from the stern torpedo tube.

At 0352hrs a torpedo left the stern's tube V. 'Target was the same tanker. After 140 seconds – 2,075 meters, hit aft 10 meters, about 30-meter-high explosion column.' The tanker's crew let off emergency rockets giving *U-402* a good view of the tanker. Von Forstner concluded that 'because sinking is not certain, [I] decide on a coup de grace.' The tanker hit was the American-flagged *Robert E. Hopkins* (6,625 GRT).

The *Hopkins* had not been zig-zagging, but running completely blacked out following radio silence guidelines. Six armed guards were on watch, manning the 20mm forward and 4in

HMS *Mignonette* (K38) was a 'Flower'-class corvette commissioned in May 1941. She was 940 tons, 205ft long, had a range of 3,500nm and a top speed of 16 knots. She was armed with one 4in Mk IX BL gun forward, two twin Lewis machine guns, two twin Vickers machine gun, two Mk II depth-charge throwers and two depth charge rails with forty depth charges. Many modifications were made to the 'Flower' class as experience was gained during the convoy battles of the North Atlantic, which were later incorporated into a modified design introduced in the latter half of the war. *Mignonette* picked up survivors from the rescue ship SS *Toward*, which was the first vessel sunk by *U-402* on the night of 7 February, as well as the *Robert E. Hopkins* and *Afrika*. (Imperial War Museum/FL5763)

gun aft. The mate, quartermaster and one lookout were on the bridge. 'The weather was clear, light clouds, sea white caps with swells, wind NW, strong force, no moonlight, dark, visibility very poor. . .' The first torpedo struck the starboard tanks beneath the cargo hold, distorting the forward gun platform. The ship was still afloat and manoeuvrable. No one saw the torpedo track or the U-boat that fired it, though they knew from radio chatter that U-boats had been in the vicinity for 48 hours.

Ten minutes after the first explosion a second rocked the *Hopkins*. A torpedo fired from tube IV struck 'in the engine room. High explosion column, red lights lit, tanker settles astern immediately. After about 20 minutes sunk. Destroyers come to the tanker to take the survivors on board.' Von Forstner's second hit 'struck very low in the engine room' on the starboard side. There was a flash and the boilers exploded and the 'hull ruptured extensively' according to the crew. The ship listed to starboard and sank by the stern. The crew abandoned ship in two lifeboats and one life raft. HMS *Mignonette* pulled alongside to pick up the survivors now that the rescue ship had been sunk. Once the destroyer arrived to pick up survivors, *U-402* turned away to look for more targets.

Von Forstner saw targets all around him, as he was now in the middle of the convoy. He carefully picked out what appeared to be another large tanker. At 0438hrs a single shot from the reloaded tube II left the boat headed for 'a large tanker of about 12,000 GRT of type: VIKTOR ROSS (11,200 GRT).' *U-402* was so close that the 'tanker did not fit in the binoculars at the shot'. One minute later an escort appeared on an opposite course and

The third vessel torpedoed by *U-402* was the Norwegian-flagged motor tanker SS *Daghild*. The 9,272 GRT ship was carrying 13,000 tons of diesel, and a deck cargo of aircraft, barges and the British landing craft HMS *LCT-2335*. At 0438hrs on 7 February, she was hit by a single torpedo from *U-402* and was abandoned by her crew. She remained afloat and was later sunk by a coup de grâce shot from *U-608* (55° 25'N, 26° 12'W - Grid AL 5143). (The Mariners' Museum P0001.003-01–PB7011)

U-402 crash dived. This was probably the *Campanula*. A depth-charge explosion rocked the boat, then the detonation of the torpedo came across. Seventeen minutes later *U-402* surfaced to survey the torpedo's work. 'Tanker lies stopped with the forecastle in the water, destroyer is with him and takes the crew off. I decide on a coup de grace.' Fourteen minutes later a single shot from the reloaded tube I was launched, but missed due to an aiming error. *U-402* 'remained in the vicinity of the tanker' until von Forstner was convinced it would sink without another shot as the tanker had settled so low 'the bridge was now in water . . . '. He turned his attention to another target as his crew feverishly reloaded the torpedo tubes.

The ship he had hit was the Norwegian-flagged tanker *Daghild* (9,272 GRT). The large tanker had previously been damaged by a torpedo from *U-404* back on 12 September 1942 as part of Convoy ON-127. Then, like now, the U-boat commander had thought the vessel sunk. But as *U-402* departed, the *Daghild* remained afloat until the 8th, when *U-608* located the abandoned vessel and sunk it with a coup de grâce shot that also sent HMS *LCT-2335*, which was lashed to the tanker's deck, to the bottom.

At 0540hrs, star shells and tracer bullets were observed along the horizon to port. This was followed by the sounds of depth charges, as well as a torpedo detonation. This may have been an attack by *U-614* on the British-flagged merchant *Harmala*, and a subsequent attack on the U-boat by the *Mignonette*, but the reported times are inconsistent with those in *U-402*'s logbook.

Forty-five minutes later von Forstner sent a message to BdU 'Contact lost, last convoy position 0512hrs square AL 4447, sank a freighter, a large tanker, left a large tanker sinking. 39 cbm. 5+2 torpedoes.' As the watch scanned the still-dark horizon, two

HMS *Campanula* (K18) was a 'Flower'-class corvette, similar to the *Mignonette*. After the *Daghild* was torpedoed, the *Campanula* caught *U-402* on the surface, and forced it to dive as she launched a series of depth charges. However, von Forstner had developed a 'sixth sense' regarding escort attacks and was always able to time a crash dive to avoid serious damage. He showed little concern for escorts and on several occasions outmanoeuvred them while surfaced. As Waters stated after the war, 'No surface escort was ever going to get him.' He was right. *Campanula* rescued survivors from the *Afrika*, sunk on the night of 7 February. (Imperial War Museum/FL6005)

The fourth vessel sunk by *U-402* was the British-flagged motor merchant ship SS *Afrika* (8,597 GRT). She was carrying 5,000 tons of steel and 6,457 tons of general cargo, including grain and explosives, when at 0636hrs on 7 February a torpedo hit hold #5 and she sank in 8 minutes (55° 16'N, 26° 31'W – Grid AL 4441). (The Mariners' Museum P0001.003-01–PB6048)

minutes later a large freighter appeared and a shot calculation was readied. 'Fire!' A torpedo was launched from tube IV at 0636hrs. The 'target appears to be an 8,000 GRT large freighter with flat forecastle and conspicuous long superstructure, bridge is set off from the superstructure, broad smoke stack. Type not found.' After 90 seconds, or a 1,400m run, a hit occurred about amidships, 'with dark explosion column. Freighter quickly takes a heavy list to starboard, shoots white rockets, crew abandons ship. Freighter begins to sink on an even keel.'

This was the British-flagged merchant *Afrika* (8,597 GRT), with the torpedo exploding in Hold #5. The vessel sank in eight minutes. The weather grew rougher during the course of the night, with high winds and rain now whipping the surging surface. This made rescue of the survivors difficult, as one of the three launched lifeboats capsized. Twenty-nine of the fifty-two crew were picked up by *Campanula* and *Mignonette*.

As von Forstner watched the *Afrika* sink to her railings, he quickly turned his attention to yet another freighter that loomed up on the horizon. Twenty-three minutes later, at 0659hrs, a torpedo exited tube II. His new target was 'a 6,000 GRT freighter, bow and stern somewhat higher than the continuous deck, type like: JERSEY CITY (6200 GRT)'. After 53 seconds, or 820m, a 'hit

The fifth vessel sunk by *U-402* was the American-flagged troop transport USS *Henry R. Mallory* (6,063 GRT). At 0659hrs on 7 February, a torpedo hit on the starboard side at the #3 hold. The explosion damaged the main steam line, destroyed the oil pump and engine-room gauges and blew off the #4 hatch covers. The stern settled quickly and she gradually began to list to port until she sank 30 minutes after the hit (55° 18'N, 26° 29'W – Grid AL 4441). (The Mariners' Museum P0001.003-01–PB13447)

15m before the aft mast. Steamer begins to burn immediately. Bright tongues of flame ignite. Out of which shoots a rocket. After the detonation the stern is under water, the crew abandoned ship, a destroyer went to the ship, which sank shortly thereafter.'

The fifth ship sunk by von Forstner in just over three hours was the American-flagged troop transport *Henry R Mallory* (6,6063 GRT). The single torpedo struck Hold #3. The explosion reportedly damaged the main steam line, destroyed the oil pump and the engine-room gauges, and blew off the #4 hatch covers. The stern settled quickly in the heavy seas and the ship gradually began to list to port. She sank 30 minutes later. The ship was carrying trucks, tanks, clothing, food, cigarettes and 610 bags of mail when she was torpedoed. On board were 9 officers, 68 crewmen, 34 armed guards, and 383 troops (136 US Army, 72 US Marines, 173 US Navy, and 2 civilians). Only three launches with 172 men cleared the sinking ship, with other men jumping into the sea in order to reach the lifeboats.

No one in the convoy knew that the *Mallory* had been hit. USS *Schenck* (DD 159), which was in the process of picking up survivors from the previously-torpedoed *Toward*, spotted lights in the distance and requested permission to investigate but was refused. It was only four hours later that the *Bibb* discovered the *Mallory*. She had picked up a strong HF/DF bearing at the rear of the convoy and pursued the possible contact. With no results, she turned to re-join the convoy and spotted a red flare shot from one of the lifeboats and began its rescue operation, picking up 205

The *Wickes*-class destroyer USS *Schenck* (DD-159) was commissioned in 1930. She displaced 1,211 tons, was 314ft long, and had a top speed of 35 knots. She was armed with four 4in/50 guns, one 3in gun and twelve 21in torpedo tubes. The latter were replaced during the war with depth-charge racks. She was also equipped with both sonar and surface-search radar. The destroyer rescued survivors from the *Toward*. (US Naval History and Heritage Command 108704)

survivors, though three later died. The rescue was screened by *Campanula*, *Mignonette* and the *Ingham* that arrived from Iceland and picked up twenty-two additional survivors, of which two later died. Out of the 494 crew and passengers, 272 lost their lives.

Still surfaced, von Forstner continued his attack. He sent out another contact keeper report as per procedure. At 0730hrs another freighter was spotted, and five minutes later another torpedo launched. His new target was 'a very large freighter, about 9000 GRT with 5 hatches, high smoke stack, type: MATHURA (8900 GRT)'. After a short run of 48 seconds, or 740m, there was a 'hit amidships, with about 30-meter-high white explosion column. Steamer shoots rockets, settles astern deeper and takes on a list to starboard.' Von Forstner 'remained close for a coup de grâce if necessary. The crew abandoned ship, 25 minutes after the hit the bow jutted steeply out of the water, steamer sank.' Star shells went up to port.

U-402's sixth victim of the night was the Greek-flagged merchant *Kalliopi* (4,965 GRT). Like the other vessels torpedoed that night, she was not zig-zagging, running blacked out and radio silent with a strong watch and deck guns manned. The visibility was poor, with a strong SSE wind and rain. Four other vessels of the convoy were in sight. The torpedo stuck the starboard side, amidships in the cargo hold, and the vessel began to list. The crew quickly abandoned ship, and the *Bibb*, having seen the star shell fired from the stricken vessel's deck, arrived to pick up survivors, of which thirty-three out of thirty-six crew were rescued.

The sixth vessel sunk on that long night by *U-402* was the Greek steam merchant SS *Kalliopi* (4,965 GRT) carrying 6,500 tons of steel and lumber. A torpedo hit the starboard side, just aft of amidships, at 0735hrs on 7 February. The explosion raised all the hatches and ruptured the side plates, causing the ship to settle aft with a list to port and she sank by the stern about 25 minutes after the attack (55° 27'N, 26° 08'W – Grid AL 4418). (The Mariners' Museum P0001.003-01–PB15049)

It was now 0835hrs, just before light as *U-402* looked for more targets. The seas continued to grow heavy as the convoy entered a rain squall. 'Want to attack a freighter about 7000 GRT from the port side,' von Forstner recorded, but he had 'too little room forward. Attack broken off and initiated from starboard.' Fifteen minutes later, a single shot from Tube III was fired but it turned out to be a 'surface runner' and missed the target. Von Forstner dived to reload the stern tube. Sound bearings were still heard over the hydrophone allowing the U-boat to maintain its attack course. About 90 minutes later *U-402* resurfaced and quickly sent a message to BdU: 'Besides reported 3 units, 3 other freighters torpedoed, 2 sunk, one left sinking. Total of 6 ships, about 45000 GRT . . .' After concluding the report with the convoy's current position, *U-402* dived because the watch spotted an approaching escort. It resurfaced, then spotted a destroyer coming out of the morning haze. *U-402* slipped beneath the waves again, and surfaced a few hours later at noon. Von Forstner had lost contact with the convoy.

Later that day BdU sent a wireless message at 1554hrs that must have energised the crew: 'Forstner well done. Stay with it and maintain contact. All boats must still come. The depth charges will run out. Remain close. The convoy is extremely important.' *U-402* and its crew had been pushed to the limit by their commander, yet the battle was not over. As the U-boat maintained contact with the convoy during the day to be in position for another night attack, the cooling water pumps leaked heavily but repairs were out of the question for von Forstner who was now locked in combat. The main pump had to continually pump water from the diesel bilge.

U-402 continued to stay surfaced in the heavy seas. A destroyer was spotted, and avoided. Von Forstner issued another convoy report. At 1604hrs he recorded in the logbook that the 'starboard diesel can only run on 5 cylinders for the rest of the convoy operation . . . Starboard thrust bearing runs hot, must temporarily reduce speed. The repaired port thrust bearing held up perfectly, again an indication of the great skill and diligence of Obermasch. Fischer, who carried out the fitting of new jaws.'

A new contact report came at 1629hrs from *U-456*. *U-402* headed in that direction and soon smoke was spotted on the horizon. Then an aircraft appeared and *U-402* dived. It surfaced again less than 10 minutes later, and again spotted an aircraft in the distance and again submerged. It surfaced 18 minutes later and was soon greeted by a steamer. However, *U-402* was struggling with mechanical problems and barely remaining operable. Due to leaking pipes, both compressors were underperforming. The diesel high-pressure lines had 'failed long ago' due to too many crash dives. All surfacing had to be done very carefully, to conserve the remaining pressure he had in the lines. After surfacing *U-402* sent off a short report with the suspected bearing of the convoy. Thirty-four minutes later, at 1934hrs a destroyer was spotted, and after manoeuvring away, a land-based aircraft was spotted. Again *U-402* dived and resurfaced 22 minutes later to continue pursuit.

BdU sent a message to Group 'Pfeil' at 2320hrs with the approach of the next evening: 'If no contact, continue to run with long legs and high speed up to darkness. Tomorrow will be too dangerous due to air. Convoy probably goes at dawn in the direction of the North Channel.'

Von Forstner was even more determined to regain contact. 'I must be close to the convoy. . .' and dived to listen with the sound gear. No sound bearings were heard and he ordered and immediate surface to head toward the last course *U-456* had reported earlier. It was now past midnight on the 8th when a 'torpedo explosion' was heard on bearing 180 degrees. Von Forstner sat in the control room and tried to work out the best possible course to the convoy. He recorded his thoughts in the logbook as follows: 'By operating direct according to plotting, however, with uncertain information (distance to the detonation location, is it at the front or the back of the convoy, convoy course) passing by [the convoy] is possible in the low visibility night. If, however, I head for torpedoed steamer and pursue from there to the convoy, I must definitely gain contact.' He decided to head toward the location of the attack, and from there hopefully pick up the convoy.

What the hydrophone operator recorded as a torpedo hit, however, was in fact a collision between the Greek-flagged merchant *Adams* and an unknown tanker in the convoy. The collision on the port side of the *Adams* was so severe that it cut a hole in the combined boiler and engine room, which subsequently flooded. Some 50 minutes later, just before 0100hrs, *U-402*'s watch spotted the damaged steamer with an escort, USS *Babbitt* (DD128), nearby rescuing the crew.

Had the inadvertent collision not occurred, it is unlikely that von Forstner would have regained contact with the convoy, but such is fate in war. An experienced and intuitive commander like him easily recognised when chance presented a moment of opportunity to be exploited with often devastating effect. *U-402* continued on course into the darkness and spotted the convoy again to starboard, about 30 minutes later. Von Forstner 'initiated approach from port on a large freighter, due to heavy visibility deterioration broke off, and moved to the other side, since it is empty, [as] surprise by destroyer there is less likely, there are probably other shadows to port.'

At 0142hrs *U-402* launched a single shot from the stern tube V at a target von Forstner recorded was 'a large freighter of about 10,000 GRT. Freighter with 4 masts, apparently heavy cargo masts, 3 hatches and long super structure, type: CUMBERLAND (10900 GRT). At the shot he fit with the length between exterior masts in the binoculars.' A hit was heard after a 98-second (1,475m) run. 'Approximately 20-meter-high explosive column about amidships. Begins to sink immediately, within 5 minutes sank over the sternpost, probably heavy cargo.' The last vessel sunk from SC-118 was the British-flagged merchant *Newton Ash* (4,625 GRT).

The final vessel sunk by *U-402* during the battle for Convoy SC-118 was the British SS *Newton Ash* (4,625 GRT) carrying 6,500 tons of grain, military stores and mail. She was torpedoed at 0142hrs on 8 February and sank stern-first in five minutes (56° 25′N, 22° 26′W - Grid AL 5143). (The Mariners' Museum P0001.003-01–PB9079)

U-402 was now out of torpedoes. Von Forstner decided to drop astern of the convoy and send out a spotting report. His first transmission to BdU was picked up on the HF/DF receiver on board the nearby *Bibb*. With a course bearing, the *Bibb*'s new SG radar took over the job of pinpointing the squawking surfaced U-boat. A contact was identified at 4,500 yards and general quarters sounded. At the range of 1,700 the *Bibb*'s commanding officer, Commander Raney, ordered star shells fired as he believed *U-402* was about to make an attack on the convoy. He had no idea von Forstner had run out of torpedoes. His gunners open fire. The concussion of the star shells knocked out the radar, and the gun flashes blinded them as inaccurate fire raked empty waves. *Ingham* was just two miles away, and her older radar set did not pick up on the surfaced *U-402* passing across her bows in the dark.[36]

Over the next 18 hours *U-402* remained in contact and transmitting spotting reports. Sea and land-based aircraft soon arrived to assist the beleaguered escorts. *U-402* was detected and again pursued alternatively by surface escorts and aircraft, causing the U-boat to crash-dive at least three times during the day. The starboard diesel gave out temporarily at 1440hrs on the 8th. Two hours later it was caught on the surface again and attacked by a B-17. Von Forstner noted in his logbook '18 depth charges, inexplicably 22 minutes after diving, no sound bearings, oil trace?' As an experienced commander, he knew there was something continually giving away his position given how frequently he was being attacked.

By the 9th *U-402* was low on fuel. He was advised by BdU to head back to port. Von Forstner responded that with only 25 cbm such a trip was 'not ensured'. Instead,

Von Forstner had put on arguably the most successful single performance of any U-boat commander since the early days of the war, sinking eight merchants and a troop transport totalling 41,718 GRT from a single convoy in less than 24 hours. The crew knew that based on their calculations von Forstner had sunk over 100,000 tons which guaranteed the award of the Knight's Cross. They made one from scratch and when the official announcement of the award was received by radio communication a celebration took place in the wardroom. Pictured here is von Forstner with the hand-made Knight's Cross and a smiling 1st Watch Officer Oberleutnant Henning Schümann. (Author's collection)

he decided on a mid-Atlantic re-supply with the U-tanker *U-460*. *U-402*'s involvement in the battle of SC-118 was over.

At 0145hrs on the 10th BdU sent the following: 'Radio Message: To Pfeil boats: Recognition for tough and hard battle in the convoy, particularly Forstner, Rudloff and Franke for success and contact keeping. However, even more boats should have approached with so numerous a group. Oberbefehlshaber.' That messaged was followed up at 0951hrs with: 'To Kapitänleutnant Baron von Forstner. Warm congratulations to you and your brave men for the award of the Knight's Cross. Your BdU and ObdM.' At 1521hrs von Forstner slipped beneath the waves for an onboard celebration arranged by his crew who made him a makeshift Knight's Cross.

The congratulations continued, this time from the Chief of the 3rd U-Flotilla which *U-402* was assigned, 'Warm congratulations to you and your men and happy homecoming.' The following day a final congratulations was sent from Großadmiral Raeder. 'Warm congratulations are conveyed on the award of the Ritterkreuz [Knight's Cross] to you and your gallant crew.'

U-402 arrived at the rendezvous point with *U-460* on the 11th and refuelled. The doctor on *U-460* came aboard *U-402* and treated 'various inflammations of the crew'. Six hours later, *U-402* decoupled the fuel lines and left *U-460* to begin a still-dangerous journey back to port. In the late evening of the 19th *U-402* was spotted on the surface by a corvette and a destroyer and attacked. *U-402* rode out the attack lasting several hours at the extreme depth of 180m (594ft). The depth charges were very accurate, but exploded high above *U-402* in the water column, causing only minor damage. After enduring some twenty-nine explosions, von Forstner recorded somewhat comically in his logbook 'on the 20th at 0013hrs last sound bearing, breaks off suddenly, destroyer seems to have stopped, departure is not heard, but that is no miracle, with my bad sound gear. However, now I can afford to wait.' He did, and the Allied vessels had long gone when he resurfaced.

Von Forstner returned to La Pallice where he arrived at night on 23 February, after 41 days at sea, to a hero's welcome. His tally against Convoy SC-118 totalled 41,718 GRT of Allied shipping damaged or sunk was the best single performance of a U-boat in over two years. Not since Kapitänleutnant Joachim Schepke in *U-100* sank a total of 50,340 GRT in four hours against Convoy HX-72 in September 1940 had a U-boat claimed such a success. It was a needed boost to the morale of the U-boat force that had witnessed growing losses for diminishing sinkings in return over the preceding years.

The following three photos show *U-402* arriving in La Pallice on 23 February 1943 to a hero's welcome. It is flying all of its pennants and '113,000' has been painted on the side of the conning tower to represent the total tonnage sunk, which was overestimated by von Forstner. The actual tonnage sunk to-date, was just under 80,000. *U-402*'s success was notable for 1943 as such single performances by a U-boat captain at this stage of the war were rare. In celebration his wife hand-knitted red pompoms for the crew and the Karlsruhe boat now became affectionately known as the 'Pompom Boat' as the crew would be seen wearing the gifts from their service caps. The pompoms were also painted atop the shield of Karlsruhe on the conning tower. (Bibliothek für Zeitgeschichte, BZ 1-52-0179-a, BZ Sahlin_245_5 *U-402*_H, BZ Rehwold *U-402*_a)

As *U-402* was being overhauled, von Forstner was promoted to Korvettenkapitän and went on tour as one of the newest recipients of the Knight's Cross. He penned a letter to the Mayor of Karlsruhe about the experience. 'I was placed in the "Holders of the Knight's Cross talk to the Hitler Youth" campaign and spoke in Braunschweig, Hanover, Wesermünde, Leer and Berlin, getting a good impression of the Hitler Youth and their leaders in the process,' he wrote.[37] He later received members of this younger generation as new crew on board his U-boat, but found their 'zeal' – meaning their ardent adherence to National Socialist dogma – problematic.

Before *U-402* ever arrived back in port, his award of the Knight's Cross was announced in the German press on 11 February. The article incorrectly assessed his total tonnage sunk as 97,000 GRT. (Stadtarchiv Karlsruhe 1/H-Reg 902)

CHAPTER 6

Turn of the Tide

No surface escort was ever going to get him.

Waters, 'Stay Tough'

On 21 April 1943 *U-402* sailed to begin its seventh patrol after another two months in drydock. The Battle of the Atlantic was at its height. A reported 741,019 GRT of Allied shipping was sunk or damaged in March for the loss of only fifteen U-boats. This was the second highest total of tonnage claimed by U-boats in nine months. April was also proving to be a favourable month for the wolfpacks, though the balance sheet was still being calculated. New crew replacements arrived, as old hands were transferred to provide experience on board other boats being commissioned. The sailors that arrived were young, often in their late teens. They were boys who were born in the mid-1920s and had grown up under the strong influence of Hitler's National Socialism. Indoctrinated through the Nazi-infused education during their mandatory time in the Hitler Youth, they viewed themselves as 'supermen'. 'These boys,' von Forstner told his wife, were all 'too willing to assume authority without the accompanying sense of responsibility and self-control.'[38]

Von Forstner viewed duty to his country through the lens of family tradition and military professionalism. He and many of the crew were educated in a pre-Nazi Germany, and while they served in Hitler's Kriegsmarine, many drew inspiration from the naval tradition from the Reichsmarine of Tirpitz, Scheer, Hipper and those pioneering U-boat officers who earned hero status during 1914–18. Von Forstner found it frustrating that he had to continually discipline the new recruits, who seemed too willing to exert authority well beyond their age or position. He exclaimed that 'whenever I had given cause for admonishment, you bet I took good care it wouldn't happen a second time!'[39] There was no room in a U-boat for a superiority complex. Everyone needed to know their job, be technically proficient in the complexity of U-boat operations, and be able to work well as a team under the pressures of both combat and the ocean's depths. All submariners in every navy must function as one cohesive unit to be effective and survive. Von Forstner was clear that he and his senior officers needed to instil the necessary professionalism into these zealous youth, and that 'If we shirk this trouble, the fault is ours and not theirs'.[40]

Building esprit de corps is critical to any unit of military personnel operating under wartime conditions. While training and discipline are critical elements to achieve this goal, it is often small gestures that can make the difference. Such was the case with *U-402*. Baroness Annamarie von Forstner made each crew member a set of red pompoms that were stitched to their sailor hats worn when ashore on leave. This unofficial addition to their uniforms was worn with pride, as noted in a US Naval Intelligence report.[41] A crewman also wrote a poem on the second anniversary of the boat's commissioning titled 'U-Pompom' to commemorate its accomplishments, thus far. The red pompoms were probably also painted above the Karlsruhe Shield that adorned the conning tower before *U-402* departed on its patrol as this grey wolf now became known as the 'Pompom Boat' throughout the port.

On the day of its departure the port diesel overheated. Upon investigation a loose flange was found lodged inside the cooling water pipe. *U-402*'s diesel engine problems continued throughout the patrol, a lingering reminder of the damage inflicted off North Carolina the previous year.

Out in the North Atlantic the battle of intelligence reached a crescendo during the month of May. Allied cryptologists had a good understanding of BdU's new U-boat deployment line situated just east of the Flemish Cap. In response to that, Convoys SC-129 and HX-237 were routed south. B-Dienst deciphered a single decrypt of HX-237 on the 2nd that became available on the 4th, which gave the new position, course and speed of the convoy. The U-boats had to relocate if they were going to intercept the convoy. BdU took immediate action.

By 7 May a patrol line 550 miles long had formed that consisted of twenty-seven U-boats. The former boats from the patrol lines 'Amsel 1' and 'Amsel 2' joined with several additional U-boats to form 'Elbe 1' and 'Elbe 2' to the north. Among these fifteen boats was *U-402*. A southern group formed under the codename 'Rhein' that extended the line to the south made of boats from the previous 'Amsel 3' and 'Amsel 4' that consisted of the remaining twelve U-boats. However, the convoy began to reroute again around these new deployment lines.

Each day B-Dienst provided an update of the new convoy

movements, and BdU ordered an adjustment. By the 8th BdU observed this move-countermove between the U-boat lines and convoy routing with concern: '. . . this quite clear by-passing of the "Amsel 4" line which existed until 7 May and the "Elbe"-"Rhein" disposition ordered that day brings to the fore the question what possibilities were given to the enemy for discovering our lines . . .'. BdU dismissed the possibility that perhaps their Enigma codes had been broken. 'It may be possible that as a general rule enemy air reconnaissance picks up all our patrol positions by location, but this cannot be assumed. It is also considered unlikely that the enemy has cracked our ciphers unless he has captured one of our boats. The possibility of his having cracked our ciphers has been cancelled out by an immediate change in the cipher setting. Other possible sources of leakage are again being checked.'

This intellectual failure on the part of Dönitz and B-Dienst to recognise the Allied ability to locate U-boats through radio transmissions and broken cyphers is well represented in David Syrett's history titled *The Battle of the Atlantic and Signals Intelligence: U-boat Situations and Trends, 1941–1945*. In his introduction Syrett correctly opines:

> At various times the BdU concluded that there was a leakage of information about U-boat operations to the Allies. From time to time they even advanced various theories, such as an Allied wiretap on phones in Norway used by the U-boat service. This was a major intelligence failure. Indeed, the reasons that BdU and other German command and intelligence authorities failed to recognise the possibility that the Allies could develop the technology to intercept and D/F high frequency radio transmissions and break complex codes are obscure. And this oversight by the Germans is even harder to understand in light of the significant role communications intelligence played in the defeat of the U-boats in the First World War.[42]

On the 8th contact with HX-237 was lost, then on the following day SC-129 shifted course, and B-Dienst alerted BdU who rerouted 'Elbe'. Contact with HX-237 was regained on the 10th, then lost. On the following day, the 11th, contact was regained on HX-237 just as SC-129 was found. No new decrypts came into B-Dienst on HX-237 on the 12th and it was BdU's intention to halt all operations against it by the morning of the 13th and focus 'Elbe' on SC-129. With the loss of contact with SC-129 and no further intercepts from B-Dienst, BdU now planned to end its operations against SC-129 on the morning of the 14th. BdU assessed that the ability for the convoys to avoid their U-boats was directly related to their 'excellent radar'. They were only partly correct as the increased deployment of ship-based HF/DF sets, and triangulation from Ultra decrypts played an equally significant role in giving away U-boat dispositions.

Ebb and Flow
Signs that the time of the wolfpacks was at its end were already obvious by the end of March, despite the fact that it was BdU's most successful month in terms of tonnage sunk. As the convoy battles continued through April and May and U-boat losses jumped threefold, the end of the wolfpack became a fact, though convoys did not immediately pass unscathed during this period of Allied ascendency.[43]

U-402 continued to have diesel problems as it passed through the Bay of Biscay. On 26 April the port E-motor bearing failed, then the diesel clutch began to slip. Repairs took nearly a day. Then on the 29th the starboard diesel clutch slipped, went out of service and had to be repaired. On 1 May von Forstner noted 'port thrust bearing out of service, until the end of repairs to the starboard clutch, running on E-motors at slow'. By the morning of the 2nd the 'starboard diesel clutch again in service, transit with starboard diesel, various drive settings with regard to repair of the port thrust bearing'. Not until the next day was the port diesel thrust bearing back in service.

U-402 was making steady, but slow, progress to its assigned area as part of 'Elbe'. Von Forstner was also having trouble sending wireless messages on the assigned circuit, and on the 5th broke with normal radio protocol to send a message to BdU: 'Port thrust bearing has failed twice. Request meeting to take over thrust part. Position 5 May at 0400hrs square AJ 9766, course, 325°, highest speed 9.5 knots. Sea 0, NNW 1, 1042 mb steady, long NE-swell. 100 cbm. Forstner.' That message was intercepted and his boat's position triangulated. *U-402* was now being tracked in near real time by the US Naval Intelligence office OP-20-G where analysts would use this data, among other U-boat plots, to vector in new anti-submarine assets that were making their debut in the North Atlantic.

During the 5th *U-402* tried to locate another U-boat to get the required part, but the rendezvous did not take place, in part due to problematic communications. Von Forstner decided to improvise and swapped the required bearing from the reverse drive to the forward drive. He recorded that 'since the bearing is already at hand, expect to be ready at about 2200hrs'. As repairs were underway, contact reports came in regarding the HX convoy. Behind the scenes, as previously noted, the eastbound SC convoy that typically transited the same route as the HX, was shifted farther south around the 'Elbe' line.

Von Forstner, however, correctly predicted the location of the convoy based on his calculation of sighting reports. He put himself in the mind of the convoy commander, to determine what his next step might be. At 1854hrs he ordered *U-402*'s previous course with the belief '. . . that the enemy seeks the coast and therefore steers a south-westerly course . . .'. He positioned himself ahead of the expected convoy and manoeuvred back and forth in his grid square. He was in an excellent attack position, if he could get past the escort screen and inside the convoy. He listened intently for other U-boats sighting reports, as his lookouts peered through the heavy rain and rolling fog for any sign of Allied vessels.

At 2155hrs he noted 'Port pressure bearing ready. The [propeller] shaft was knocking obviously, as it was hot from [running] as high speed with full charging to starboard [engine] at 11 knots.' Nearly two hours later he encountered his first escort of the patrol, which forced him to submerge. 'Scare or bluff depth charges' were dropped, as von Forstner referred to them. The entire day of 6 May proved frustrating as the search for the convoy proved fruitless.

Even while depth charges were being dropped, and U-boats manoeuvred to survive and attack, normal military routine continued. On the morning of the following day BdU sent a short message announcing promotions among the various U-boat crews deployed in the North Atlantic. Among the sailors were two crewmen on *U-402*, now promoted to Oberfähnrich. Such routines helped maintain morale out in the North Atlantic.

The remnants of the 'Amsel' line were ordered to reform into 'Elbe' and were repositioned to the south-east accordingly, including *U-402*. As *U-402* headed in that direction, the starboard diesel again gave trouble and work commenced on the clutch. On the 8th the new group 'Rhein' was formed, and von Forstner was ordered to join that group operating on its northern edge, but he radioed back that he could not comply because of the problems with the starboard diesel. By evening of the following day von Forstner received the order to move back to the southern edge of the 'Elbe' line. *U-402* reached its assigned position at 1722hrs on the 10th where von Forstner ordered a test dive, then began his routine sweep.

At 2140hrs BdU radioed the U-boats of 'Elbe' that a 'slow convoy expected tomorrow with certainty, pay strict attention'. B-Dienst provided the detection. *U-402* adjusted its position, based on orders from BdU, and headed due north.

Some 11 hours later on 11 May, von Forstner reached his assigned position at 0715hrs and began to patrol back-and-forth on a north-south course. At 1042hrs in slight seas, and an overcast sky, *U-402*'s lookouts spotted smoke on the horizon, followed by large masts. Von Forstner gave the order to dive as it was daylight, but he had a hard time managing trim and he was not able to re-locate the target by periscope. He resurfaced the boat and spotted what he believed was a large 'approximately 6,000-ton freighter with 3 masts bearing 150°T, 4000m away, bow left, broad target angle. Due to moderate visibility set flag is not recognised, possibly they are neutrality markings on the hull.' He ordered the boat to dive, then surfaced again and, with the steamer already out of sight, determined that any pursuit was 'hopeless' due to his restricted speed.

During the course of the day, the seas grew heavy with a sea state of 6. At 1840hrs the watch spotted '2 smoke clouds in sight bearing 270°T, came to easterly course, speed increased, shortly thereafter a mast comes out, quickly becomes larger, destroyer mast, the prepared Short Signal is not transmitted, because Luis [*U-504*] has just reported, and for me there is still an opportunity for a surprise submerged attack'. Now an experienced tactician, von Forstner clearly recognised the value of silence in his effort to stalk his quarry without giving away his position.

U-402 immediately dived, and came to a northerly course in order to approach the expected convoy from starboard. However, *U-402*'s submerged handling proved very difficult due to the problems with the engines. Below half-speed the boat could not be held at periscope depth, and even at three-quarters speed it frequently cut under the surface, as *U-402*'s depth-keeping characteristics deteriorated after the bearing conversion.

Despite these challenges von Forstner maintained his pursuit. Forty-five minutes later two destroyers came into view that did not detect *U-402*. By observing their courses, von Forstner concluded that he was inside the escort screen, and that the merchant vessels were just ahead. As usual, his tactical intuition proved correct.

Aces Duel

SC-129 was escorted by the six 'Flower'-class corvettes and two smaller ASW trawlers of B2 Group under Donald Macintyre's command. The escorts departed Argentia to escort SC-129 on its crossing. The two destroyers spotted by *U-402* were HMS *Whitehall* (D94) and HMS *Clematis* (M36), who picked up nothing on their gear during their sweep.

Macintyre was one of the most experienced escort commanders and U-boat killers in the Royal Navy at that time. He was a professional, much like von Forstner, drilling his men as often as possible, for he understood that seconds meant the difference of achieving a kill or letting a U-boat slip away into the protection of the depths. 'Naval successes', he wrote, 'are almost invariably the result of teamwork and training' and most importantly 'failures by the humblest member of the team can ruin the efforts of all'.[44]

Royal Navy captain and highest-scoring U-boat killer Donald Macintyre. He sunk von Forstner's close friend Otto Kretschmer in 1940 and was still wearing his binoculars in 1943 during the battle of Convoy SC-129. His Escort Group B2 was not able to prevent *U-402* from sinking merchantmen under his protection, and Macintyre seethed with anger. (Imperial War Museum/A16868)

While a strong sense of tactical professionalism was a shared characteristic between Macintyre and von Forstner, so was a past acquaintance. As Macintyre stood on the bridge of HMS *Hesperus*, he took a moment to survey the horizon using a pair of German Zeiss binoculars.

This unusual piece of personal gear had belonged to none other than von Forstner's classmate and friend, Otto Kretschmer. Macintyre had depth-charged and critically damaged *U-99* two years earlier while in command of HMS *Walker*. When *U-99* started to sink, Kretschmer, along with forty of its 43-man crew, jumped into the water and were pulled from the sea by the destroyer's crew. As Kretschmer was pulled on to the deck, he still wore his Zeiss binoculars, which were quickly retrieved and presented to Macintyre. Now the very binoculars that perhaps von Forstner once used while 3rd Watch Officer during his brief training stint on *U-99*, were now being used to scan the surface for him.

At 1958hrs von Forstner observed his first target and at 2004hrs and commenced a submerged attack with a single shot from tube I. The target appeared to about a 5,000 GRT freighter with 'two masts and one smoke stack, bridge positioned free'. After 47 seconds (730m) a torpedo detonation was heard, but due to the continued troubles with trim, the periscope was awash and the hit was not seen.

This vessel hit was the Norwegian-flagged SS *Grado* (3,082 GRT). The torpedo slammed into the port side of the foreship and she sank by the bow in about 50 minutes. The master, thirty-two crew members and four gunners abandoned ship in three lifeboats.

U-402 torpedoed the Norwegian-flagged steam merchant SS *Grado* (3,082) carrying 1,000 tons of steel and 3,000 tons of lumber at 2000hrs on 11 May. The vessel sank by the bow 50 minutes later (40° 30'N, 32° 30'W – Grid CE 1547). (The Mariners' Museum P0001.003-01–PB7886)

The second and last vessel sunk by *U-402* during the battle of SC-129 was the British-flagged SS *Antigone* (4,545 GRT) carrying 7,800 tons of grain, 255 tons of general cargo and 250 trucks. A torpedo hit the vessel at 2008hrs, but the actual sinking was not observed by *U-402* due to the periscope undercutting the waves. (The Mariners' Museum P0001.003-01–PB14233)

Sixteen of them were picked up by the British rescue ship *Melrose Abbey* while the remaining men were retrieved by two escort vessels.

A second target was quickly acquired, the firing solution calculated, and a single shot from tube II launched at 2008hrs. The new target appeared to be a 4,000 GRT freighter with two masts and one smoke stack. After 41.2 seconds (640m) a torpedo detonation was heard, but again no observation was made due to the continued cutting-under of the periscope. The second vessel sunk was the British-flagged SS *Antigone* (4,545 GRT). Three of her crew members were lost. The master, thirty-five crew members and seven gunners were picked up by the *Melrose Abbey* and later landed at Gourock on 20 May.

A few minutes later, von Forstner was able to make an all-around sweep of the area and spotted five steamers, along with his first torpedoed vessel that 'lies stopped with heavy list to port forward'. His second hit 'not made out with certainty, periscope again cut under'.

HMS *Gentian* (K90), a 'Flower'-class corvette, quickly picked up *U-402* on her sonar and pulled out of line from behind a steamer and began a series of heavy depth-charge attacks that did serious damage to the U-boat and almost sent it uncontrollably down into the depths. *U-402* was able to level off at nearly 600ft, close to its crush depth, and slowly began to rise. The damage caused by *Gentian*'s depth charge attack ended *U-402*'s ability to conduct further offensive action against SC-129. (Imperial War Museum/A6086)

U-402 had little time inside the convoy. At 2021hrs the boat's hydrophone operator reported an approaching escort that had not been observed through the periscope, as it was likely 'hidden by a steamer'. HMS *Gentian* (K90) had picked up the U-boat on sonar and was on its way to drop its deadly payload. Von Forstner, never daunted by an escort, ordered the boat to dive deep to avoid detection and continue on the same course as the convoy. For the third time during the patrol, the port thrust bearing failed when the boat went to three-quarters speed submerged. Then the motor stopped as the depth charges came.

At 2023hrs the first depth-charge series exploded at 40m. The sound of pinging from ASDIC was heard, but the corvette clearly was having trouble locating *U-402* as the following series of depth charges were 'poorly placed'. Von Forstner ordered silent running, followed by a series of evasive course changes. The U-boat's drain pumps were turned on several times that night to handle some of the leakage on board. The boat continued to have trouble maintaining its depth. Yet, despite the circumstances, the crew clearly heard the audible sounds of their quarry sinking into the depths, as steel plates crumpled and boilers ruptured. It was a reminder to the crew of what could happen to them.

About an hour later, von Forstner gave the order to slowly surface, but as the boat did, the ASDIC pings began anew, and the hydrophone operator clearly heard the sounds of a 'turbine' that confirmed the escort was still present. *U-402* went deep again. A half an hour later, at 2325hrs, the order was again given to slowly raise the boat. Depth-charge explosions were heard, but at a distance, so *U-402* continued its slow approach to the surface.

Now there was confusion as to how close the corvette actually was. Knocking and strong vibrations were felt inside the U-boat and it was believed it was a depth charge. The 1st Watch Officer climbed into the conning tower in anticipation of opening the upper hatch once the boat surfaced. He yelled down to von Forstner that 'he heard strong propeller sounds'. Von Forstner, now well aware of his boat's equipment deficiencies, noted in his logbook 'cannot rely on the [hydrophone], because it did not even register the steamers at 700m and now [we have] the knocking of the starboard shaft at higher speed settings; even more unfavourable conditions . . .'. Again, he ordered the boat to go deep.

But the descent did no go as intended and *U-402* began to slip uncontrollably into the depths. At 120m (396ft) ballast tank 5 was blown, but the boat did not stop sinking. The creaking and groaning of bursting pipes echoed throughout the boat as it descended past its test depth. Von Forstner gathered most of the crew into the control room and calmly led them in prayer. The boat soon reached 180m (594ft), and von Forstner ordered all ballast tanks blown one final time. The boat finally slowly levelled off, suspended at the very point of no return. The main ballast tanks 1 and 5 were flooded and *U-402* began to slowly respond accordingly to trim control.

After an investigation as to what happened the chief engineer reported that the 'port regulating and reserve fuel oil tank indicates outboard pressure', suggesting it was blown open and the cause of the loud bang and negative buoyancy of the boat. Von Forstner recorded 'venting of ballast tank 3 via the blowing piping is not possible, because it under pressure probably by the leaking of one blow valve by which the main blow valve cannot be opened. The auxiliary drain pump cannot be used to pump the bilge water because it is under pressure from a leaking hull valve.' *U-402* again began to surface, but over the next 45 minutes the crew again struggled with buoyancy, as the boat began to settle back into the depths.

Finally, at 0155hrs on the 12th, *U-402* surfaced. Despite of the boat's mechanical difficulties, von Forstner ordered pursuit of the convoy in moderately heavy seas and a cloudy sky. While surfaced he got a good look at the exterior of the boat and noted that the 'main ballast and reserve fuel oil tank 2 on the portside had a 3-meter-long tear'. However, due to the overwash 'work on the over deck is not possible'. Work on the 'supercharger clutch of the starboard diesel is not successful. I decide to first complete repair of the port thrust bearing, because the starboard diesel must be stopped during work on the clutch, I must have at least the port diesel in service.' Later that day, the decision was made that *U-402* was not mechanically sound enough to operate offensively and had to return to port. It rendezvoused with the U-tanker *U-459* on 15 May in order to refuel before heading back to La Pallice on the 26th.

The only vessels sunk from SC-129 were the two struck by torpedoes from *U-402*. Macintyre wrote of that day, 'But now I was in a fury. Not only had a U-boat penetrated our defences in broad daylight but, for the first time in the nine months I had been with B2 Group, ships from a convoy escorted by us had been sunk. We were all very proud of our record which had thus been marred, and vengeance was called for. A thorough search for the culprit proved unsuccessful . . .'[45] At that moment in time, the best U-boat captain on patrol and best U-boat hunter afloat had faced off in the North Atlantic, and their chance meeting was a draw.

Von Forstner demonstrated that potential success was still achievable in the North Atlantic by an experienced U-boat crew lead by a capable commander with an ability to visualise the naval battlefield through his enemy's eyes. Arguably, Macintyre's limited losses were due as much to *U-402*'s technical difficulties as they were to B2 Group's proficiency. As correctly noted by BdU Chief of Operations at the end of von Forstner's logbook for his seventh patrol: 'A patrol of the tried and tested Kommandant who was rewarded with a clear victory for his tough and aggressive effort. Possibilities for [further] success for the boat were impaired by the accumulation of machinery malfunctions and failures.'

One naval commander's ability, however, could not win an entire campaign. The wolfpack strategy was an arithmetic equation, whereby Dönitz attempted to increase his success by massing the highest number of torpedoes per Allied vessel as possible. If his wolfpacks could not locate the convoys, then they no longer served any tactical purpose no matter how gifted a single commander might be. The amount of Allied tonnage sunk or damaged in the Atlantic dropped significantly from 741,019 GRT in March 1943 to only 266,884 GRT in May, while at the same time U-boats destroyed leaped from twelve to forty-one.[46] The significant drop in tonnage sunk or damaged was enough to raise questions about the viability of the wolfpack on its own, but the comparative losses in U-boats proved too much. Faced with the loss of 25 per cent of his operational U-boats, Dönitz ordered a halt to wolfpack operations in the North Atlantic.

CHAPTER 7

Go Fetch

> To accomplish [a U-boat kill by an aircraft], it would seem that the ideal combination would be the control of an explosive carrier by radio energy directly from an aeroplane.
>
> Georg-Günther von Forstner, *The Journal of a Submarine Commander* (1916)

The damage *U-402* had suffered in its most recent depth-charging was significant and it had to spend considerable time in drydock. The U-boat fleet also underwent extensive modifications now that the threat of radar-equipped aircraft had spread across the North Atlantic battlefield. All this translated into *U-402* undergoing repairs and modification for three months.

Dönitz ordered a series of modifications to the armament of U-boats to deal with the new threat. The 88mm deck gun was removed, as it no longer had practical value. In the case of *U-402*, it had never once been fired in anger. The aft portion of the conning tower was expanded, and extended, to include a lower gun deck. This was officially known as the Turmumbau IV, but the crew called it the 'Wintergarten'. The enlarged upper platform was equipped with two twin 20mm C38 anti-aircraft guns, and on the lower platform was either a quadruple 20mm 38/43 Flakvierling with a shield or a single 37mm cannon, as in the case of *U-402*. A new high-explosive shell, known as the Minengeschoss (mine shell), was developed and introduced to the U-boat fleet. This was equipped with a Hexogen filling three times the size of that of the old ammunition and delivered greater destructive power.

Macintyre gave full credit to the evolving role of airpower that emerged as the prime threat to U-boats from May 1943 until the end of the war. He wrote '. . . where Coastal Command [aircraft] played its most important role, in spite of the half-hearted way it often went about it, was *in the vicinity of convoys*. Untrained in cooperation with the Navy as our aircraft were, the remarkable fact is that only nineteen merchant ships out of the huge numbers

The escort carrier USS *Card* (CVE-11) carried twelve TBM Avengers and sixteen FM-2 Wildcats. The FM-2s were an improved model of the F4F that included an upgraded R-1820 powerplant, some with water injection to give more power for take-off from small-deck escort carriers. The ship formed part of the hunter-killer Task Group 21.14 that was vectored toward U-boat concentrations in the mid-Atlantic from spotter reports and intelligence gained from Ultra intercepts. The introduction of escort carriers into the Battle of the Atlantic was a significant factor in the end of wolfpack tactics. The Avengers were equipped with both a 500lb bomb and the new acoustic homing torpedo called 'FIDO', but referred to as a 'mine' to maintain its secrecy. Doctrine called for the aircraft to drop the 500lb bomb in order to force the U-boat to dive, then to drop the 'mine', to home in on the propellers then detonate, destroying the U-boat underwater. (US National Archives Records Administration)

sunk during the war, were lost when both air and surface escort were present . . .' He continued, 'therefore it was a very great step forward when the escort carriers began to come forward and the naval aircraft, manned by crews properly trained for the job, could accompany convoys throughout their voyage or could be sent to aid an escort heavily beset'.[47]

High Hopes

To deal with Allied airborne radar, and to a lesser extent escorts equipped with radar, a new warning receiver was deployed on U-boats. The FuMB 9 Hagenuk Wellenanzeigegerät 1 (W.Anz.g1),

which was later contracted to Wanze I passive search receiver, replaced the older Metox mounted on the 'Biscay Cross'. Wanze I could scan frequency ranges from 120cm to 180cm through fine tuning on the Runddipol (round dipole) 'Bali' mounted on the starboard side of the conning tower. This initial receiver was not waterproof and had to be fitted manually when the U-boat surfaced. *U-402* may also have received the FuMO 30 active radar set added to the port side of conning tower casing as evidenced by the last aerial photographs taken of the U-boat, though this is not confirmed. In addition to the passive search receivers, new Aphrodite radar decoy balloons were issued to the U-boats. These 91cm-diameter balloons were filled with hydrogen and floated above the surface while tethered to a floating raft. The line attached to the balloon was 50m long, and had three strips of aluminium foil attached to the line to act as radar reflectors. The device had to be assembled on the upper deck, and had a lifespan of three to six hours after deployment.

Finally, the new T5 Zaunkönig G7 acoustic homing torpedo was delivered. Its main targets were escorts. It could be fired as a homing torpedo against vessels steaming at 10 to 18 knots. Armed with a combined contact and magnetic pistol it could be used against destroyers, corvettes and other shallow-draught vessels.

All of this new technology came with new tactics. The employment of the T5 was meant to sink some of the now increasing number of escorts, in order to reduce their ability to force U-boats to break contact, and create an opening through their screen into the convoy. Additionally, U-boats were now expected to engage aircraft on the surface and provide collective air defence. The coming deployment to the North Atlantic was to be the first since the withdrawal in May, and the first where all these new technical improvements and tactics were to be employed. Expectations ran high at BdU.

As *U-402* went through its conversion, von Forstner departed for extended leave to his home on the tree-lined cobblestone street along Klosteralle, in Hamburg. While home he became sick with a throat ailment, and was admitted to hospital. When he was discharged, he penned a letter to the Mayor of Karlsruhe on 22 July 1943. 'Dear Sir,' he began, 'Yesterday, I was finally released from this field hospital, where I had been for nearly 3 weeks with a bad throat problem.' Like many military professionals who are pulled away from the front in time of war, he noted that 'It's a dumb feeling; the boat is clearly at its support base – and I'm in the hospital.' He added, 'I'm still not completely up and about, but

I hope that in early August under my wife's good care I will be back in good sorts. Then there will be nothing more keeping the boat from going out again; the tests, etc. were already carried out by a comrade.'

Interestingly, von Forstner noted how his two successes during the last patrol were remarkable because 'it is precisely the lamest boat that managed to get off two shots', while the other 'healthy boats' returned from patrol 'without a streamer'. Clearly, he was referring to the significant technical problems *U-402* had experienced. The fact that no other U-boat that engaged Convoy SC-129 achieved a success resonated with von Forstner as an ominous sign of the changing tide of the war.

There was also more bad news to report. Walter Friebolin, who had transferred off the boat after its third patrol, had been killed when his new U-boat, *U-526*, struck a mine while returning to its port in France. 'Shortly after our arrival, we learned the sad news that Bootsmannsmaat Friebolin, who was previously on board, had not returned from a trip against the enemy on another boat.' Friebolin was a connection between *U-402* and the city of Karlsruhe, as von Forstner reminded the Mayor. 'You might remember his parents, his brother and his fiancée, who live in Wössingen and were also invited to the meeting room for a reception at one point because of him. The circumstances were particularly tragic; the boat had already been under the escort of the minesweeper for a long time and supposedly ran into a mine right next to the pier.'

The war was not going well for Germany by mid-1943. This was made all the clearer when the RAF and the US Army Airforce launched Operation 'Gomorrah' shortly after von Forstner left the hospital on 24 July. Over the course of the next eight days approximately 3,000 Allied aircraft dropped 9,000 tons of incendiary bombs on Hamburg. The very dry summer greatly contributed to the ensuing firestorm that destroyed 250,000 homes, killed 42,000 people and left some 37,000 wounded.

All the homes in von Forstner's neighbourhood went up in flames, with the exception of the one he and his wife lived in, as well as their neighbour. As the firestorm raged in the city that first night, von Forstner said to his wife 'This is beastly. Out there is bad enough, but if someone starts attacking me, at least I can fight back with all that I am worth, and you bet I do! But here you can only sit tight and hope for the best – a sitting duck to shoot at . . . and to think, that whatever we do out there, we cannot prevent this!'[48]

Shortly after the devastating raids, von Forstner was called to a naval briefing full of Nazi propaganda designed to reinforce the 'will to fight' in the wake of the bombing. He came home that afternoon in a 'sullen and depressed mood' and uncharacteristically exploded in the privacy of his home:

> 'This is really the limit! We are called to a briefing to be told that we should hate and despise the enemy, otherwise we cannot do our duty. My sense of responsibility needs no bolstering by such sentiment. The mere suggestion is an outrage. Why should I hate the enemy? They are standing by their country as I am by mine. Despise them? What for? None of us out there in his right senses would dream of underestimating what we are up against – indeed, if we did, it might well prove our undoing. What is more, how very stupid it would be – belittling the enemy means but detracting from one's own achievement, if you have been lucky enough to get the better of him.'[49]

On his last day of leave, with the firebombing still in his mind, von Forstner said his goodbyes to his wife.

> Whenever I realise that I have lost the game and have absolutely no chance left, you may rest assured that I won't do anything foolish – and I shall try to save my men and myself. The war will be over for us, and there will be more than enough for us to do after the war is ended. However, should it happen that the boat is sunk, and we are trapped, do not torment yourself with visions of slow suffocation. I have sufficient means for the entire crew to prevent this. But that is a last resource, as you know me well enough to be certain that I shall not make use of it unless I must.[50]

His words were certainly meant for her peace of mind.

The modified *U-402* sailed from La Pallice on 4 September 1943 with orders to head to BE 5820. A sealed envelope with additional instructions were handed to von Forstner to be opened on order of BdU. *U-402* joined another twenty boats to become part of the 'Leuthen' line, marking the first return to the convoy battle of the North Atlantic since Dönitz ordered their withdrawal in May. There were high hopes, but first *U-402* had to pass through the Bay of Biscay, which had become a daunting task in recent months.

Between 20 July and 2 August, ten U-boats were lost and one heavily damaged out of seventeen that crossed this body of water. BdU ordered all crossings temporarily halted as U-boats had to hug the Spanish coast without regards to territorial waters until the new Wanze radar search receivers were deployed.[51]

U-402 was being tracked by Allied aircraft based upon the sighting reports logged by BdU. We will never know for certain without *U-402*'s logbook, but given the proximity of its track to these aircraft sighting reports, it is possible that *U-402* was identified by radar-equipped aircraft at least three times while crossing the Bay of Biscay.

On 7 September two Wellingtons from 172 Squadron at RAF Chivenor located *U-402* using radar at a distance of 6 miles. Flying Officer T. Armstrong dropped to 200ft in a moonlit and cloudless sky and switched on his Leigh Light that illuminated *U-402* cruising on the surface. He dropped six depth charges from 50ft, but scored no hits. *U-402*'s crew returned fire from their flak guns equipped with the new HE shells. Armstrong circled and conducted a strafing run against the U-boat having expended all of his depth charges, not realising until he later landed that his aircraft had indeed been hit by the U-boat's return fire. He then spotted another Leigh Light turn on at a very low altitude. The now-alert crew of *U-402* opened fire in the direction of the beam and began to exchange fire with the new Wellington. *U-402*'s gunners were able to shoot it down almost directly over the boat. The aircraft crashed into the sea and burned on the surface for about 20 minutes as leaking fuel caught fire. Armstrong had no option but to return to base. The other Wellington, captained by Flying Officer C J Payne, and its crew were all lost.

On the following day, the 8th, another Wellington, 'M' from 612 Squadron, picked up a radar return 4 miles out and the commander, Flying Officer J M Bezer manoeuvred his aircraft in for a closer look. At 0515 GMT they tracked over the blip at 600ft and the rear gunner spotted *U-402*'s wake. The Wellington flew on for 3 miles before it made a turn and dropped to 100ft. At three-quarters of a mile from its target the Leigh Light went on, as the alert crew of *U-402* opened fire 'from what appeared to be from three positions'. The front gunner of the aircraft attempted to return fire but his 'armament jammed'. Six depth charges were released from 50ft, just as shells struck the Wellington. Reportedly '. . . the Perspex shattered cutting the pilot's cheek, others hitting the port engine and nacelle, starboard petrol tank and wing, tailplane and fuselage, the radar was also knocked out'.[52]

Bezer managed to fly the stricken aircraft back to base, even though it had lost its starboard engine. Everything that could be jettisoned was, to keep the aircraft aloft. The Wellington crash-landed at Portreath in Cornwall without further injury to its crew after a 90-minute flight. Clearly the new armament and HE shells proved effective defence, though it is not known what type of warning *U-402*'s crew received from the new Wanze detector.

As the new 'Leuthen' line formed across the great circle route, BdU gave specific orders to converge on westbound convoys only, and only engage eastbound merchants as targets of opportunity. Standing Order No. 13 was issued, reminding U-boats to stay submerged during the day and only surface at night to recharge batteries. BdU wanted to preserve the element of surprise before the attack. However, timely Enigma decrypts allowed the Admiralty to re-route Convoy ONS-202 around the line. Yet, in the fog of war, navigation variances unique to war at sea so often gave rise to chance encounters that wrought havoc with the best-calculated plans.

The destruction of *U-341* on 19 September by RCAF Liberator 'A' 586 of 10 Squadron in the vicinity of ONS-18 meant that the forming wolfpack line was farther north than BdU planned, but inadvertently right where the re-routed convoy was now headed. On the 20th *U-270* spotted the frigate HMS *Lagan* (K259) and damaged her using the new T5 torpedo. These two events caused the Admiralty to bring together Convoys ON-202 and ONS-18 for greater protection. The combined convoys numbered some sixty-seven merchant ships and forty-eight escorts.

On the same day, at 0400hrs *U-290* sent in a spotting report and BdU gave the new U-boat group the order to engage the convoy. How close von Forstner may have got to the convoy is unknown, though he reported a missed T5 stern shot on a pursuing destroyer at 2300hrs that night. *U-402* continued its pursuit of the convoy in heavy seas and foggy conditions, picking up a destroyer on the hydrophones on the 22nd, and later fended off an attack by a 'flying boat'.

Interestingly, there was no recorded report by BdU of the following anti-aircraft action attributed to *U-402*. In clearing skies, RCAF Liberator X of 10 Squadron RCAF launched a devastating air attack on the surfaced *U-270*. The U-boat was badly damaged by near-direct hits by four 250lb depth charges that bracketed the bow and ruptured the pressure hull. The crew of the U-boat continued to fire at the aircraft with its new flak armament, even as it settled low in the water. Once the crew went below and the boat submerged, the Liberator dropped two more 600lb bombs.

The U-boat was forced to withdraw and was unable to dive until makeshift repairs were completed by the 25th.

U-402 was surfaced some seven miles away and von Forstner witnessed the punishing air attack on *U-270*. He directed his boat toward the scene as his crew opened fire on the Liberator in an aggressive way that alarmed the aircraft crew. Typical of von Forstner's personality, the U-boat closed the range and turned toward the aircraft, as if chasing it, while his crew continued to throw up shells until *U-402* withdrew into a fog bank and he ended the counter-attack.[53]

While no ships of ONS-18 were sunk, ON-202 paid a heavy toll with the return of the U-boats. Ten vessels were sunk totalling 41,277 GRT and two damaged for 14,352 GRT. This included four escorts. Only three U-boats were lost. But the elation at BdU was short-lived. On the 23rd 'Leuthen' was called off. BdU recorded in its diary that day: 'Through operations lasting for three days under the most difficult weather and defence conditions, the demands made on the boats' crews have reached their limits. A further operation in fog might lead to losses of boats, since their capacity for operations is exhausted.' Reinforced with fresh U-boats from France, the former boats from 'Leuthen' were now renamed 'Rossbach' and directed toward a series of eastbound convoys. Based in part on B-Dienst intercepts, BdU assessed that the eastbound convoys were now alerted and would re-route, but that the westbound convoy already en route would not. If the twenty U-boats of 'Rossbach' maintained radio silence there might be a chance of intercepting either a follow-on ON or ONS convoy.

U-402 headed north-west and reached its position in the new patrol line on the 27th. Nothing else is known of *U-402*'s operation during the convoy battle that ensued, except that on 1 October the U-boat was caught on the surface and 'fended off' an aircraft with defensive fire.

'Rossbach' was called off on 5 October. The U-boats sunk a total of two additional Allied vessels, a Polish destroyer and an American steam merchant ship, but lost six of their own – all sunk by aircraft attack. A telling toll in a changing operational environment now that the escort carriers were operating in the North Atlantic. BdU also noted the waning value of B-Dienst intelligence when it noted in its war diary that 'the operation provided a further illustration of the difficulty of interception on the strength of radio intelligence, unsupported by visual reconnaissance'.

U-402 was already down to 52cbm of diesel on 24 September, and was expending on average 8cbm a day based on the calculation of expenditure from the 22nd through the 24th while it repositioned and searched for the convoy. Normally the average fuel oil capacity maintained on board a Type VIIC at the time of departure for a patrol was 105–110cbm. On 4 October BdU directed U-boats low on fuel to head south and rendezvous with the U-tanker *U-488*.

U-488 headed north-east to its rendezvous point, where it arrived on 12 October. The next morning, *U-488* was ordered to shift again to the north in heavy seas, with a warning from BdU: 'Beware of carrier air'. In the late afternoon of the 12th, von Forstner reported the presence of enemy aircraft to BdU at 1906hrs. He also reported that he was noticed, but his transmission provoked no attack. Aircraft from the escort carrier USS *Card* (CVE-11) were active in the area as part of the new hunter-killer TF 21.14, which had already attacked *U-488* and *U-731* without success.

A Prediction Comes True
USS *Card*'s air group was made up of twelve Grumman TBF Avengers and sixteen FM-2 Wildcats of VC-9. Each Avenger was launched with a 500lb bomb used to force a U-boat to submerge and a new secret Mark 24 'mine' that was actually an acoustic homing torpedo designed to lock on to the sound of a U-boat's propeller as it dived where it would eventually strike the boat, destroying it below the surface. It was first deployed in May 1943 with the nickname of 'FIDO', an allusion to the often used saying employed with one's canine companion: 'Fido, go fetch.' Indeed, the Mk 24 did just that.

Von Forstner continued to look for *U-488* in the rendezvous square on the 13th. At 1026hrs he radioed BdU 'Am being attacked by aircraft'. Indeed, he was. Lieutenant (jg) Fowler took off from the deck of USS *Card* at 0816hrs GCT in TBF Avenger #10 and was on the first leg of the second sector of his anti-submarine patrol when he sighted the fully-surfaced *U-402* three miles away on his starboard bow. Fowler immediately climbed, and circled to starboard astern of *U-402* in preparation to drop his 500lb bomb to force von Forstner to dive. However, the release was not armed, and Fowler had to circle and make another run, by which time *U-402* had submerged and instead he dropped the Mk 24 acoustic homing torpedo 450ft ahead of the swirl caused by the boat's wake. According to Fowler's report, 'About a minute and a half later, what is believed to have been the explosion was seen by the

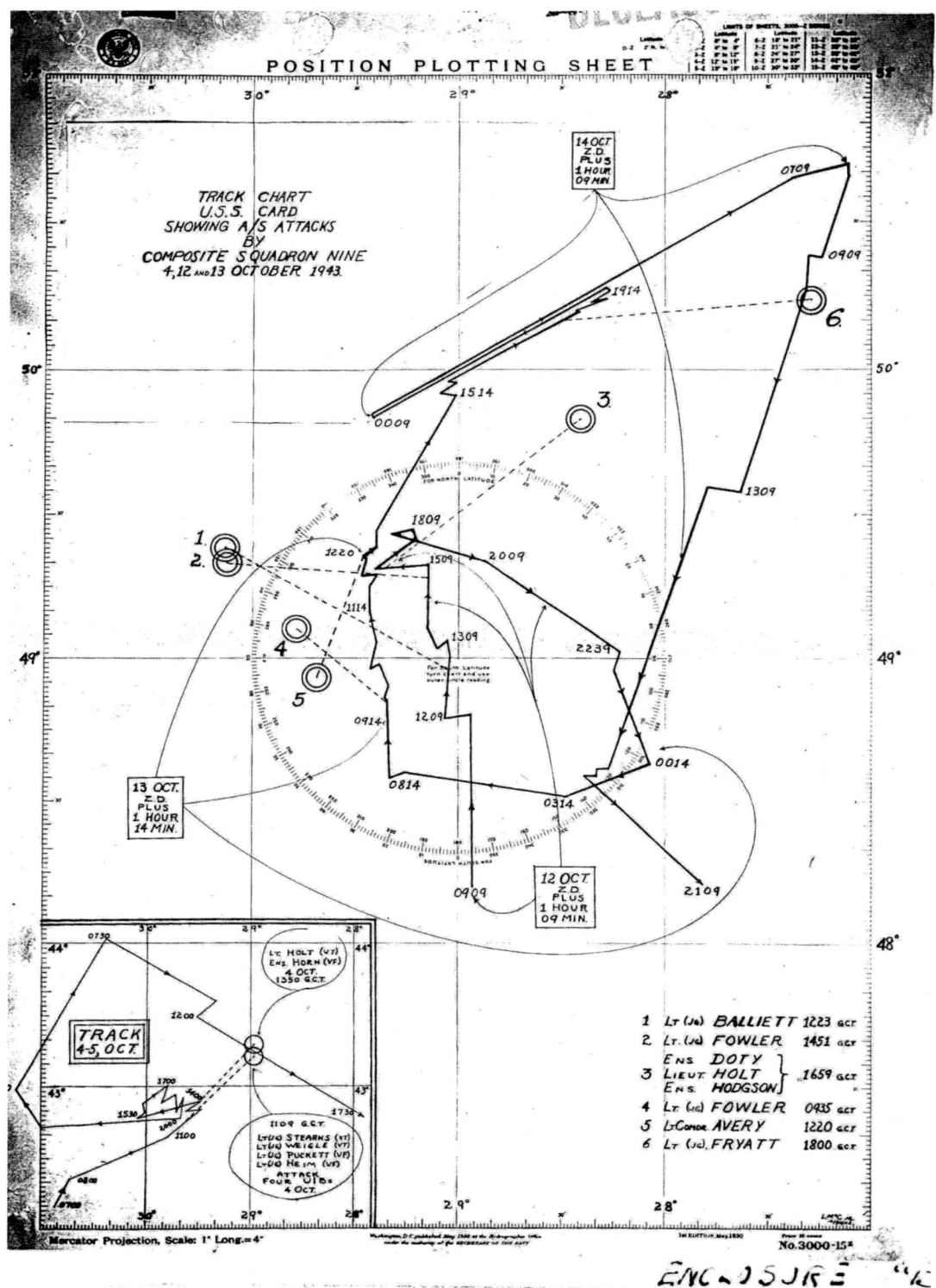

Left: This position plotting sheet reveals attacks by aircraft from USS *Card* against U-boat targets on 12–13 October. The *Card* was vectored into the area based on Enigma intercepts that revealed that U-tankers were operating. Destruction of the Type XB boats was critical to ending U-boat's long station time in the mid-Atlantic. They also provided an opportunity to attack U-boats trying to refuel. At 1223hrs GMT on 12 October, *U-488* (XB) was attacked without any damage (1). At 1451hrs, *U-488* was attacked again, and the acoustic homing torpedo failed to find its target and the U-boat escaped (2). At 1659hrs that same day *U-731* was unsuccessfully attacked (3). On the morning of 13 October at 0435hrs *U-378* was unsuccessfully attacked (4). At 1220hrs *U-402* was caught on the surface, attacked and sunk (5). Later that afternoon at 1800hrs *U-603* was attacked and also survived (6). The aircraft never used radar in this attack to avoid detection by U-boats and maintain surprise. (US National Archives Records Administration)

radioman', though Fowler himself saw 'no results of damage'. The gunner, R A Burton, stated that 'the sub was black and of fairly large size. Although I saw no deck guns or crew there was some anti-aircraft action that appeared to be of 40mm and 20mm. I saw no indication of an explosion at all. Throughout the attack I was using my gun camera but none of the pictures turned out. After circling for a short time, we were called back to the ship.'

At the moment Fowler reported spotting *U-402*, TBF Avenger #9 under the command of Lieutenant Commander Howard M Avery was catapulted at 0929hrs GCT to assist Fowler. He arrived at the attack site and reported that 'on investigation, the slick was 300' long and 20 to 30' wide. At the downwind end, the yellow and white spoiler boards from the mine were scattered in the slick area.' With no U-boat in sight, Avery was ordered to remain on station.

What damage, if any, *U-402* incurred from the initial attack is not known. The boat remained submerged for some time, then resurfaced some hours later. At 1313hrs BdU received another short-signal from *U-402* that was its last: 'Am being attacked by aircraft.' In heavy seas and scattered rain squalls, Avery spotted the resurfaced *U-402*, 12 miles south-east of Fowler's previous engagement. He now initiated his attack at 1209hrs GCT. Due to heavy seas breaking over the bow, Avery thought the U-boat was submerging, so he immediately 'turned toward it losing altitude preparatory to dropping his mine. He closed on the U-boat from astern on course 2100T losing altitude and speed. At about 500 yards he realised the U-boat was not submerging and that he was too close to break off the attack, so he continued on course and strafed the conning tower with his two .50 cal. wing guns. He passed the U-boat close aboard on the starboard side, jerking violently as he retired.'

Avery believed he had surprised *U-402* because there was little or no return anti-aircraft fire during his strafing attack. As he passed the U-boat again, Avery 'observed men in the conning tower and one man training his gun after him'. Soon 'sporadic bursts of high explosive AA fire, believed to be from 37MM guns were observed behind and short of the plane, at about the correct altitude'. Avery abruptly altered his course to throw off the gunners. One can imagine von Forstner in the conning tower, awash with spray and battered by wind, assessing the situation tactically, calculating his best next move, as he often did. There is no doubt that he believed he could fight off any single aircraft.

At 1217hrs GCT Ensign B C Sheela flying TBF #12 arrived

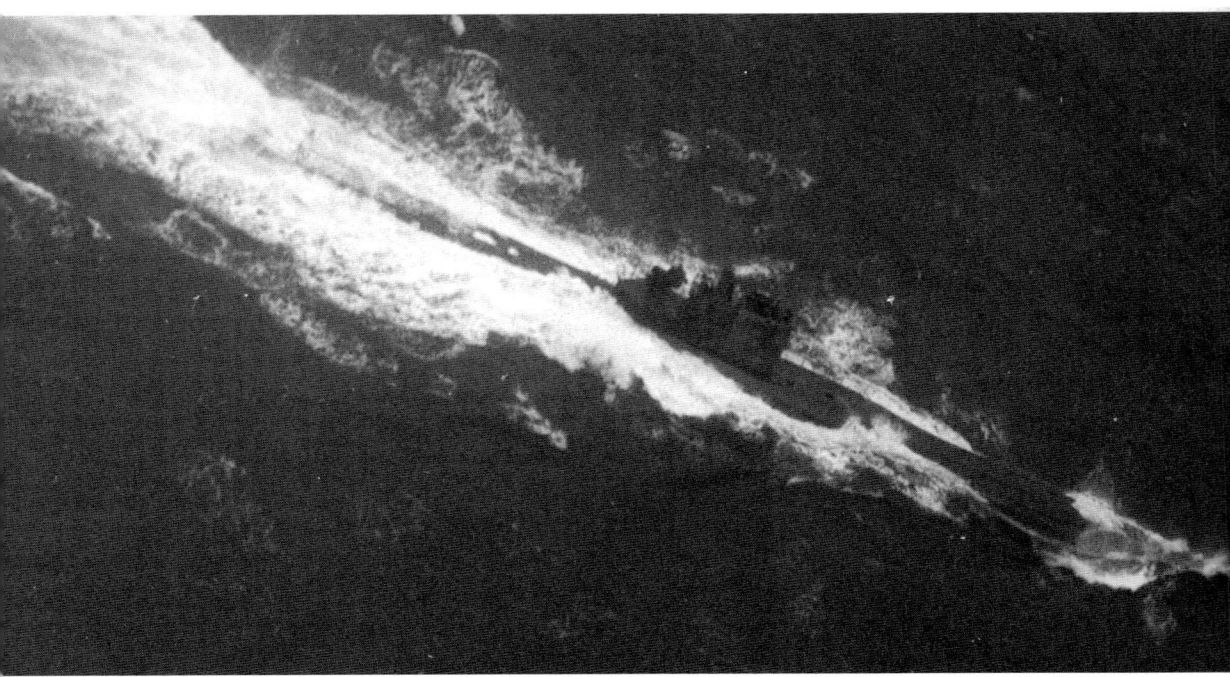

U-402 was photographed during the attack by Lieutenant Commander Avery. We see its final modifications that occurred during its last overhaul. The 88mm deck gun was removed as was its watertight ammunition container. The aft conning tower was expanded and extra anti-aircraft guns were added. It is painted a uniform dark grey. (US National Archives Records Administration)

on the scene. He immediately climbed to a position astern of *U-402* and attacked from about 150ft. *U-402* turned hard to port, but it probably did not see the new aircraft as it approached through the clouds. Sheela released his 500lb bomb at 1,500ft. The bomb was over the mark, and exploded about 800ft ahead of *U-402*, about 100ft to starboard.

Von Forstner had had enough surface action after the arrival of the second aircraft. He realised the odds were now against him with two aircraft overhead and ordered a crash dive. *U-402* straightened its course and began to submerge. Avery saw his chance. He immediately put on full power, closed to about 1,000 yards, lowered his wheels, and cut off his throttle to lose speed for the 'FIDO' drop. *U-402*'s stern was still above water at a high angle of dive and remained visible for another 5–6 seconds before it slipped below the surface. The mine was released 25 seconds after the conning tower had disappeared, and struck the water 100ft up from *U-402*'s track and about 75ft to starboard. The acoustic homing torpedo could be seen adjusting course to the sound of *U-402*'s screw as it turned to port. 'About 20 seconds later Ensign Sheela and Falwell, gunner in Lieut. Comdr. Avery's plane, saw the explosion about 200' up track and 100' to starboard of the point of entry.' On the surface all that could be seen was an 'oil slick and three cylindrical objects appeared in the residue of the explosion

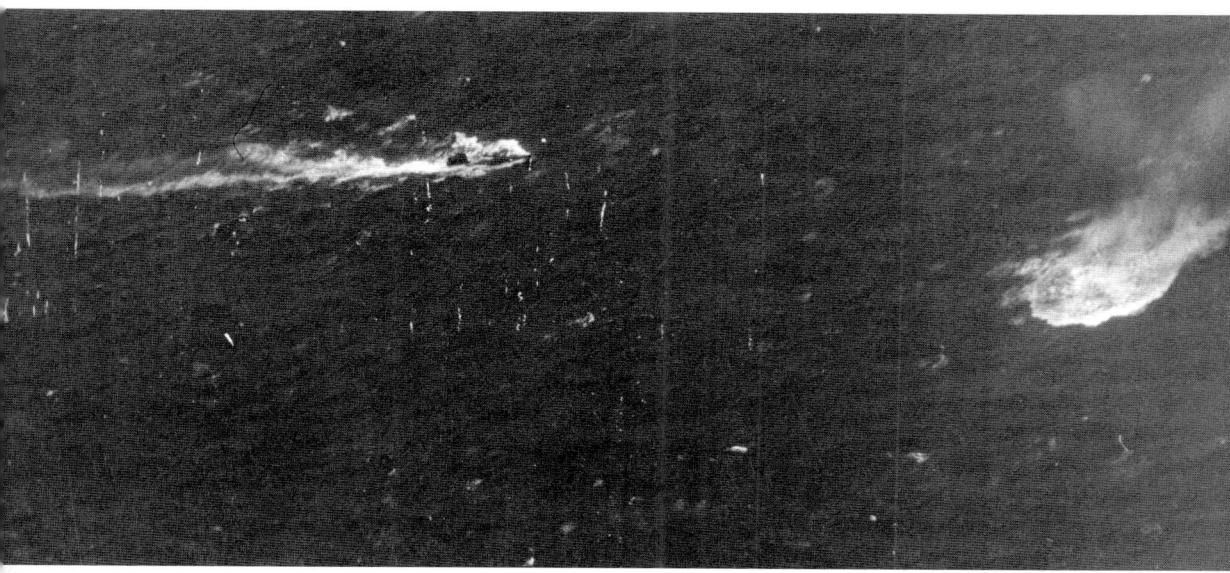

Here Ensign B C Sheela flying TBF #12 drops his 500lb bomb ahead of the U-boat to force it to submerge, which it already appears to be doing. (US National Archives Records Administration)

about 5 to 6 minutes later, and it is believed that the U/B was definitely sunk'.[54] Von Forstner and the crew of *U-402* succumbed to the very weapon his uncle predicted a quarter of a century earlier – a air-dropped guided bomb.

Six months later, on 18 April 1944, the Mayor of Karlsruhe's secretary penned a letter to Baroness von Forstner. 'Dear Madame,' it began,

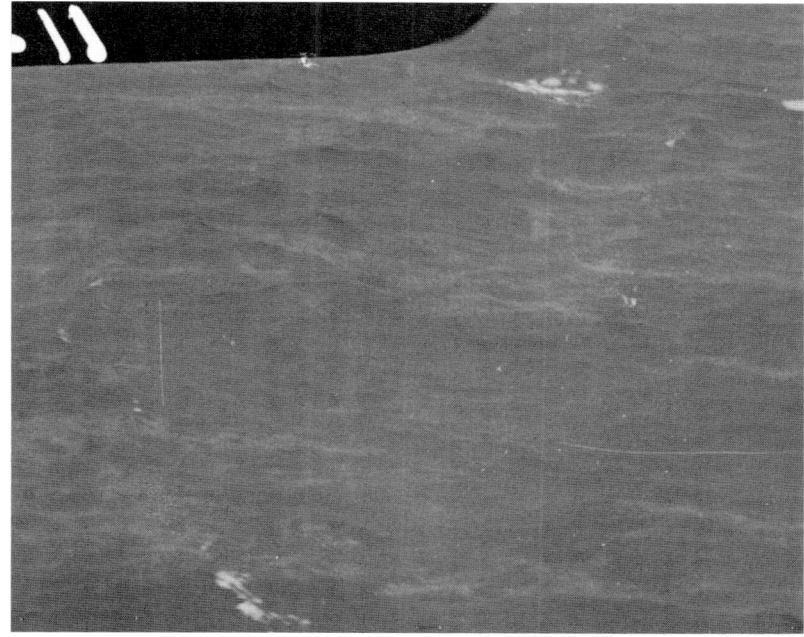

The remnants of the 'FIDO' track can be seen as remnants of air flasks bob to the surface. The 'FIDO' found its mark and exploded on the aft section of the U-boat, rupturing its hull and sending it careering into the depths with all hands lost. (US National Archives Records Administration)

Lieutenant Commander Howard M Avery is pictured receiving the Legion of Merit on the deck of the *Card* from Admiral Royal E Ingersoll who was Commander-in-Chief US Atlantic Fleet at that time. (Courtesy of US National Archives Records Administration)

Since we have not received any news from our U-boat since the end of last year, we are most greatly concerned about our dear comrades on the boat. I am therefore taking the liberty of asking you kindly whether you, Madame, have received any news from the U-boat or at least know where the men of the U-boat are? I assume that you yourself are doing well and that you are still in Nesow. I also hope that you have at least received some sort of good news from your spouse.

The Baroness responded in early May.

Thank you very much for your kind letter of the 18th of this month. Unfortunately, even today I cannot tell you anything more than I wrote at the time to the mayor, which is that our boat was declared missing on October 22nd, 1943. To date, nothing is known about the boat and its crew except for what little one can conclude from the last radio transmissions of the boat, which, putting it carefully, makes it impossible that the crew was taken prisoner. We have been waiting for over 6 months – and can do so even today with the hope to which we as people are entitled, because the time lag after which a report through the Red Cross or personal letters from prisoners reaches the homeland is greater and greater. Thus, even today, we are not yet in any way allowed to give up on the boat's crew. I am convinced that even today we cannot do that, because for the comrades that we, trusting in the wonderful leadership of God, continue to hope for in the distance, this waiting time is also interminably difficult and they need our thoughts and wishes and the hope and trust of our confident hearts – how could we give up on them! News has come from other boats even after a much longer waiting period, so we are definitely entitled to wait and hope for a long time to come.[55]

Von Forstner's wife concluded the letter, 'With great sorrow, I heard about the attack on Karlsruhe a few days ago; I do know from my own experience only too well what such attacks mean. As soon as I hear any more news about the crew/individual crew members, I will let you know. Might I ask you to wait with us some more.' No amount of waiting would bring back von Forstner or the crew of *U-402* from the depths of the North Atlantic.

CHAPTER 8

Conclusion

On Eternal Patrol

> The land begins to disappear in the distance, and as we gaze at the bobbing buoys that vanish in our wake, we hope that after a successful journey they will again be our guides as we return . . . .
> Georg-Günther von Forstner, *The Diary of a Submarine Commander* (1916)

U-402 was sunk in the approximate position 48.56N, 29.41W on 13 October 1943, taking fifty souls to the ocean floor along the mid-Atlantic ridge – a depth of over 20,000ft. During its wartime career it was responsible for sinking fifteen vessels (71,036 GRT) and damaging three (28,682 GRT), as well as knocking one Coastal Command Wellington aircraft out of the sky and damaging two others. Total tonnage sunk or damaged was 99,718.

How many German soldiers' lives were spared by sending Allied war material and supplies to the ocean's bottom can never be known, but this remained Dönitz's prime motivation to continue U-boat deployments through the end of the war. Not every Allied armed merchant sunk entailed loss of life. While some crew and passengers were killed by the initial detonation of a torpedo, and others succumbed to harsh North Atlantic conditions, most were able to abandon ship and be rescued. For survivors, solace only came years later in knowing their enemy had met a similar fate. As Peter Halstead, crewmen on the *Dalcroy* sunk by *U-402* stoically recalled in a post-war interview, 'I don't remember how many ships he sunk in that convoy, but he did quite well. Anyway, we got his submarine later in the war.'[56] All told, *U-402*'s combat actions cost the lives of 517 Allied crewmen or soldiers, to include the five airmen of the shot-down Wellington. Two crewmen, it must be remembered, of the *Cythera* were rescued, both apparently surviving their time in German prisoner-of-war camps.

Within the world of U-boats that von Forstner served, he was considered an 'ace'. Only sixty other U-boat captains sank more vessels than he did during the war. He was awarded the Iron Cross 2nd Class on 18 February 1942, 1st Class on 7 August 1942 and the Knight's Cross on 3 February 1943. He joined an elite group of undersea warriors and continued his family's tradition, surpassing his uncle's First World War tally of twenty-four vessels sunk (54,587 GRT), two damaged (10,511 GRT) and two taken as prizes (3,226 GRT) while in command of *U-28*. Von Forstner's performance in the North Atlantic convoy battles set him apart from many of his peers. He demonstrated that tactical intuition and technical proficiency, combined with tenacity, created chances to penetrate a convoy's defences. However, one U-boat commander alone could not win the campaign in the North Atlantic.

As a naval cadet who entered service in 1930, von Forstner was no National Socialist. He certainly wanted to see Germany ascendant again in the aftermath of the Versailles Treaty, as arguably most officers of his age did, but his enlistment into the navy was motivated by family tradition, not vengeance. No less than ten families whose fathers or uncles had served in the First World War U-boat service saw their sons or nephews do the same in the Second.[57]

Von Forstner's actions during the war, while necessarily aggressive, were proportionate and measured. He proved to be a consummate naval professional who fought his battles not as the overused caricature of the 'wolf', but rather that of a medieval knight of old. He certainly gained the respect of Captain Waters, an adversary who served as a watch officer on board the USCGC *Ingham* in the battles for Convoys SC-107, SC-118, SC-12, and SC-122. Waters offered high praise to von Forstner and the other U-boat men he fought. 'Long after the passions of battle have cooled, the bravery, the fighting spirit, and the dedication of the men who fought in the U-boats and the Kriegsmarine compel the respect of other fighting men,' Waters wrote. He directed the following passage toward his fellow Allied navy veterans who fought the 'U-boat menace' in an attempt to bridge the divide of enemies, through the common ground of service to one's country. 'That they served a government bent on an evil design was their misfortune and later shame,' Waters began, 'but like us, most of them fought for their country and their people, professionals carrying out their duties with little knowledge and even less control over the political direction of the war.'[58]

During his post-war research Waters befriended former German U-boat commanders, as well as the eminent German naval historian Jürgen Rohwer. Most rewarding was the relationship he established with von Forstner's former wife, who remarried after the war, dropped the 'Baroness' and become Frau Annamarie Rapp.

The aftermath of war can bring former enemies together through the shared bond of loss and understanding that few others, looking back on such tumultuous times from the safe distance of the present, can never fully comprehend. Waters sent Annamarie a copy of his article about von Forstner titled 'Stay Tough' that was published in US Naval Institute *Proceedings* in December 1966. She responded with a short letter of her own that included a set of hand-made red pompoms she once made for each member of her husband's crew back in 1942. The letter read:

> I find it quite difficult to express my appreciation and gratitude in a fitting manner, the more so since I have said all I possibly could in my previous letters. Maybe, though, that the little red pompoms, or Bommel!, which I enclose herewith will tell you more accurately than so many words how I feel about your article. Let me add that I should, surely, not give them to you could I not be certain, after all this time, that Captain and Crew of *U-402* would be glad to make this gesture, thus welcoming the gallant recorder of their deeds, and kindred spirit (for how else could he have understood their operations, and the spirit behind it all so well), among their friends.

A fitting tribute that still resonated with Waters' son when I contacted the family nearly 50 years after this letter was written.

From Submersible to Submarine

> To attack the submersible is a matter of opportunity.
> Georg-Günther von Forstner, *The Journal of a Submarine Commander* (1916)

The Battle of the Atlantic did not end with the loss of *U-402*. Its destruction demonstrated the ascendency of aircraft in the battle against the surface-bound submersible, which all too many historians forget that the U-boat was. Now equipped with radar, armed with acoustic homing torpedoes, and vectored toward U-boat concentrations through a combination of decrypted signals and direction-finding gear, carrier-based aircraft became the primary U-boat killer. All that can be asserted is that the tactical construct of the wolfpack, not the U-boat itself, was defeated during 'Black May' 1943 despite the scores of published histories that suggest otherwise. The U-boat, as a representative example of the submersibles of the day, demonstrated the ability to survive in the face of all the advantages in technology and tactics fielded by the Allies. In order to destroy a U-boat, it had to be found. This became increasingly difficult by the end of the war.

In secret development since May 1943 was a new device destined to transform submersible and undersea warfare forever. Born from the necessity of survival came the Schnorchel (snorkel) that soon enabled submersibles to never have to surface to refresh their air, recharge their batteries or even run their diesel engines. The introduction of the snorkel countered the threat of attacks by Allied aircraft overnight. It reduced U-boat losses by air attack by a factor of ten by the autumn of 1944. In addition came advances in anti-sonar and anti-radar technology a generation ahead of the Allies. New U-boat designs were being produced with hull forms meant exclusively for continuous underwater operation. Even a new hydrogen-peroxide propulsion system was developed that achieved underwater speeds in excess of 20 knots, foreshadowing the post-war introduction of Air-Independent Propulsion (AIP) systems. The dawn of the true submarine was at hand; one that did not need to surface to recharge batteries or refresh oxygen, and was exceedingly hard to track and destroy. With the wolfpack defeated, a single U-boat could not change the outcome of the war no matter how well it could avoid Allied detection. However, the advances made in technology and tactics by the German submersible force set the stage for the evolution into the true submarine and its employment as a strategic weapon and instrument of intelligence collection in the post-world war.

If *U-402* had survived and returned to port von Forstner and his crew would have seen their boat undergo yet another period of transformation, whereby survival meant no longer fighting it out with aircraft on the surface, but never having to surface at all, with the introduction of the snorkel and the concept of 'Total Undersea War' the device introduced into the U-boat force.

Of Wrecks and Sanctuaries

> Therefore, hardly a single ship will be salvaged, and the sea will retain all those ships it has swallowed in the

CONCLUSION

course of this war carried out by all the nations of the earth.

Georg-Günther von Forstner, *The Journal of a Submarine Commander* (1916)

Thousands of Allied vessels and hundreds of German U-boats came to rest on the bottom of the ocean across both sides of the Atlantic. Most, though not all, are in deep water. Underwater search technology has recently become more accessible, and more precise, allowing the exploration of depths that only a generation or two ago were thought impossible.

No scientific or maritime archaeological survey of the North Atlantic where the majority of convoy battles took place during the war has occurred to date, but one can hope that increasing interest will generate such historic missions in the near future. The men who fought here deserve their battlefield mapped, surveyed and remembered to the same extent that land battles enjoy today. Such a venture brings with it not just historical rewards, but a look at how man's weapons of war have been given a second life in the ocean's depths.

In the case of *U-581*, which was sunk in 1942 while attacking the *Llangibby Castle* along with *U-402*, its wreck site has become a wellspring of new undersea life. *U-581* was located by the Rebikoff Foundation in the year 2016 at a depth of 870m, south of the Island of Pico. The wreck sprouted a deep-sea coral reef. Specimens taken in the summer of 2018 revealed an entirely new species currently being researched by the IMAR Institute of the University of the Azores. Imagine what life might be found among

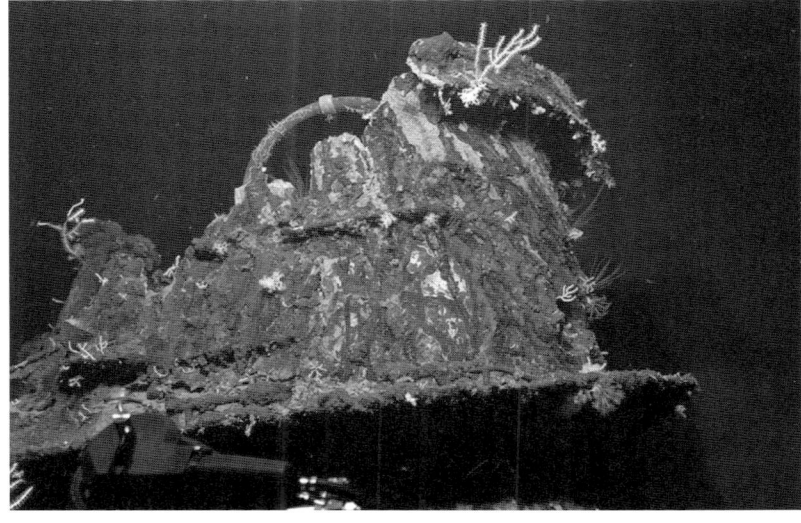

The conning tower of *U-581* as it looked in 2016. Note that the U-boat's symbol of a crab louse is still visible underneath the forming rust. (Courtesy of the Rebikoff Foundation)

The author sketching the twisted remnants of the *Ashkhabad*'s bow section in 2013. (Courtesy of Lauren Heesemann)

the other deep-water wrecks in the battlefield of the North Atlantic?

In the summer of 2013, I participated in the National Oceanic and Atmospheric Agency (NOAA) maritime archaeological survey of the sunken freighter SS *Ashkhabad* in support of the Monitor National Marine Sanctuary off the coast of North Carolina. The *Ashkhabad* was sunk by *U-402* in April 1942. It was a surreal experience to map a sunken vessel my grandfather's U-boat torpedoed while he was on board. It made his wartime experience more than just a story, a document, or even a photo. Here I could touch the hull of a wreck that luckily witnessed no human loss, and which now served a second life as an artificial reef to a wide range of marine flora and fauna within a marine sanctuary.

When the survey was complete, I drove up to New Jersey to visit my maternal grandparents, both of whom were in their mid-90s. I wanted to show my grandfather the underwater video I had made of the wreck site, not being quite sure of what reaction it might elicit. I sat down, opened my laptop, explained the purpose

CONCLUSION

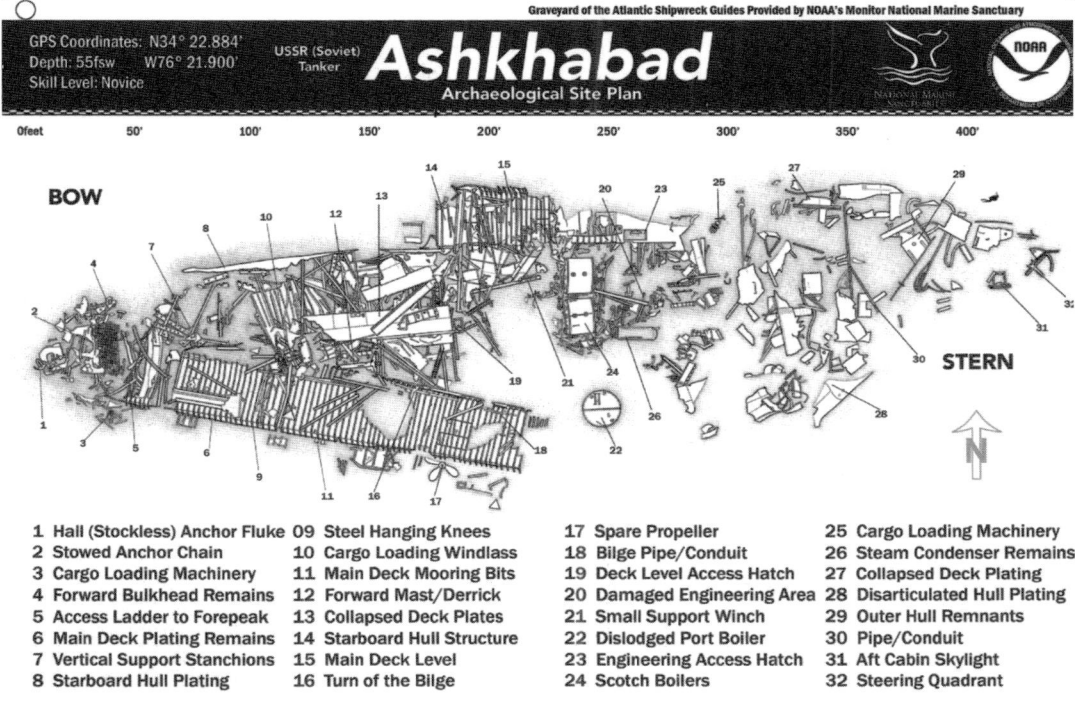

A dive card of the *Ashkhabad* produced by NOAA with the assistance of BAREG. Cards like these provide a history of the sunken vessel on one side and a current depiction of the wreck site on the other. (Author's collection)

of the survey and played the colour video. I knew my grandfather no longer could recall specific dates or events that occurred during his time on *U-402*, some 70 years ago, and I certainly did not expect it to bring back any meaningful memories. As my grandfather watched the video, a rare smile formed on his otherwise stoic German face. Then he took a breath, and a man of few words stated in his thick accent: 'Das is unbelievable!' He laughed, turned to my grandmother and stated to her 'Mama, look at das fish!'

The wreck itself, just as the war he was drafted into more than seven decades before, was of little interest to him – if it stirred any memory of the far-away combat action at all. But the bright-coloured fish, like the narwhals he saw on his first patrol in the North Atlantic, certainly drew his attention. It was a window into an underwater world he only imagined as a submariner. For many who served on or below the sea during the war an inherent love of its majestic beauty and respect for its awesome power took root in their soul. It was no different with my grandfather. This was the last we ever spoke of his wartime experiences before he passed away in 2015 at the age of 96.

The small band of avocational divers and professional maritime archaeologists who bonded during the survey of the *Ashkhabad* later formed the non-profit Battle of the Atlantic Research and Expedition Group (BAREG). After eight years of operation our group has surveyed numerous sunken wrecks from the Battle of the Atlantic along the coast of North Carolina, and visited many others along the shores of North America and Europe. Our efforts have helped maintain awareness of the sacrifices made by the merchant marine and naval veterans of both sides in the conflict. It is far too easy to look out to the Atlantic from the safety of shore and forget that below its often-majestic surface, some 3,500 Allied merchant ships, 783 U-boats and 222 warships of both sides, as well as the frames of hundreds of aircraft engaged in the battle for supremacy of the sea lanes, rest on the sea floor. Over 100,000 souls from both sides were lost, victims of the longest military campaign in human history.

U-402 memorial at the U-Boot Ehrenmal. (Author's collection)

APPENDIX A

Evolution of a U-boat

As the Battle for the Atlantic progressed the Type VIIC began to undergo modifications that reflected the changing operational environment. The first change was the removal of the net cutter from the bow of Type VIICs commissioned from 1941 onward, as evidenced in *U-402*.

In 1943 the after bridge was widened and extended to include a lower gun deck. This was known as the Turmumbau IV officially, and as the 'Wintergarten' to the crew. The enlarged upper platform was equipped with two double-barrelled 20mm C38 anti-aircraft guns, and on the lower platform was a single 37mm cannon. The FuMB 9 Hagenuk Wellenanzeigegerät 1 (W.Anz.g1), which was later contracted to Wanze I 'Bali' passive detector, replaced the older Metox mounted on the 'Biscay Cross'. Wanze I could scan frequency ranges from 120 to 180cm through fine tuning on the Runddipol (round dipole) mounted on the starboard side of the conning tower. This initial receiver was not waterproof and had to be mounted manually when the U-boat surfaced. *U-402* may also have received the FuMO 30 active search radar added to the portside, outer conning tower casing as evidenced in the final aerial photographs taken of the U-boat, though this is not confirmed.

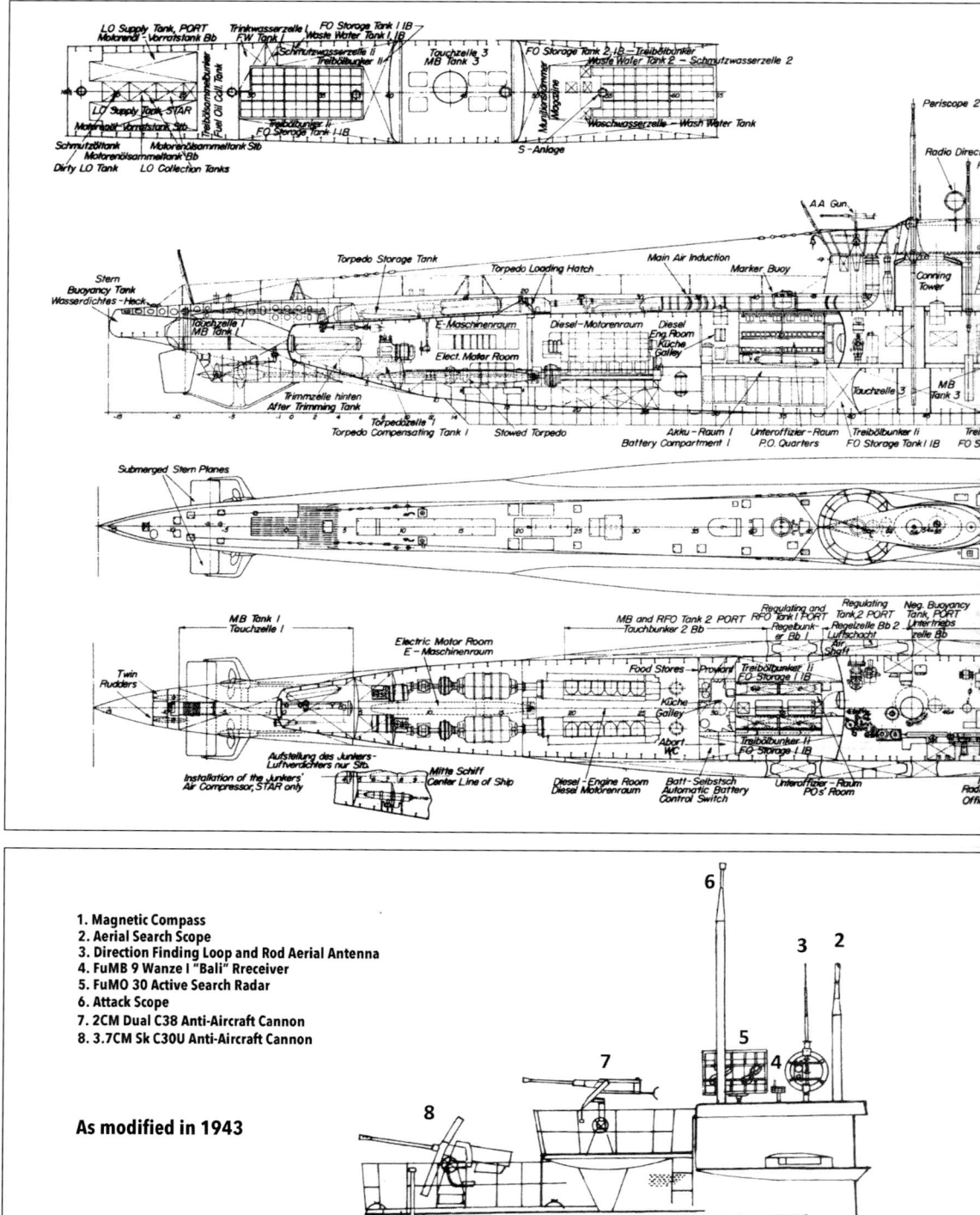

APPENDIX A

As commissioned in 1941

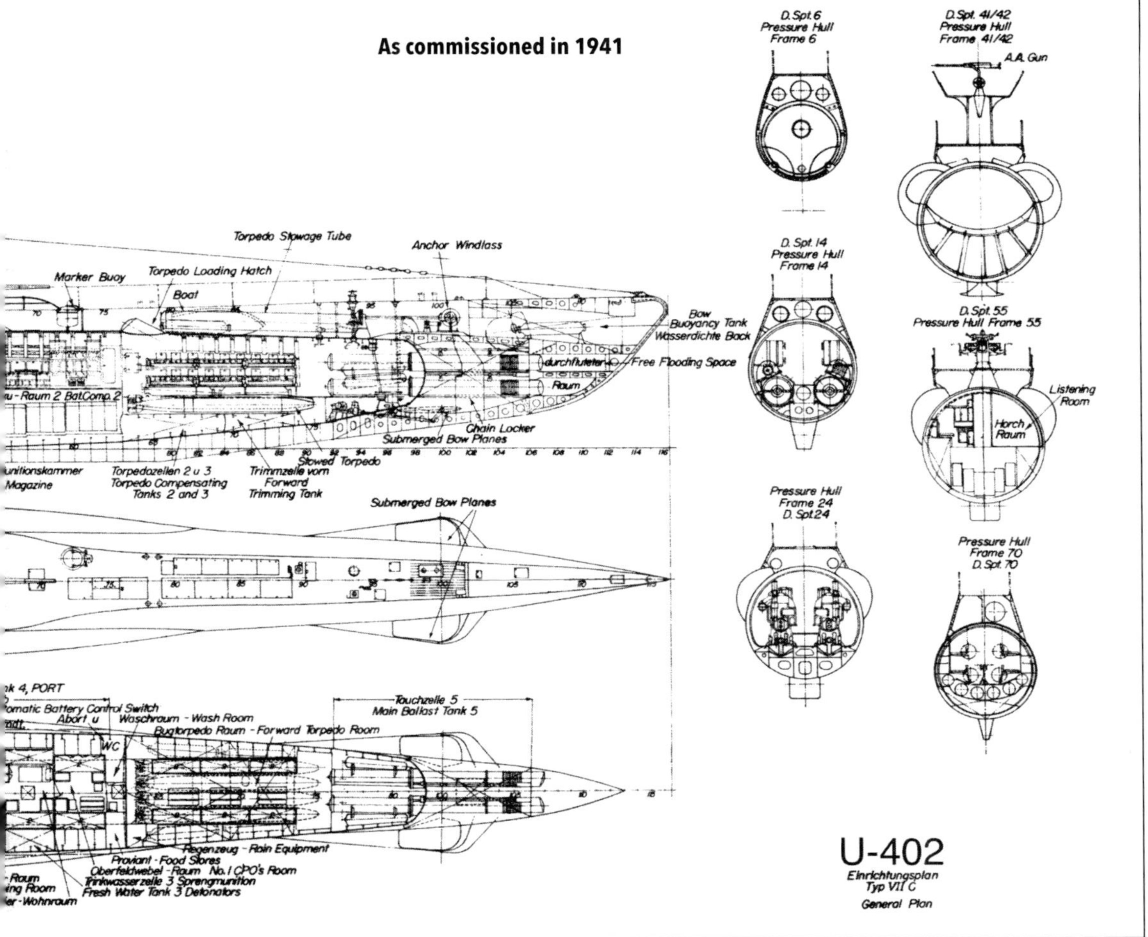

D.Spt.6 Pressure Hull Frame 6

D.Spt. 41/42 Pressure Hull Frame 41/42
A.A. Gun

Marker Buoy
Torpedo Loading Hatch
Torpedo Stowage Tube
Anchor Windlass
Boat
Bow Buoyancy Tank
Wasserdichte Back
durchflutetar
Free Flooding Space
Raum
Chain Locker
Submerged Bow Planes
Stowed Torpedo
Munitionskammer
Magazine
Torpedozellen 2 u 3
Torpedo Compensating Tanks 2 and 3
Trimmzelle vorn
Forward Trimming Tank
Submerged Bow Planes
u-Raum 2 BatComp.2

D.Spt.14 Pressure Hull Frame 14

D.Spt. 55 Pressure Hull Frame 55
Listening Room
Horch Raum

Pressure Hull Frame 24
D.Spt.24

Pressure Hull Frame 70
D.Spt.70

ak 4, PORT
omatic Battery Control Switch
Abort u. Waschraum – Wash Room
WC
Bugtorpedo Raum – Forward Torpedo Room
Touchzelle 5
Main Ballast Tank 5
Regenzeug – Rain Equipment
Proviant · Food Stores
Oberfeldwebel · Raum No.1 CPO's Room
Trinkwasserzelle 3 Sprengmunition
Fresh Water Tank 3 Detonators
Raum
Wohnraum
Room

U-402
Einrichtungsplan
Typ VII C
General Plan

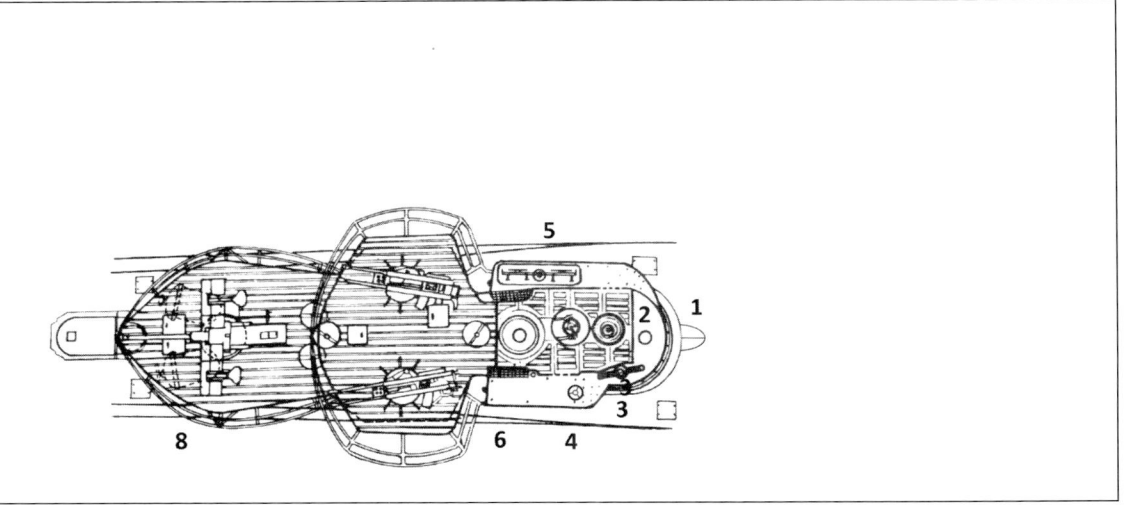

191

APPENDIX B

Crew

(+) Killed 13 October 1943

Commander:		**Date of Birth**
Korvettenkapitän Siegfried Freiherr von Forstner (+)		9 Sep 10

Watch Officers:

IWO Oberleutnant zur See	Adolf-Wilhelm Freiherr von Hammerstein-Equord (May 41–Oct 41)	11 Mar 18
IWO Oberleutnant zur See	Kiehn (Nov 41–Jul 42)	?
IIWO Leutnant zur See	Otto Hübschen (May 41–Aug 42)	6 Dec 19
IWO Oberleutnant zur See	Henning Schümann (Aug 42–Mar 43)	17 Apr 19
IIWO Leutnant zur See	Karl-Wilhelm Pancke (Sep 42–Mar 43)	8 Mar 21
IWO Oberleutnant zur See	Wolf-Rudiger Methling (+)	19 Oct 18
IIWO Leutnant zur See	Hans Engelien (+)	24 Nov 20

Watch Officer School (Temporarily Assigned):

Fähnrich zur See Jochen Frintrop	(?)
Fähnrich zur See Ottmar Heydecke	(?)
Fähnrich zur See Dieter Forstmann	(?)

Engineering Section:

Oberleutnant Ing Hans Meyer-Oswald (03.41–05.42)	10 Mar 17
Oberleutnant Ing. Hermann Hartke (+)	23 Oct 19
Obermaschinst Eugen Fischer (+)	11 Dec 15
Obermaschinst Heinrich Prause (+)	21 Feb 15

Ship's Doctor

Marineoberassistenzartzt Dr Gerhard Wagner (+)	22 Feb 17

Quartermaster Section:

Obersteuermann Wilhelm Prokop (+)	9 Jan 14
Leutnant zur See Hermann Schwartz (+)	5 Apr 22
Gefreiter Herbert Schwuchow (04.41–07.42)	20 Feb 19

Non-Commissioned Officers

Grieskorn, Johann (+)	Obermaschinenmaat	13 Jul 18
Hohberger, Willi (+)	Obermaschinenmaat	6 Sep 18

Koch, Max (+)	Obermaschinenmaat	10 Nov 14
Lakischus, Kurt (+)	Obermaschinenemaat	30 Mar 19
Lemmersdorf, Wilhelm (+)	Oberbootsmannsmaat	13 Jul 19
Quitzsch, Walter (+)	Oberfunkmaat	9 Jan 22
Storz, Edgar (+)	Obermaschinenmaat	13 Sep 19
Bochynski, Wilhelm (+)	Bootsmannsmaat	6 Sep 20
Brieskorn, Johann (+)	Obermaschinenmaat	13 Jul 18
Coye, Hans (+)	Maschinenmaat	3 Oct 21
Friebolin, Walter	Bootsmannsmaat (Apr 41–May 42)	16 Sep 21
Hilgendorf, Georg (+)	Bootsmannsmaat	4 Aug 20
Kollinger, Franz-Robert (+)	Funkmaat	24 Feb 22
Mai, Walter (+)	Mechanikermaat	18 Nov 20
Scholl, Willi (+)	Maschinenmaat	20 Apr 21

Ship's Company:

Blank, Herbert (+)	Matrosenobergefreiter	21 Aug 22
Farin, Friedrich (+)	Matrosengefreiter	19 May 22
Garnatz, Rudolf (+)	Maschinenobergefreiter	10 Aug 22
Gieß, Rolf (+)	Matrosenobergefreiter	10 Nov 20
Kassur, Heinz (+)	Maschinenobergefreiter	7 Feb 24
Makurath, Johann (+)	Matrosenobergefreiter	23 Oct 23
Ostant, Willi (+)	Maschinenobergefreiter	13 Jul 23
Rauch, Heinrich (+)	Matrosenobergefreiter	28 Jan 23
Reckling, Helmut (+)	Maschinenobergefreiter	21 Aug 22
Seifert, Bruno (+)	Matrosenobergefreiter	2 Sep 21
Sommer, Gunter (+)	Funkobergefreiter	16 Mar 24
Strohbach, Siegfried (+)	Matrosenobergefreiter	29 May 20
Thom, Gerhard (+)	Maschinenobergefreiter	23 Aug 23
Thielisch, Ernst (+)	Mechanikerobergefreiter	27 Sep 22
Wente, Kurt (+)	Maschinenobergefreiter	31 Oct 20
Zipfel, Andreas (+)	Maschinenobergefreiter	22 Apr 23
Becker, Willi (+)	Maschinengefreiter	30 Aug 23
Eppert, Wilhelm-Heinrich (+)	Matrosenobergefreiter	15 Apr 23
Gierspecht, Gunter (+)	Maschinengefreiter	22 Jan 24
Grönberger, Heinz (+)	Matrosengefreiter	28 Oct 24
Haack, Gerhard (+)	Maschinengefreiter	10 Oct 21
Hammer, Egon (+)	Matrosengefreiter	5 Oct 23
Hermanns, Abram (+)	Maschinengefreiter	16 Sep 23
Kleber, Martin (+)	Matrosengefreiter	1 Nov 24
Kullmann, Franz (+)	Funkgefreiter	30 Dec 24
Schleutermann, Paul (+)	Mechanikergefreiter	20 Dec 23
Vogt, Karl (+)	Mechanikergefreiter	29 May 25
Spinner, Richard (+)	Matrose	2 Nov 24

APPENDIX C

Pompom Life

This poem was written by an unidentified crewman from *U-402* and sent to the Mayor of Karlsruhe after the seventh patrol.

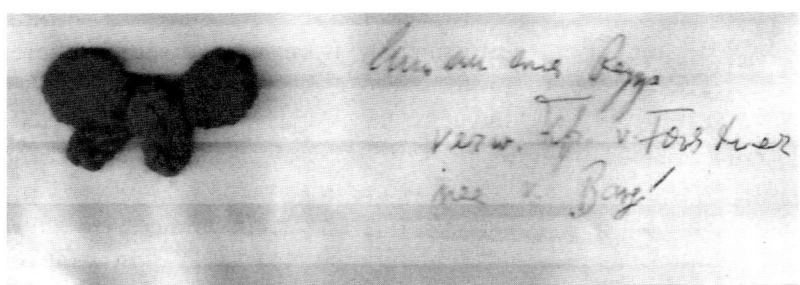

A handmade red 'pompom' presented by von Forstner's wife to Captain Waters (Ret.) after the war. This is the only known photo of one of the handmade pompoms produced for the crew of *U-402*. (Waters' collection)

Pompom Life

On the occasion of the
birthday
of the
Pompom
May 21, 1943.

<u>Pompom Life</u>

Oh dear Pompom people! Today, we are celebrating the birthday of our boat, which started travelling two years ago on Danzig's roads.

    At the beginning of February, a totally new crew came to the Danzig Wharf. They met each other, work began, and in fact, it turned into one crew. The crew arose, soldered together by the commandant, who instilled into it the true Pompom spirit. Far over the Atlantic from east to north, it became known thanks to its sinking record. Karlsruhe was made our sponsoring city when it was known that Forstner had a U-boat. We carried '*Fidelitas*' as a charm, to our joy and the British hatred. In a lot of hours, great danger hung over us; that is quite true.

    With the construction over, the training over, the Pompom

now headed toward the Atlantic. We went through the Skagerrak to Norway, but we had bad luck and roared out. That meant 'back,' back to the shipyard in Kiel, but the laze-about time was also quickly past. Back to Norway – with luck on our side, we did not need to return to Kiel. Then out into the Atlantic on a great journey; that was definitely Pompom style.

The first undertaking was unsuccessful – six weeks on patrol, nothing seen, nothing heard. So it was off to St Nazaire on the coast of France to get armed for the next trip. The second trip was supposed to go to the Americas, but a convoy found the Pompom. We shot at one. But that was shit; it ran away from us, the old bastard. The unstructured hunt continued to the Azores; unfortunately, it ran into something there. So back to France, an annoyed mood, doubting our luck. St Nazaire took the boat again and also put up with the large amount of work needed to equip us for the third trip, which set off for the Americas with a great start. Luck was on our side, the war god was gracious and two steamers with 12,000 tons were handled. We sent a well-equipped coastal defence ship into the deep. A fan went off, but it was stranded – now the fish had enough to eat. From the third, we took two Yankees home; they were glad that they were left to live. It was in the bow area where they lived and quite some crazy jokes they made.

But what the third trip brought in joy, the fourth one made up for. The mood was expansive on the third trip, but on the fourth one, it was nearly dreary. The goal of the fourth trip was the same as for the third one – to the Americas. We just suffered more. An airplane saw us and bombed us, so we thought the end was coming. The boat was well built, the Pompom stayed intact and we were soon on the way back. We put the 3,030 nautical miles behind us to quickly find La Pallice. So there was once again a new city to explore, La Rochelle, a very wonderful town, not big, but looked at overall, very famous. But everyone said, 'Not long on land' and soon the pompom went out on its fifth run. Now we went up to Newfoundland – putting up with the bad weather. From a convoy, we offed six steamers in a frantic battle. Now going home quickly with high RPM – that was the return trip for the undertaking. With flapping pennants, that's how we were welcomed by the flotilla chief, some nuns and a lot of people we knew. People started looking at the Pompom in general, at the boat, its crew and the commander. And now we were out on leave; people were glad to be living once again in their own houses. But it quickly passed; the time was over and soon the Pompom was ready again. And back into the North Atlantic. Will we be granted as great success this time as well with multiple tons? The trip was started with this desire. In a situation compounded by vessel damage, the Pompom suddenly came to a great blow in one night, because it happened that we sent six steamships to the deep.

52,000! – that's an accomplishment. But it went on; a seventh followed the next night and raised the number to 63 – heavens to Betsy for once. It was something to cheer about, it was something great. The Pompom had again shown what the boat and its crew could do in the [convoy] tracks that were so important to the Brits.

– It didn't take long for a radio transmission to come awarding the Knight's Cross to the old guy. Homemade in the vessel, we had the award ceremony in the bow area. That was the crowning of the sixth trip. Although overall the fight was quite hard, happy faces could be seen because we were supposed to be going back home. At the tower stood the number that we had reached – 113,000 tons!

– A great welcome, a quick look, a short speech and happy music from the flotilla chief and other officers, and then we were able to touch land again for the first time.

– But not just in port, but on land as well, there were numerous busy hands making sure that the Pompom could be received overall. In the pubs, one saw a lot of resplendent green. Eight weeks of free time, 8 weeks of free time, then we were out again, and it was time for the Pompom to start running again through the Bay of Biscay and then the ocean. After the senior commander, we then went back and the two thrust bearings went on top. So the Pompom was completely crippled before it got to the convoy at all. We were unsuccessful, so we were forced to go further down south. And here we were successful! After a relatively short time, two steamers were found again.

Two 'eels' and two explosions on them, and then came destroyers that didn't want to spare us and dropped depth charges, again and again and there was indeed a large hole. Indeed, it looked that way from the outside. Well, let's see what they say about it at home.

Pompom spirit – Pompom. *Fidelitas* maintains watch, thinking of you, in good times and bad. Today, all of us old and young Pompom people thank you.

APPENDIX D

Patrol Summary

Patrol	Departure	Arrival	Length	Vessel Hit	Date	(S)unk or (D)amaged	Tonnage
1	26 Oct 41 – Kiel	9 Dec 41 – St Nazaire	45 days	n/a	n/a	n/a	n/a
2	11 Jan 42 – St Nazaire	11 Feb 42 – St Nazaire	32 days	*Llangibby Castle*	16 Jan 42	D	11,951
3	26 Mar 42 – St Nazaire	20 May 42 – St Nazaire	56 days	*Empire Progress*	13 Apr 42	S	5,249
				Ashkhabad	30 Apr 42	S	5,284
				USS *Cythera*	2 May 42	S	602
							11,135
4	16 Jun 42 – St Nazaire	5 Aug 42 – La Pallice	51 days	n/a	n/a	n/a	n/a
5	4 Oct 42 – La Pallice	20 Nov 42 – La Pallice	48 days	*Empire Sunrise*	2 Nov 42	D	7,459
				Rinos	2 Nov 42	S	4,649
				Dalcroy	2 Nov 42	S	4,558
				Empire Leopard	2 Nov 42	S	5,676
				Empire Antelope	2 Nov 42	S	4,945
							27,287
6	14 Jan 43 – La Pallice	23 Feb 43 – La Pallice	41 days	*Toward*	7 Feb 43	S	1,571
				Robert E. Hopkins	7 Feb 43	S	6,625
				Daghild	7 Feb 43	D	9,272
				Afrika	7 Feb 43	S	8,597
				Henry R. Mallory	7 Feb 43	S	6,063
				Kalliopi	7 Feb 43	S	4,965
				Newton Ash	8 Feb 43	S	4,625
							41,718
7	21 Apr 143 – La Pallice	26 May 43 – La Pallice	36 days	*Grado*	11 May 43	S	3,082
				Antigone	11 May 43	S	4,545
							7,627
8	4 Sep 43 – La Pallice	13 Oct 43 Sunk	40 days	n/a	n/a	n/a	n/a
						Total	**99,718**

Notes

[1] Unless otherwise noted, all times are Berlin summer time, GMT +2.
[2] Karl Dönitz, *Memoirs: Ten Years and Twenty Days* (Annapolis, Maryland: Naval Institute Press, 1990), p 4.
[3] An analysis of 717 front-line U-boats lost during the war reveals that 40 per cent were sunk due to direct or indirect actions of aircraft, compared to a loss of 30 per cent due to surface action alone. Axel Niestlé, *German U-boat Losses During World War II: Details of Destruction* (London: Frontline Books, 2014), Appendix 2.
[4] Von Forstner's mother passed away in 1919. His father remarried and his second wife gave birth to two sons, both of whom later lost their lives serving in the army during the war.
[5] Timothy P Mulligan, *Neither Sharks nor Wolves, The Men of Nazi Germany's U-boat Arm, 1939-1945* (Annapolis, Maryland: Naval Institute Press, 1999), p 111.
[6] Marischal Murray, *Union-Castle Chronicle 1853-1953* (London: Longmans, Green and Co, 1953), p 229.
[7] www.convoyweb.org.uk.
[8] www.uboatarchive.net, BdU KTB, 16 Jan 1941.
[9] David Syrett (ed), *Publications of the Navy Records Society, Vol. 139, The Battle of the Atlantic and Signals Intelligence: U-boat Situations and Trends, 1941-1945* (Aldershot: Ashgate, 1998), p 6.
[10] The *Barbarigo* departed Bordeaux, France on 30 April 1942 with orders to cross the Atlantic and patrol along the coast of Brazil. Italian submarines were not suited for the rough waters of the North Atlantic, so Dönitz ordered them to patrol the in the calmer waters of the South Atlantic. On 20 May, Grossi spotted the cruiser USS *Milwaukee* and destroyer USS *Moffett*, incorrectly identifying the former as a *Maryland*-class battleship. Grossi ordered two torpedoes fired at the 'battleship', and while submerged, he and the crew discerned sounds that believed to be their torpedoes striking and sinking the 'battleship'. The crew of the *Milwaukee* never spotted the torpedoes and continued on without realising an attack occurred. Grossi's report on the sinking reached his command back in Bordeaux, where doubts were raised on its accuracy. However, the supposed sinking was widely publicized in both the German and Italian press and Grossi was awarded the Gold Medal of Military Valor and promoted to Capitano di Fregata (Commander). After the war an investigation into the incident determined that Grossi and his crew acted in 'good faith', but Grossi was stripped of his award and rank.

[11] Syrett, p 8.

[12] C.B. 4051 (42) 'U581' Interrogation of Survivors, April 1942. N.I.D. 01730/42 (http://www.uboatarchive.net/Int/U-581INT.htm) and 'The History of U-581' (http://dubm.de/en/the-history-of-u-581/).

[13] Leutnant zur See Walter Sitek swam 6.4km (4 miles) to reach a point on Pico Island near the village of Guidaste where he was rescued by the local inhabitants. He then managed to make his way to neutral Spain and in May 1942 and returned to Germany. Sitek went on to command *U-17* (Type IIB), *U-981* (Type VIIC) and the electro-boat *U-3005* (Type XXI). He survived the war.

[14] BdU War Log 16-30 November 1941 PG30300b, NARA/T1022/4063 (http://www.uboatarchive.net/BDU/BDUKTB30300B.htm)

[15] *The German Navy's Use of Special Intelligence, Task C IV h* (US National Archives and Records Administration, reference citation unknown), p. 85.

[16] These lifeboats were survivors from either the American steamer *Steel Maker* torpedoed by *U-654* or the British merchant *Empire Dryden* sunk by *U-572*, both of which had been sunk earlier that day. Both groups of survivors were later rescued.

[17.] Navy Casualty Case Files, USS Cythera Box 20, National Archives at College Park, College Park. MD cited on http://www.navsource.org/'.

[18] Interview of Mr James E Brown, conducted by Mr Mike McCarthy in 1991 (www.uboat.net/allies/merchants/ship/1586.html).

[19] John M Waters, Jr., CAPT., US Coast Guard (Ret.), *Bloody Winter*, revised paperback ed. (New York: A Jove Book, 1986), pp 275–6.

[20] Brown interview.

[21] For a detailed account of late-war U-boat operations off the North American coast, see Aaron S Hamilton, *Total Undersea War: The Evolutionary Role of the Snorkel in Dönitz's U-boat Fleet, 1944-1945* (Barnsley: Seaforth, 2020), pp 225–304.

[22] United States Airforce Historical Research Agency, Expenditure of Depth Charges. Reported filed 14 July 1942.

[23] Kiehn later transferred off *U-402*.

[24] Jochen Frintrop, Hörzu, 'Mit "Feindsender" auf Feindfahrt' (29 May 1987), p 7.

[25] David G. Thompson, 'Villains, Victims, and Veterans: Buchheim's *Das Boot* and the Problem of the Hybrid Novel-Memoir as History', *Twentieth Century Literature* 39, no. 1 (1993), pp 59–78.

[26] Ibid, p 73.

[27] The 'Leigh Light' was a powerful 24-million-candle carbon arc searchlight that measured approximately 610mm in diameter. It was fitted to Coastal Command aircraft and was turned on to illuminate a surfaced U-boat at night during the final approach of the aircraft that used aerial radar to initially close with the surfaced enemy. This gave the bomber a visual target to attack.

[28] Waters, p 16.

[29] Ibid, p 46.

[30] Tenth Fleet Convoy Routing, NARA, RG 138, Box 124.

[31] Waters Papers, copy in the author's collection.

[32] *The German Navy's Use of Special Intelligence*, p 85.
[33] Ibid, p 97.
[34] Ibid, p 98.
[35] Niestlé, p 76.
[36] Waters, p 174.
[37] Letter from von Forstner to the Mayor of Karlsruhe, dated 22 July 1943.
[38] Waters, p 271.
[39] Ibid.
[40] Ibid, p 272.
[41] Ibid.
[42] Syrett, p xiii.
[43] *The German Navy's Use of Special Intelligence*, p 103.
[44] Ed Offley, *Turning the Tide, How a Small Band of Allied Sailors Defeated the U-boats and Won the Battle of the Atlantic* (New York: Basic Books, 2011), p xii.
[45] Captain Donald Macintyre, *U-boat Killer: Fighting the U-boats in the Battle of the Atlantic* (London: Cassell Military Paperback, 2000), p 123.
[46] Statistics of this sort tend to vary from source to source. I used those available on https://uboat.net.
[47] Macintyre, pp 100–01.
[48] Waters, pp 273–4.
[49] Ibid, p 273.
[50] Ibid, p 274.
[51] Günter Hessler, *The U-boat War in the Atlantic 1939-1945* (London: Ministry of Defence, HMSO, 1992), Chapter VII, pp 12–13, Section 359 and 360.
[52] Norman Franks and Eric Zimmerman, *U-boat versus Aircraft* (London: Grub Street, 1988), pp 84–5.
[53] Marc-André Haldimann, 'End of a Charmed career' (undated and unpublished article), p 5. Note that there are factual errors in Haldimann's reconstruction of the final events of *U-402*. He asserts that an attack occurred on the U-boat on 12 October, but this did not happen.
[54] ASW-6 Report No. 28 (13 October 1943): Antisubmarine action aircraft Report (ASW-6) written by Lt (jg) Fowler, submitted by Lt Comdr Avery and endorsed by Capt A J Isbell, NARA.
[55] Exchange of letters between Mayor's Office of Karlsruhe and Baroness Annamarie Forstner, dated Letter from von Forstner to the Mayor of Karlsruhe, dated 18 April and 25 April 1944.
[56] Peter Halstead, Oral History, recorded by Toby Brooks, Imperial War Museum, Record Number: 31729.
[57] Mulligan, p 26.
[58] Waters, pp 276–7.

Select Bibliography

A large portion of material sourced for this book came from personal papers, interviews, and undated primary documents without archival references acquired since research began in the early 1990s. Efforts were made to source the original documents where possible, but where this was not possible, the author notes that they are available in his personal collection of papers.

PRIMARY DOCUMENTS
Germany
Deutsche Dienststelle (WASt), Berlin
Service history for Herbert Schwuchow.

Deutsches U-Boot Museum, Cuxhaven
U-402 U-Blatt. File contains usual details about the U-boat, crew list, assorted awards and articles.

Stadt Karlsruhe, Kulturamt, Stadtarchiv & Historische Museen
U-402 Patenschaftsprogramm file, 1/H-Reg 902. File contains all correspondence related to *U-402* between the Mayor's office, von Forstner and his wife.

United Kingdom
Imperial War Museum
Peter Halstead, Oral History, recorded by Toby Brooks, Imperial War Museum, Record Number: 31729.

United States
National Archives and Records Administration, College Park, Maryland
Record Group 38. Records of the Office of the Chief of Naval Operations.
Intercepted Enemy Radio Traffic and Related Documentation 1940-1946, *U-402* Ultra Intercepts, Box 123–24.
Record Group 242.
T1022. Records of the German Navy, 1850-1945.

Kriegstagebücher (KTB) & Stehender Kriegsbefehl Des Führers/Befehlshaber der Unterseeboote (FdU/BdU).

Documents in Author's Collection
10th Fleet Convoy Routing, SC 107. United States Coast Guard's Historian's Office.
10th Fleet Convoy Routing, SC 118. United States Coast Guard's Historian's Office.
10th Fleet Convoy Routing, SC 129. United States Coast Guard's Historian's Office.
The German Navy's Use of Special Intelligence, Task C IV h, US National Archives and Records Administration, Record Group and Box unknown. Author's collection.
Combat Intelligence Report on the Torpedoing of the Russian S/S/ 'Ashkhabad'. 2150 Q., April 29, 1942.
Summary of Statements by Survivors of SS 'Ashkhabad', 5, 284 gross tons, owned by the USSR, Op-16-B-5 file, dated May 11, 1942.
Convoy SC-107, F-3714, Routing and Communication Dispatches. Original source likely Naval Historical Center, now Naval History and Heritage Command.
Report on Convoy SC-107, Telephone Conversation with Comnaveu. 19 November 1942.
Convoy WSC-118, F-3714, Routing and Communication Dispatches.
Convoy SC-129, F-3714, Routing and Communication Dispatches.
Report of T.G. 21.14 Anti-Submarine Operations – 25 September to 9 November 1943, inclusive.

Captain (Ret) John M Waters, Jr. Collection of Papers
Extensive collection of original documents and personal notes related to battles of Convoys SC-107 and SC-118. Included in this collection is correspondence with Prof. Dr Jürgen Rohwer, and others. Copies are in the possession of the author.

BOOKS
Delize, Jean, *U-Boote Crews. The day-to-day life aboard Hitler's submarines* (Paris: Historie & Collections, 2007).
Dönitz, Karl, *Memoirs: Ten Years and Twenty Days* (Annapolis, Maryland: Naval Institute Press, 1990).
Dörr, Manfred, *Die Ritterkreuzträger der U-Boot-Waffe. Band 1:*

A–J (Osnabrück: Biblio Verlag, 1988).

Forstner, Georg-Günther von, 'The Journal of Submarine Commander von Forstner' in *U-boat War 1914–1918, Volume 2. Three Accounts of German Submarines During the Great War* (Leonaur, 2010).

Franks, Norman and Eric Zimmerman, *U-boat versus Aircraft* (London: Grub Street, 1988).

Hamilton, Aaron S, *Total Undersea War: The Evolutionary Role of the Snorkel in Dönitz's U-boat Fleet, 1944–1945* (Barnsley: Seaforth, 2020).

Högel, Georg, *U-boat Emblems of World War II, 1939–1945*. Translated from the German by Ed Force (Atglen, PA: Schiffer Military History, 1999).

Hessler, Günter, *The U-boat War in the Atlantic 1939–1945* (London: Ministry of Defence, HMSO, 1992).

Macintyre, Captain Donald, *U-boat Killer: Fighting the U-boats in the Battle of the Atlantic* (London: Cassell Military Paperback, 2000).

Mulligan, Timothy P, *Neither Sharks nor Wolves, The Men of Nazi Germany's U-boat Arm, 1939–1945* (Annapolis, MD: Naval Institute Press, 1999).

Murray, Marischal, *Union-Castle Chronicle 1853–1953* (London: Longmans, Green and Co, 1953).

Niestlé, Axel, *German U-boat Losses During World War II: Details of Destruction* (London: Frontline Books, 2014).

Offley, Ed, *Turning the Tide, How a Small Band of Allied Sailors Defeated the U-boats and Won the Battle of the Atlantic* (New York: Basic Books, 2011).

Stachelhaus, Uwe, *U-526, Dokumentation über ein Deutsches U-Boot und seine Besatzung* (Mülheim an der Ruhr: Privately published, November 2012).

Syrett, David (ed), *Publications of the Navy Records Society, Vol. 139, The Battle of the Atlantic and Signals Intelligence: U-boat Situations and Trends, 1941–1945* (Aldershot: Ashgate, 1998).

Urbanke, Axel, *Suppliers of the Grey Wolves: The Story of the German Submarine Tankers, 1941–1944* (Bad Zwischenhahn: Luftfahrtverlag Start, 2013).

Waters, Jr., Captain John M US Coast Guard (Ret.), *Bloody Winter*, revised paperback ed (New York, NY: A Jove Book, 1986).

Westwood, David, *Anatomy of the Ship. The Type VII U-boat* (Annapolis, MD: Naval Institute Press, 1984).

Y'Blood, William T, *Hunter Killer: US Escort Carriers in Gallant Battle Against the Nazi U-boat Menace* (New York: Bantam Falcon Books, 1992).

ARTICLES

Frintrop, Jochen. Hörzu, 'Mit "Feindsender" auf Feindfahrt' (29 May 1987).

Haldimann, Marc-André., 'End of a Charmed career'. Undated and unpublished.

Thompson, David G, 'Villains, Victims, and Veterans: Buchheim's *Das Boot* and the Problem of the Hybrid Novel-Memoir as History', *Twentieth Century Literature* 39, no. 1 (1993), pp 59–78. Accessed June 9, 2021.

Waters, J., Captain John M, 'Stay Tough', US Naval Institute *Proceedings* (December 1966).

Waters, Jr, Captain (USGC, RET.) John M, 'A Ship for All Seasons', *Naval History* (Winter 1988).

LETTERS AND CORRESPONDENCE

Letter to the author from Prof. Dr Jürgen Rohwer dated 7 November 1994.

Letter to the author from Prof. Dr Jürgen Rohwer dated 4 January 1995.

Letter to the author from Otto Kretschmer dated 29 April 1995.

WEBSITES

https://uboat.net/

Interview of Mr. James E. Brown, conducted by Mr. Mike McCarthy in 1991.

http://uboatarchive.net/

C.B. 4051 (42) 'U581' Interrogation of Survivors, April 1942. N.I.D. 01730/42

ASW-6 Report No. 28 (13 October 1943): Antisubmarine action aircraft Report (ASW-6) written by Lt. (jg) Fowler, submitted by Lt. Comdr. Avery and endorsed by Capt. A. J. Isbell.

http://dubm.de/

'The History of U-581'

Patrol Charts

U–402 Patrol 1 (26 October–9 December 1941) – page 206

U–402 Patrol 2 (11 January–11 February 1942) – page 208

U–402 Patrol 3 (26 March–20 May 1942) – page 210

U–402 Patrol 4 (16 June–5 August 1942) – page 212

U–402 Patrol 5 (4 October–20 November 1942) – page 214

U–402 Patrol 6 (14 January–23 February 1943) – page 216

U–402 Patrol 7 (21 April–16 May 1943) – page 218

U–402 Patrol 8 (4 September–13 October 1943) – page 220

U-402 Patrol 1 (26 Oct - 9 Dec 1941)
A. Patrol area
B. Patrol area 16-23 Nov
C. Approach point 24 Nov

PATROL CHARTS

KNIGHT OF THE NORTH ATLANTIC

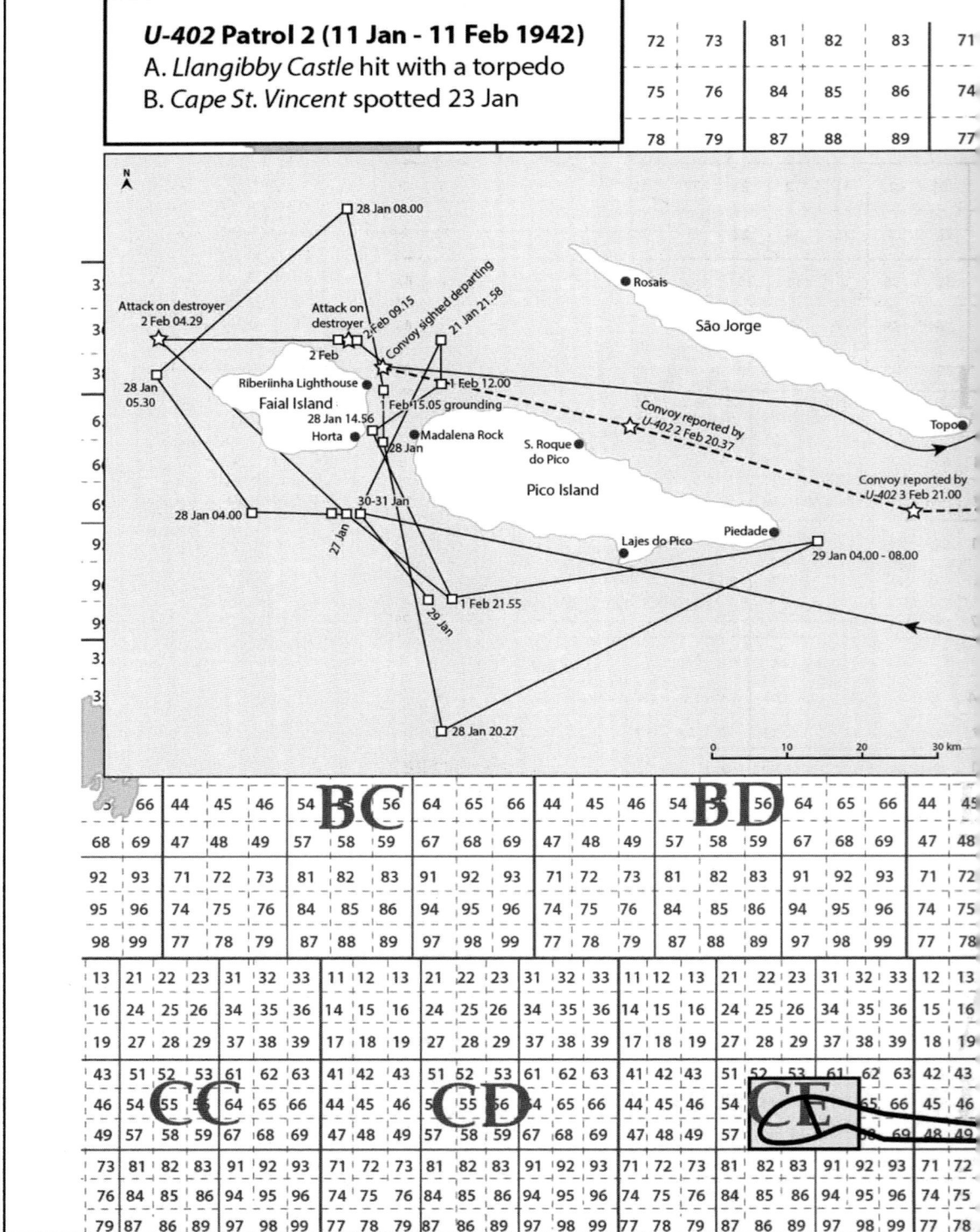

PATROL CHARTS

KNIGHT OF THE NORTH ATLANTIC

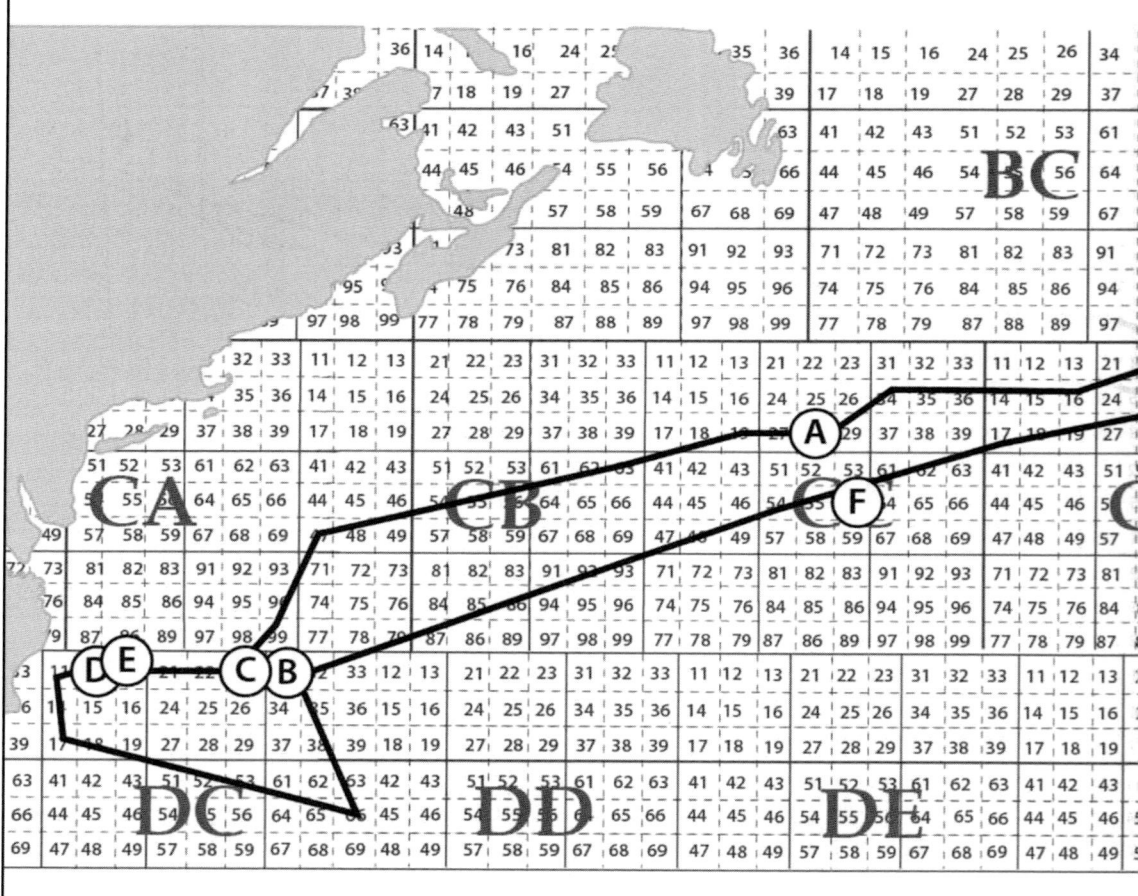

U-402 Patrol 3 (26 Mar – 20 May 1942)
A. *Empire Progress* sunk on 13 Apr
B. Four life boats with sails spotted 20 Apr
C. Land based aircraft spotted on 23 Apr
D. *Ashkhabad* sunk on 30 Apr
E. *Cythera* sunk on 2 May
F. Unsuccessful attack on steamer on 9 May

PATROL CHARTS

KNIGHT OF THE NORTH ATLANTIC

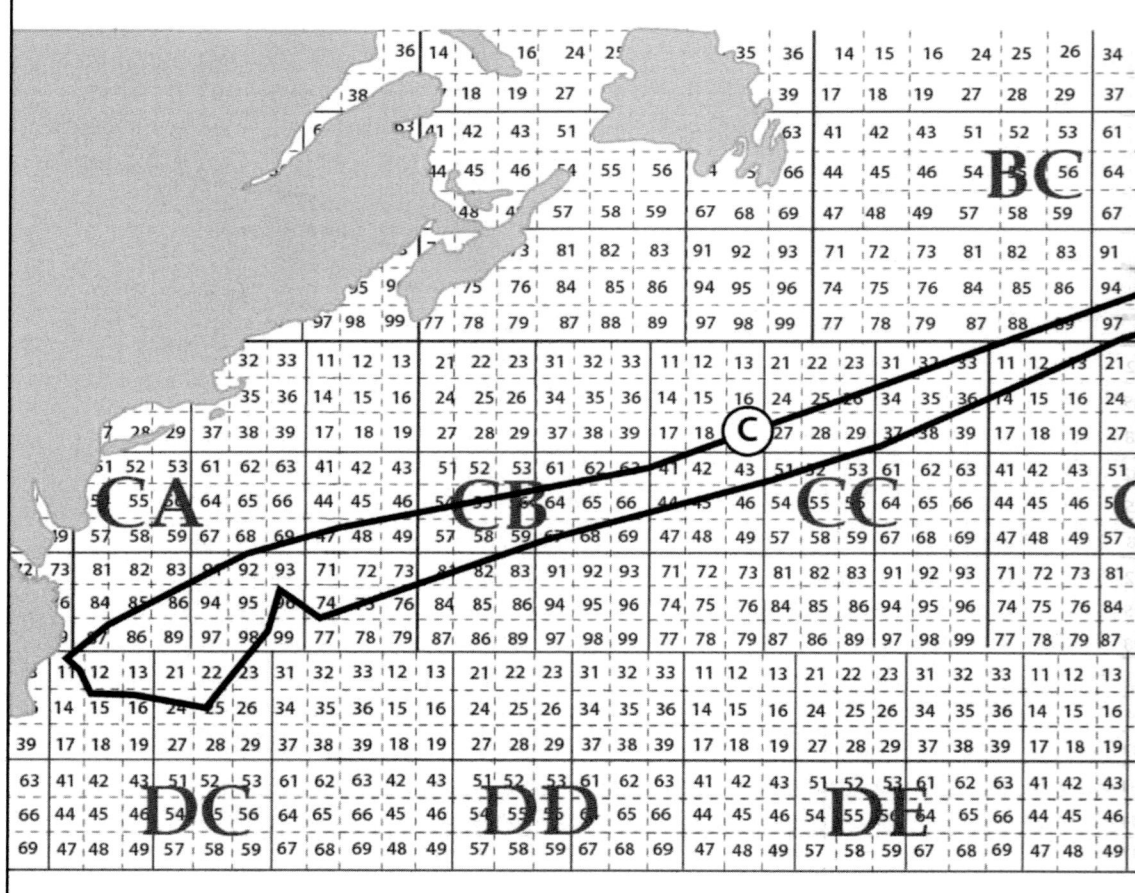

U-402 Patrol 4 (16 Jun - 5 Aug 1942)
A. Initial patrol area 25 Jun
B. Resupply with *U-460*
C. Encounter with *Serpa Pinto* 6 Jun
D. Attack by aircraft on 14 Jul

PATROL CHARTS

U-402 Patrol 5 (4 Oct - 20 Nov 1942)
A. One merchant sunk on 2 Nov
B. Four merchantmen sunk on 2 Nov
C. Refuel with U-117

PATROL CHARTS

U-402 Patrol 6 (14 Jan - 23 Feb 1943)
A. Refuel with *U-460* on 15 Feb
B. Five merchantmen sunk or damaged on 7 Feb
C. Two merchantmen sunk on 7 Feb

PATROL CHARTS

217

U-402 Patrol 7 (21 Apr – 26 May 1943)
A. Two merchantmen sunk on 11 May
B. Meeting with *U-459* on 17 May

PATROL CHARTS

U-402 Patrol 8 (4 Sep - 13 Oct 1943)
A. *U-402* fends off aircraft attack on 22 Sep
B. *U-402* fends off aircraft attack on 1 Oct
C. *U-402* attacked twice by aircraft and sunk on 13 Oct

PATROL CHARTS

221

Ship Name Index

Abbreviations

Warships are identified by their navy
Canada/Royal Canadian Navy – RCN
Free French – FF
Germany/Kriegsmarine – KM
UK/Royal Navy – RN
USA/United States Navy – USN

Merchantmen are identified by their country
France – Fr
Greece – Gr
Netherlands – Ne
Norway – Nor
Portugal –Pr
Russia – Ru
Spain – Sp
United Kingdom – Br

Abelia (RN) 133
Afrika (Br) *142*, 144, 197
Amherst (RCN) 124
Annik (Nor) 136
Antelope (Br) 125, 197
Antigone (Br) 163, 197
Arvida (RCN) 121
Ashkhabad (Ru) 12, 90–3, 186, *187*, 188, 197

Babbitt (USN) 149
Barbarigo (RM) 62, *198*
Beverly (RN) 133, 136
Bibb (USCG) 124, 133, 135–6, *137*, 138, 145, 146, 150
Bismarck (KM) 82

Campanula (RN) 133, 143–4, 146
Campbeltown (RN) 82
Card (USN) *168*, 175, *177*, *180*, 187
Clematis (RN) 161
Croome (RN) 69, 71, 72
Cythera (USN) 94, *95*, 96, 101, 181, 197, 199

Daghild (Nor) 143, *144*, 197
Dalcroy (Br) 123, 181, 197
Deutschland (KM) 22

Emden (KM) 21
Empire Antelope (Br) 125, 197
Empire Dryden (Br) *199*
Empire Leopard (Br) 125, 197

Empire Progress (Br) 86, *87*, 197
Empire Sunrise (Br) *121*, 122, 197
Exmoor (RN) 69, 70, 72

Forfar (RN) 23

Gentian (RN) 164
Gneisenau (KM) 31
Grado (Nor) 162, 197

Harmala (Br) 143
Hertfordshire (RN) 91, 92
Henry R Mallory (Am) *137*, 145, 197
Hesperus (RN) 133, 162

Ingham (USCG) 9, 11, 124, *137*, 138, 146, 150, 182

Jeypore (Br) 118, 119

Kalliopi (Gr) *137*, 146, *147*, 197
Kamerun (KM) 29

Lady Elsa (RN) 90
Lagan (RN) 173
Llangibby Castle (Br) 54, 57–62, 65–7, 69, 71–5, 79, 185, 197
Lobelia (FF) 133

Mignonette (RN) 133, 142–4, 146
Milwaukee (USN) 198
Moffett (USN) 198

Navemar (Sp) 62
Newton Ash (Br) *137*, 149, 197

Oklahoma (USN) 97

Restigouche (RCN) 119, 121, 122
Reuben James (USN) 52
Rinos (Gr) 123, 197
Robert E Hopkins (Am) 141, 142, 197
Robert Ley (KM) 27, *28*, 29
Roper (USN) 104

Salmon (RN) 22

223

Serpa Pinto (Pr) 107
Scharnhorst (KM) 31
Schenck (USN) 124, 145, *146*
Semmes (USN) 92
St. Zeno (RN) 92

Thames (Ne) 69
Tirpitz (KM) 45, 82,
Toward (Br) 133, 141, *142*, 145, 146, 197

U-1 (RM) 20
U-7 (RM) 20
U-17 (KM) *199*
U-23 (KM) 22
U-28 (RM) 20, 182
U-59 (KM) 24
U-69 (KM) 50
U-71 (KM) 43, 116, 118
U-84 (KM) 118, 121–3
U-85 (KM) 57, 104
U-87 (KM) 57
U-89 (KM) 116, 118
U-96 (KM) 112
U-99 (KM) 23-4, 54, 123, 162
U-100 (KM) 151
U-105 (KM) 87
U-107 (KM) 105
U-116 (KM) 105
U-117 (KM) 127
U-131 (KM) 69
U-132 (KM) 113-4, 116, 118, 128
U-136 (KM) 98-9, 102
U-149 (KM) 43
U-173 (KM) 107
U-187 (KM) 134, 136
U-201 (KM) 50, 93
U-215 (KM) 111
U-262 (KM) 134, 140
U-266 (KM) 139
U-267 (KM) 135-6, 139
U-270 (KM) 173–4
U-290 (KM) 173
U-332 (KM) 49, 50
U-341 (KM) 173
U-357 (KM) 133
U-381 (KM) 118-9, 127
U-402 (KM) 3, 9–15, 18-9, 21, 24–5, 27, 28, 30–7, *38*, *39*, 40–4, 45, 46, 47–52, 54–64, 66–9, 71–76, 78-9, 81–95, 98–104, 106–16, 118, 120–8, 130–52, 154–6, 158–63, 164–67, 169–75, 177–81, 183–7, 188, 189, 194, 199–201, 205

U-404 (KM) 143
U-434 (KM) 41, 45, 47
U-437 (KM) 118, 119
U-438 (KM) 118
U-442 (KM) 118
U-454 (KM) 118, 127
U-455 (KM) 105
U-456 (KM) 132, 148
U-459 (KM) 166
U-460 (KM) 106, 107, 151
U-488 (KM) 175, 177
U-492 (KM) 13
U-504 (KM) 160
U-522 (KM) 119, 120, 126
U-526 (KM) 11, 104, 170, 203
U-552 (KM) 119, 120, 123–4
U-564 (KM) 55
U-571 (KM) 116, 118
U-572 (KM) 62, 66, 74, 199
U-576 (KM) 106, 111
U-581 (KM) 54, 55, 57, 58, 60, 62, 67, 71–74, 185, 199, 204
U-593 (KM) 105
U-594 (KM) 132
U-608 (KM) 135, 143
U-609 (KM) 116, 134–36
U-614 (KM) 143
U-624 (KM) 138
U-632 (KM) 135
U-654 (KM) 67, 87, 9
U-658 (KM) 116, 118
U-701 (KM) 111
U-704 (KM) 116, 118, 120
U-731 (KM) 175
U-852 (KM) 97
U-3005 (KM) 199
UB-68 (RM) 16

Vanessa (RN) 124, 132
Venus (KM) 37
Vimy (RN) 133, 135

Walker (RN) 24, 141, 162
Westcott (RN) 68, 69, 72
Whitehall (RN) 161
Wilhelm Gustloff (KM) 28